T0064076

Bakassi Peninsula

Bakassi Peninsula

The Untold Story
of a People Betrayed

Okon Edet

PARTRIDGE
A Penguin Random House Company

Print information available on the last page.

To order additional copies of this book, contact
Toll Free 800 101 2657 (Singapore)
Toll Free 1 800 81 7340 (Malaysia)
orders.singapore@partridgepublishing.com

www.partridgepublishing.com/singapore

DEDICATED TO

Mma Obot Antigha Oku;
My Mother

Chief (Dr.) Archibong Edem Young,
Madam Iquo Effiom,
Miss Ukpong Edem Young,
Master Cyril Effiong Bassey,

And to

All who fell in the struggle for Bakassi Peninsula
That they die not in vain.

Wine is strong,
A king is stronger,
Women are even stronger,
But truth will conquer all.

(The Book of Esdras)

FOREWORD

Despite the country's loss at the International Court of Justice, at The Hague, it is still widely believed in Nigeria that its centuries-old territorial entanglement in the Bakassi Peninsula, was badly managed to undermine its sovereignty in the territory, and thus, gravely scarred its standing as a regional power.

For many Nigerians, therefore, the basic Bakassi Peninsula narrative has been that of a serial administrative, legal and political missteps, while for the Usakedet aboriginal population, the shifty character of the international politics, as played out in their homeland, brought them a long night of nightmares.

This is what one would easily come away with, in reading through Mr. Okon Edet's *Bakassi Peninsula: The Untold Story of a People Betrayed*. The book is exquisitely multi-sided; partly historical, political; international diplomacy, with all the legal trappings and contexts, as well as a whiff of autobiographical sketches, in which the writer delicately captures brief beautiful scenes of the social climate of the Usakedet cosmos.

Himself an active professional at the international diplomacy scenes, but with strong and unyielding attachment to his autochthonic Usakedet natives of the Bakassi Peninsula, the author was thus better placed to watch, participate, record, canvass opinions and push some viewpoints, during the ever-changing phases, mode and mood of the bilateral engagements of both Nigeria and Cameroon in the marine resource and hydrocarbon-rich peninsula, through the years.

The unvarnished upshot has been the *Bakassi Peninsula: The Untold Story of a People Betrayed.* The author treats the behind-the-scenes tales with unparalleled passion, courage and candour, but careful to set great store by way of his presentation of the finer details and dynamics, in every effort to ensure justice for his people who have lived and engaged in economic and socio-cultural reproduction, since the 15th Century, even as the two contending nations pursued their historicity and legal ownership claims over the Bakassi Peninsula.

His views on certain historical issues, made touchy in recent times, because of the negative interplay of some contrived in-group perception and attitude, and mutual socio-cultural snobbery, are as strong, brave, as they are dispassionate and unsentimental.

The author, for instance argues, most powerfully that the universe of the 'Calabar Nation,' which, by his thesis, encompasses all other sub-nationalities like the Efiat, Ibibio, Okobo, Annang, Oron, etc, has been made small, through the unwitting discriminatory attitude and tendencies of the Efik, despite self-evident socio-cultural and traditional affinities, among these peoples of the same linguistic family. Such attitude, he infers, had led to the plight of the Usakedet people, themselves, Efik in every account, but left in the lurch, by the 'Efik World,' during the Bakassi Peninsula ownership struggle.

Here then is a rather seminal offer that may not only help to illumine some of the darker side of the Bakassi saga, but would also possibly help to answer those pesky questions on many issues, particularly appertaining to the Usakedet history, sociology, politics, culture, religion and world view.

But above all, the author grapples with the thinking, or rather the hunch, that there are things that are still uncertain with regard to his ancient homeland. The book itself is pleasantly deep, sweep, wide and breath-taking. Easy to follow through the even keel presentational style, I certainly believe this to be a delightful and valuable text for all peoples connected with the many tales of the Bakassi Peninsula; a book for the international audience, and a book for all seasons.

Akpan John
Calabar, Nigeria. 2015

PREFACE

Africans bear the family burden like a cross. Tradition saddles you from birth with a duty to care, protect and defend your family once you come of age. This duty to care, protect and defend is not limited to your father, mother, brothers and sisters. It extends to your numerous cousins, nieces, nephews, uncles, aunties etc, indeed to your clan and tribe. Ironically, these are the very same duties you owe your country. So what happens when the interest of your family, clan or tribe appears to be in conflict with the interest of your country? *Bakassi Peninsula; the Untold Story of a People Betrayed,* essentially highlights the dilemma of this situation and illustrates how compounded the problem could be when your father and mother are drawn into different sides of a conflict.

Bakassi Peninsula; the Untold Story of a People Betrayed is 'un petit peu de tout' a little bit of everything. It is politics; it takes a cursory look at the back-stage efforts of an individual to bring his motherland; Bakassi Peninsula back to Nigeria; his fatherland and brings to light the difficulties encountered on that tortuous road. *Bakassi Peninsula; the Untold Story of a People Betrayed* is history. It provides a brief history of the Bakassi Peninsula and its peoples. *Bakassi Peninsula; the Untold Story of a People Betrayed* is also law. It offers a few legal opinions on the Bakassi Peninsula ownership controversy between the Federation of Nigeria and the Republic of Cameroon and attempts to provide an overview of legal instruments that have shaped the Bakassi Peninsula from colonial times to date. *Bakassi Peninsula; the Untold Story of a People Betrayed* brings to the reader un-edited extracts of the judgement of the International Court of Justice conferring sovereignty over the Bakassi peninsula to Cameroon and makes available select reactions to that judgement by Cameroonians and Nigerians. Finally, *Bakassi Peninsula; the Untold Story of a People Betrayed* is the voice of the voiceless; the untold story of a people betrayed; our struggle and a requiem for the Bakassi Peninsula

This book should be a valuable resource on Bakassi peninsula. It should be compelling reading for students, politicians, lawyers, policy makers, diplomats and the academia. Above all, *Bakassi Peninsula; the Untold Story of a People Betrayed,* should be a must for everyone who was involved or may still be involved with Bakassi peninsula affairs especially those who might otherwise have had insights other than that contained in *Bakassi Peninsula; the Untold Story of a People Betrayed.*

Let me also take this occasion to express my gratitude to my professional colleagues who may have in one way or the other contributed ideas, criticism, advice and encouragement in the course of my writing this book. My very special thanks in this regard go to Dr. Obasola Fatunla, Ambassador Femi Rotimi, Ambassador Bassey S.B., Ms Roseline Asuquo and Mr. Kashim Musa Tumsah, MFR

I owe immense gratitude to my family for being my source of strength and inspiration and for their encouragement and support. Let me particularly acknowledge the editorial assistance of my son and my nephew; Barr. Henry Edet Okon Edet and Edet Ekpe Etim. My heartfelt appreciation goes to my friend, Mr. Akpan John, a brilliant writer, who edited the manuscript and produced the foreword.

CONTENTS

CHAPTER ONE
Bakassi Peninsula; Yesterday and Today

Sandwiched between the Republic of Cameroon and the Federation of Nigeria somewhere along the Gulf of Guinea coast, the Bakassi Peninsula was probably one of the most back-water and obscure corners on earth; its people most forgotten, until suddenly Bakassi peninsula became overnight one of the most widely known names in Africa and perhaps in the entire world. For millions of people around the world but particularly for Nigerians and Cameroonians, Bakassi peninsula became a household name as a result of the outbreak of hostilities between Nigeria and Cameroon over ownership of the oil rich Bakassi Peninsula in December 1993. The Gulf of Guinea; the primary access route to and from three major oil producing countries, Angola, Equatorial Guinea and Nigeria would receive increased attention as a result of the Bakassi crisis.

Many believe that between twenty-five and thirty percent of United States oil imports come from the region. Recent oil discoveries in Ghana, Cote D'Ivoire and Liberia have further increased the geostrategic importance of the Gulf of Guinea and made it a critical region not only for oil producing countries but for international shipping as well. What happens in a Bakassi peninsula that is located in the heart of the Gulf of Guinea cannot, but be of immense interest to world powers. Hardly surprising the United Nations, United States, United Kingdom, France and Germany witnessed the Greentree

Agreement between Nigerian and Cameroon. There could be no clearer way to send down the message.

However, in spite of its geostrategic importance and the huge interest in the region, only a negligible percentage of people had any knowledge about the location or indeed the inhabitants of the Bakassi Peninsula. A much smaller number still could boast of ever stepping their foot on Bakassi Peninsula soil. As a result, very little was known about this exotic land of our birth at the inception of the Bakassi Peninsula crisis. Such a situation would undoubtedly give room for exploitation by unscrupulous groups and individuals. Bakassi Peninsula would prove to be no exception. As a result of this situation, unscrupulous individuals, administrators, racketeers, dishonest politicians and an unspecified number of ethnic groups some of whom did not even share land or maritime borders with the Bakassi Peninsula would become engaged in activities whose primary objective would be to hijack Bakassi Peninsula and its abundant resources. You would think that Christopher Columbus had just discovered a new piece of land in the Americas. Thus, while Nigeria and Cameroon were locked in the battle for ownership of the Bakassi Peninsula on several fronts, unknown to the world, a more vicious conflict was raging and continues to rage even after the crisis between various communities in Nigeria and Cameroon over ownership of the very same Bakassi Peninsula.

Owned by a people of Nigerian heritage; the Usakedet people, known in Cameroon and in colonial records as 'Isangele' and overwhelmingly populated by Nigerians, Bakassi peninsula comprises a small mainland where the native population and customary owners of the peninsula live and a largely mosquito-infested mangrove swamp terrain that is criss-crossed by creeks and rivers that project into the Gulf of Guinea between Rio del Rey on the east and Akpayefe River on the west where a sizeable population of fishermen communities;

strangers in the Bakassi Peninsula live in make-shift shelters. Until the exploration of oil became a prime concern in Bakassi Peninsula, the only viable economic activity in the territory was fishing. Not surprisingly, hundreds of fishing settlements called 'ine' in Efik language dot the banks of creeks and rivers that traverse the Bakassi Peninsula landscape. Until the outbreak of hostilities in Bakassi Peninsula nobody ever claimed to come from these 'ines'. No body ever claimed to come from these fishing settlements.

Bakassi Peninsula crisis would change all that and Bakassi fishing settlements would overnight metamorphose into the ancestral homeland of Ijaw, Ibibio, Oron, Efik, Ilaje, Okobo, Atabong, Efiat, Yoruba and Igbo fishermen communities in the peninsula. Bakassi Peninsula fishermen communities who come from across Nigeria and beyond would seek to be recognized and treated as indigenous Bakassi Peninsula natives. They would lay porous ownership claims over the Bakassi Peninsula. Serious efforts appear to have been undertaken to suppress the fact that the Bakassi Peninsula has a native population. Deliberate efforts also appear to have been made to suppress the fact that these indigenous people are the customary owners of the Bakassi Peninsula. To sustain this falsehood, migrant fishermen communities; strangers in the Bakassi Peninsula who live on make-shift structures in the mangrove swamp forest would be given undue recognition and promotion. Huge effort and sometimes strange methods seem to have been deployed to keep these vital facts away from public domain while significant energy was invested in efforts to transform fishermen communities; strangers in the Bakassi Peninsula into landlords of the peninsula.

This situation would alarm the Usakedet people; customary owners of the Bakassi Peninsula and make them extremely nervous. This was not what I expected when I embarked on the mission to reunite my motherland with my fatherland. I could not understand how fishermen communities who share so much in common with Usakedet people; tradition, culture and linguistic affinity and who had lived in harmony for centuries with the Usakedet people would suddenly want to confiscate the ancestral homeland of their host and benefactors. It was obvious Usakedet (Isangele) people would never accept such an outcome. I needed to do something to change that perception, to stand any chance of taking the struggle I had embarked on some twenty-three years earlier to a logical conclusion. Thus, from the very beginning of the Bakassi crisis, Nigeria created a crisis within a crisis in the Bakassi Peninsula that was unlikely to advance Nigeria's cause in its effort to regain sovereignty over the Bakassi Peninsula.

There were two other sticking points. First, the territory of the Usakedet (Isangele) people extends far beyond the Bakassi peninsula. It includes Ngosso, Jock and Erong Peninsulas and projects up to certain points east and northwards along the Ndian and Andonkot Rivers. Nigeria was only contesting ownership of the Bakassi peninsula. So what was going to happen to the other territories owned by Usakedet people? If Nigeria regained control of the Bakassi Peninsula alone, the Usakedet people would lose Ngosso, Jock and Erong peninsula. That would be unacceptable. Secondly, there was also the extremely frightening rumour that Nigeria had plans to claim part of the Bakassi Peninsula and abandon the customary owners of the peninsula to Cameroon.

Finding solutions to such thorny issues at the inception of the Bakassi crisis was never going to be easy but I was determined to steer the boat out of troubled waters at least for the time being. So I thought it wise not to push too hard for the inclusion of other Usakedet territories in Nigeria's claim at that stage. That I thought would be better done at the later stages of the conflict. I felt raising the question of Ngosso, Jock and Erong Peninsulas at the inception of the Bakassi crisis could complicate the case for the Bakassi Peninsula, convinced that a successful resolution of the Bakassi Peninsula ownership tussle would pave the way if not hasten the way for a quick resolution of the other two peninsulas. Based on this thinking I thought we should put the issue on hold. As for the rumoured exclusion of Usakedet people from Nigeria's claim over the Bakassi Peninsula and the ownership controversy with fishermen communities, I decided to take these issues head on.

Meanwhile, fishermen communities led by unscrupulous politicians of Efik heritage who were never ever resident in the Bakassi Peninsula were not taking things lying down. From their homes and comfort in Calabar, they manipulated and exploited fishermen communities. In their haste and desperate bid to walk away with the enormous resources of the Bakassi Peninsula they would resort to cheap blackmail and other forms of questionable strategies against anyone who dared challenge their ownership claim over the peninsula. And because I happened to lead the fight against unscrupulous politicians bent on expropriating Bakassi peninsula resources, I had to take most of the heat. They called me names; a Cameroonian; a spy for Cameroon and took unimaginable steps to damage my career. They may have succeeded. I retired from service unsung, empty-handed and impoverished but that did not deter me. I was prepared to pay a higher price in defence of my people. What was perhaps unsettling was the realisation that some of my own people did collaborate with the very people I was bitterly fighting against.

Fishermen communities in Bakassi peninsula are the customary tenants of the peninsula. They are no strangers to their overlords; the Usakedet (Isangele) people. Usakedet people and fishermen communities have lived in harmony for centuries in the Bakassi Peninsula. Neither fishermen communities nor the Efik Kingdom is ignorant of the history of Bakassi peninsula. It seemed fraudulent and mischievous for the Efik world and fishermen communities, for some strange reason to claim ignorance and try to change the history of the peninsula and its peoples at the inception of Bakassi crisis. Centuries of interaction had established the relationship between Usakedet people and fishermen communities to be that of landlord and tenants-in-chief. Colonial records make this point adequately clear. It is sad that an Efik world that is renowned for its noble character and integrity would be so unwilling or unable to speak the truth at a time they were most needed. Usakedet people felt extremely betrayed. As a result of Efik inaction, unscrupulous politicians would succeed in making Nigeria believe; at least so it seemed that the Bakassi Peninsula actually belonged to fishermen communities. And once Nigeria had bought into the lie, policies began to emerge that were clearly designed to dispossess Usakedet people; customary owners of Bakassi peninsula of their territory.

Even in Cameroon where Usakedet (Isangele) people had always been recognized as customary owners of the Bakassi Peninsula, the outbreak of the Bakassi Peninsula crisis seemed to coincide with a sudden and surprising upsurge of an incredible number of Cameroonian ethnic groups claiming ownership of the Bakassi peninsula. Prominent among the group were the Balondos, Bakweris, Doualas and Bamuso (Idombi) people. What one found most baffling about some of these Cameroonian claims was that most of these ethnic groups neither shared maritime nor land borders with the Bakassi Peninsula. Both in Nigeria and Cameroon, people not only seemed ready to rewrite Bakassi Peninsula history, they, for reasons that remain a matter of conjecture also seemed quite economical with the truth about the Bakassi Peninsula.

I received news of the landing of Nigerian soldiers in Bakassi peninsula while in the Middle East with excitement and great expectation. If I had had my way, I would have actualised my dream some twenty-three years earlier when I and a few Bakassi natives quietly began to work behind-the-scenes on our dream project to see the Bakassi Peninsula revert to Nigeria. In the Bakassi peninsula, the language you spoke, the clothes you wore, the food you ate, the name you bore, the games you played, the dances you danced and the songs you sang were all Nigerian. Indeed, your entire existence was Nigerian and except for one village; Efut Inwang (Bateka) in the Bakassi Peninsula that traces its origin to Cameroon, over ninety percent of the native population of the Bakassi Peninsula has nothing in common with the people of Cameroon. Yet the Bakassi Peninsula was said to be in Cameroon. That, I found quite intriguing at an early age.

Bakassi Peninsula presents yet another peculiar phenomenon comparable only to the equally peculiar phenomenon of the oil rich nations of the Middle East. Over ninety percent of the entire population of the peninsula comprises largely of stranger elements, mainly fishermen. You could say the same of Kuwait or many Gulf States for example where substantial percentages of their population consist of migrant workers from across the world. In the Bakassi Peninsula the fishermen population come from across Nigeria and as far away as Ghana and Senegal. The Bakassi Peninsula is host to a large number of Ijaws, Ibibios, Okobos, Atabongs, Efiats, Ilajes, Ibos, Hausas, Yorubas, Ghanaians and Efiks. Their main occupation is fishing. The remaining ten percent or less of the population, with the exception of Efut Inwang village shares common ethnic affinity, tradition and culture with the Efik speaking peoples of Nigeria. Yet, the Bakassi Peninsula was said to be Cameroon. That, I thought was strange and needed to be changed. Bakassi Peninsula had to be Nigerian. Something needed to be done and for several years, I quietly worked behind- the-scenes for the day that would happen.

With such statistics, I could never stop wondering how the Bakassi Peninsula could ever have been said to be Cameroonian. Something, I thought was wrong. Something, I believed needed to be done.

What? I had no idea but for several years I gladly worked behind-the-scenes to see the day that the Bakassi Peninsula would again belong to Nigeria. Could the landing of Nigerian soldiers in Abana fishing settlement on December 23, 1993 signal the beginning of the realisation of that dream?

In the euphoria of the moment I found myself recalling how simple and beautiful life in the Bakassi Peninsula had been before Cameroon moved into the territory in the early seventies. As a child born and raised in the Bakassi Peninsula, I could vividly recall with nostalgic passion, time and time again when fishermen communities in the Bakassi Peninsula would retire to Usakedet (Isangele) at the end of the fishing season to meet their loved ones and relations; to have fun, make merriment, fetch water and make all forms of preparations for the beginning of the next fishing season. At such times, the villages of Odon, Amoto and Efut Inwang (Bateka) would be in great festive mood. The town square in Odon was usually the centre of attraction. The town square would usually be crowded with all sorts of people; dancers, drummers, singers and wrestlers who displayed diverse skills before a seemingly mad crowd that would not stop clapping, cheering and yelling in excitement and appreciation.

Occasionally however, these joyful moments would be punctuated by screams of horror from some poorly illuminated homestead. A man had just caught his wife or girl friend cheating on him and was meting out corporal punishment. A young man was attempting to adduct a teenage girl and the girl and her parents were protesting vehemently. But all that hardly seemed to distract attention from activities in the village square where the multitude assembled therein generally seemed to turn a tolerant eye as if to say 'don't worry, we understand.' Nobody, it appeared wanted anything to interfere with the moment's fun. They were sure they would get details of whatever had happened much later or perhaps the next day with sufficient embellishment.

Living in Bakassi peninsula at the time was great fun. Those were moments of great love stories too. Young men would go for each other's throat in a senseless fight for the love of the charming heart of an Usakedet (Isangele) Amazon. Yes amazons for that's exactly what those women actually seemed. They knew how to roll those eyes, make that eye contact, give that smile and display those glittering teeth that set men's heads rolling and gave the people their name. Little wonder people of Usakedet extraction are found in literally every Efik hamlet. So excellent were relations between the indigenous population and fishermen communities in the Bakassi Peninsula that the fishermen population left their footprints ingrained on the sandy beaches of Bakassi peninsula. They sired a good number of children in the peninsula. Today, many Usakedet indigenes of my generation including yours sincerely are products of that romantic era between mainly Efiat fishermen and Usakedet women.

When the fishing season returned, the fishermen would return to the numerous fishing settlements, prominent among which are Abana, Atabong, Ine Atayo, Inua Mba, Ine Ekoi, Tinkoro, Okom kiet, Andonkot, Usiak Ifia (Rio del Rey), etc and to the many other less prominent fishing ports that litter the Bakassi Peninsula landscape. Then the women-folks would go after the fishermen using all forms of pretexts. Usually, they went to sell food and buy fish and crayfish. Again, I must recall with strong nostalgic passion and a great sense of loss my childhood days spent on the sandy beaches of Abana and Atabong fishing settlements, always in company of my beautiful aunt Mma Oyo who had made those two fishing settlements her favourite places of visit. Life then seemed so endlessly beautiful. The fishermen population would come to the mainland during off seasons and the mainland would go to the fishermen during fishing seasons.

It was such a simple harmonious existence that everyone seemed happy and satisfied. I have never stopped relishing those childhood glorious memories, accompanying my aunt and later my foster father to fishing ports which only the attainment of school age had forced me to abandon. I do still sincerely miss those innocent, good old days.

But all that beautiful life gradually began to fade away as soon as Cameroon moved into the Bakassi peninsula. As soon as Cameroon effectively occupied the peninsula in the early seventies, she began to dismantle Usakedet way of life and assimilate the people. Yaounde to date still frown at names Usakedet natives bear, the songs they sing, the way they dance and indeed everything about Usakedet tradition and culture because Usakedet way of life is too Nigerian. This is not to say Cameroonians do not appreciate Usakedet tradition and culture. On the contrary, going by the number of awards Usakedet cultural troupes have won in Cameroon, Cameroonians are fascinated by Usakedet tradition and culture. The only problem appears to be that Usakedet dances and way of life are too Nigerian. As soon as Cameroon moved into the Bakassi Peninsula, she began to rename fishing settlements. Fishing settlements that for centuries had borne Efik names that reflect the origin, history, tradition and culture of the people were renamed to reflect Cameroonian origin even though you hardly could find a single Cameroonian fishing settlement or fishermen in the Bakassi Peninsula.

Yaounde remains quite uncomfortable with the fact that Usakedet (Isangele) people; customary owners of Bakassi peninsula and over ninety percent of the population of Bakassi peninsula are Nigerians or of Nigerian extraction. Yaounde is casting for Cameroonians to effectively occupy and own the Bakassi Peninsula. Cameroonian officials; civil or military posted to the peninsula seemed to be on a holy mission to try to modify that demography. And so, like an army of occupation, they have religiously tried to ensure that they too leave their footprints on the sandy beaches of the Bakassi Peninsula. And their efforts have yielded wonderful results. They have fathered a good number of children in the Bakassi Peninsula in the years leading up to the Bakassi crisis and are continuing to do. In fact, Cameroon has succeeded in creating a new generation of Bakassi native population who today can rightly be said to be Cameroonians.

Since the arrival of Cameroon in the peninsula, Bakassi native population has been subjected to a number of indignities and pressures. Usakedet people in particular have to a significant extent yielded to subtle Cameroonian pressures. Gradually Usakedet tradition and culture is falling apart. Usakedet people are beginning to abandon their Efik heritage; trading their Efik names for English, French or some corrupt versions of Efik names. It no longer seems proper and fashionable for Usakedet people to give their new born babies names their ancestors bore because the names are too Nigerian. The older generation faced with the dilemma have found smart ways to go round the problem. They have simply abandoned or added suffixes to their Efik names. Thus, Usakedet people who bear Efik names like Edet, Effiong, Effiom and Okon, etc that are commonly borne in the Bakassi Peninsula are changing their names to Edetson, Effiongson, Effiomson and Okonson, etc. Beautiful Efik names like Andim have simply become Andip while names like Nyong have become Njong. The younger generation has reacted even more strangely. They too have found some bizarre way to deal with the problem. They now give their children French, English or some ancestral names whose origins are obscure. Some have found even more extreme and ridiculous ways to deal with the problem. They now simply turn short sentences, phrases or common expressions into names or invent strange new names for their new born babies. The Efik language is of course under attack. Both the Efik language and the local dialect are gradually making way for some heavy accent Pidgin English and some patois called French as a result of pressure.

The younger generation of Usakedet people is not only looking funny, it is having difficulties communicating in Usakedet dialect.

Until lately Cameroon officials sent to work in the Bakassi Peninsula had been known to fuel centuries-old dispute between Bateka; the only village of Cameroonian origin in the Bakassi Peninsula and Odon; a village of Nigerian heritage over which of these villages first settled in the Bakassi Peninsula. The idea behind this interminable-who-first-came to the Bakassi Peninsula conflict appears to be an attempt to get recognition from Cameroonian authorities as true Cameroonians and veritable owners of the Bakassi Peninsula. Bateka indigenes are known to miss no occasion to let newly posted Cameroonian officials to the Bakassi Peninsula know that Odon indigenes are Nigerians. The irony of the situation is that most of these so-called Bateka indigenes are also Odon natives by blood. And with over-zealous security agents constantly harassing and exploiting the fishermen population, life in the Bakassi Peninsula prior to the outbreak of the Bakassi crisis seemed like a horrible nightmare.

That in essence was the situation when the people woke up one morning to discover that the Bakassi Peninsula was on fire; that their homeland had not only become the centre of world attention; it had indeed also become a major theatre of war. Few may have been taken aback by the development. Numerous complaints from fishermen communities and rising tension seemed to have finally forced Nigeria to send in troops into the Bakassi Peninsula to protect her citizens. This unresolved Bakassi peninsula border problem had remained potentially the most explosive factor in Cameroon-Nigeria relations for decades. A major dimension of the border dispute had to do with the protection and welfare of Nigerians living in the Bakassi Peninsula estimated to be between 90 and 98 percent of the total population of the peninsula. Bakassi peninsula inhabitants were glad that their nation was at last taking steps to protect her people. Hitherto, Nigeria had tended to look the other way, ignoring numerous complaints of harassment and molestations levelled against Cameroonian security agents in the Bakassi Peninsula. Now, it seemed Nigeria was prepared to go the extra mile.

Elsewhere, Nigeria's motive for intervention remained questionable. Not a few believed that Nigeria's intervention in the Bakassi Peninsula may not have been unconnected with the enormous petroleum deposits and rich marine life in the peninsula. A significant percentage of the fish, crayfish and shrimps consumed in both Cameroon and Nigeria and beyond come from the peninsula. No one knows exactly how much oil the Bakassi Peninsula holds but its proximity to abundant oil fields in the Niger Delta region of Nigeria makes one believe the peninsula holds the promise of deposits of millions of barrels making experts believe that the Gulf of Guinea could one day supplant the Middle East as America's primary source of energy.

Cameroon was said to have been exploiting oil in the Bakassi Peninsula including in the neutral corridor with Nigeria for decades. Cameroon's oil installations were equally said to constitute navigational hazards for Nigerian vessels because they obstructed the channel leading to the Nigerian port city of Calabar. Such considerations were believed to have stirred tension between both nations and provided Nigeria reason to intervene in the Bakassi Peninsula. Others differed and held the view that the motive behind Nigeria's intervention in Bakassi peninsula was economic but that the timing was essentially due to the fact that General Sani Abacha, Nigeria's beleaguered military President of the time, realising that dissatisfaction was growing against his regime at home went casting around for anything that, on the one hand would distract public attention from his regime and on the other hand increase the popularity of his regime. General Abacha, they insisted simply wanted to shore up falling domestic support and that, they claimed was how the idea of 'a victorious-little-war' in Bakassi peninsula was born.

For me and the few Bakassi indigenes who for several years had quietly worked behind-the-scenes to see Bakassi peninsula revert to Nigeria and thus make our dream come true, the outbreak of hostilities between Nigeria and Cameroon, although was going to disrupt the hitherto quiet and uneventful existence of our people seemed to offer the best opportunity for the realisation of that dream. As far as I was concerned Nigeria's motive did not matter. I was glad that Nigeria seemed ready to take back the Bakassi Peninsula that had belonged to her in the first place. Previous efforts to get Nigeria pay greater attention to the situation in the Bakassi Peninsula had proved unsuccessful. Now, even the Efik nation whose people largely occupy the peninsula and who previously had shown little or no interest in the plight of the Bakassi Peninsula seemed enthusiastic about the prospect of the peninsula coming back to Nigeria. I felt certain that with the support of the Efik nation and Nigeria's might behind the action, my dream stood a great chance of being realised.

I saw the outbreak of hostilities in the Bakassi Peninsula as a momentous event; a divine intervention to free Bakassi peninsula and our people. I could visualise Bakassi indigenous population already celebrating their return to Nigeria. The landing of troops in the Bakassi Peninsula was an opportunity I would not miss. I would not fold my hands this time around and watch things happen. I would not just stand by and watch events unfold. Somebody needed to take control of the situation before anything happened. If nobody did, anything could happen. I was determined to be that somebody. After all, I had for some twenty-three years been on this mission. Now was the time to exploit the situation to the fullest. But fishermen communities were already threatening to complicate matters for me by claiming ownership of my motherland.

I could not let that happen. It would be a tragic betrayal of my people. I needed to do everything possible to check that threat and stop the spread of that false impression. But how was I to achieve this without creating another conflict? I could not and the resultant conflict between fishermen communities politicians and my Usakedet people; customary owners of Bakassi peninsula would throw the struggle for Bakassi peninsula between Nigeria and Cameroon off balance; relegate it to the background and set the stage for a vicious fratricidal war that might not only have survived the Bakassi ownership saga between Cameroon and Nigeria but that might have in some way affected the final outcome of the Bakassi Peninsula ownership tussle between Cameroon and Nigeria.

CHAPTER TWO

Bakassi Peninsula is no *'terra nullius'.*

Before now, the only ambition I ever had was to get my motherland out of Cameroon, not because of any dislike or hatred for Cameroon. As a matter of fact, I spent the early years of my life in the then Southern Cameroons. I was and remain totally convinced that the continued existence of customary owners of the Bakassi Peninsula; the Usakedet people in Cameroon is very much threatened. I believe that unless something dramatic is done to put an end to the indignities and subtle pressure Cameroon is putting on Usakedet people or some drastic measures brought to bear on Cameroon to protect Usakedet tradition and culture, Usakedet survival as a people in Cameroon cannot be guaranteed. I remain convinced that unless the current trend of events in the Bakassi peninsula is reversed, Cameroon would put an end to Usakedet as a people sooner rather than later. Anyone who has closely followed events in the Bakassi Peninsula in the last four or five decades would agree that the customary owners of the Bakassi Peninsula; the Usakedet people are endangered species in Cameroon. I remain convinced that Usakedet people need to get out of Cameroon in order to retain their identity as a people of Efik ancestry. Bringing Bakassi peninsula back to Nigeria seemed the only way to bring that about.

As already noted destiny often seemed to smile favourably at me. The landing of Nigerian troops in the Bakassi Peninsula seemed like divine intervention. My ambition seemed set to be achieved. But the action of fishermen communities laying spurious ownership claims over the Bakassi Peninsula was beginning to threaten if not frustrate that ambition. Unless that threat was decisively dealt with, fishermen communities laying false ownership claims over the Bakassi Peninsula could kill my dream and life ambition. I needed to do everything possible to correct the emerging erroneous impression that Bakassi peninsula was a 'terra nullius' a 'no man's land'. Fishermen communities and their politicians were somehow under the erroneous impression that Nigeria was in Bakassi peninsula solely to protect Nigerian fishermen. That was partially correct but could not be the primary justification for Nigeria's presence in the Bakassi Peninsula. If it were so, Nigeria would be all over the Gulf of Guinea coastline because Nigerian fishermen occupy virtually the entire Gulf of Guinea coastline. Fishermen communities and their politicians would rather want the world to believe what they believed because it served their purpose. Fishermen communities preferred the other view because it made them feel important and gave them dominion over Bakassi natives and their resources.

I had to check that threat. If I did not tackle the threat fishermen communities were posing in the Bakassi Peninsula, the impression could gain popular acceptance and cause considerable harm to generations of Usakedet people. It could lead to the complete loss of the territory and its enormous resources to fishermen communities; strangers in the Bakassi Peninsula. That would be a price too dear to pay for Usakedet people's re-integration into the Federation of Nigeria. Besides, it could totally derail the struggle for the Bakassi Peninsula. I know Usakedet people well and was certain they would never give up the Bakassi peninsula. I could never be party to such a plot. It would be a tragic betrayal of my people. In the circumstance, I had no option than to fight this falsehood with every weapon I could find in defence of my people. As the only home-grown university graduate at the time from the Bakassi Peninsula, I felt it behoved on me to provide that defence for my people. I saw it thus as a duty that rested squarely on my shoulders. I could not afford to betray or disappoint my people.

But how was I to do battle without weapons? Besides being told from birth that the Bakassi Peninsula belonged to Usakedet people and occasionally as a teenager, being part of the teams sent out to collect all forms of taxes and tenement rates from fishermen communities in the Bakassi Peninsula and beyond, I had never seen a single document saying Bakassi peninsula belonged to the Usakedet people. Now, it seemed I would need to produce such evidence in the face of counter-claims from fishermen communities. I had no idea where to find such evidence but after days worrying about the problem, I decided to travel to the Bakassi Peninsula to discreetly talk to some trusted elders to see if I could get help. I had to be extremely careful. By this time Cameroon, through a vigorous assimilation policy already had many friends and sympathisers among Bakassi people.

On arrival I discreetly spoke to a few elders I could trust without much success. I was about to leave in disappointment when someone suggested I talked to Pa Leonardo Batista de Souza Salvador whom I had never met before. Leo, as Pa Leonardo Batista was fondly called was about eighty-four years old. He was the first Usakedet man who had been to the Whiteman's land. Everyone believed he had received a good education and Pa Leo gave everyone the impression that he was learned. No one knew exactly what he had studied but he spoke several languages although no one knew exactly which ones and how many. The simple fact that he could never speak the Usakedet dialect without adorning his speech with interjections of strange foreign words made Usakedet people believe he was truly learned.

Born in the Bakassi Peninsula of a Portuguese father and Usakedet mother, Leo disappeared from the Bakassi Peninsula at a tender age.

No one, including his mother knew precisely the whereabouts of Leo. Many believed his Portuguese father who had spent years living among Bakassi natives took him away probably to Europe to educate him and make him a gentleman without his mother's knowledge. No one, including his own mother knew of Leo's whereabouts for decades. Then one day, Usakedet people watched in disbelief as Leo disembarked from a ship that sailed into the Bakassi Peninsula from Lisbon. He looked confused and unable to communicate in Usakedet dialect. By this time his poor mother who could have helped him settle down in his motherland had long passed away. Leo nevertheless proved to be an intelligent man and before long, Leo would again pick up his mother tongue and begin to communicate effectively in Usakedet dialect. The only problem was his strange habit of constant interjection of strange foreign words and expressions such 'man talk, man fear', 'man poporapo', 'obey before complain' 'karamba!' 'coma' 'merdes' 'maluco' 'filha da puta' 'puta que pariu', etc into his Usakedet dialect. That sometimes made it hard for Usakedet people to understand him. But no such interjections were made when he spoke English. With time his real name Leonardo Batista de Souza Salvador was forgotten and Leo only occasionally remembered. He simply became known as 'man talk, man fear'; a christening he seemed to adore. Since such christening never seemed to bother him, the name 'man talk man fear' simply stuck.

And Leo gradually gained the people's trust and confidence and established himself as a truly learned man by beginning to unveil some of the astonishing knowledge and experience he had acquired during his long stay probably in Europe. He held long conversations with the people in which he told them exciting stories about the great mysteries of Asia and China. He talked to them about the great powers; Great Britain, France, Germany, the United States of America and the Soviet Union. Leo told Usakedet people exotic tales about Jerusalem, Egypt and even Babylon. He spoke with much enthusiasm about the great wars without saying clearly whether he fought in those wars or not. He talked to the people about everywhere and about everything. Leo seemed like a great consultant; some kind of a professor emeritus.

And Usakedet people reciprocated. They not only learnt to love and respect Leo, they adored him and soon made him their confidant gladly consulting him on every little problem. In Saint Michael's Catholic Church in Odon village, Leo led in the singing of Latin hymns although he never was a member of the church choir. The choir simply sang along with him to avoid disharmony and confusion in God's own House. They would stop singing when he stopped. On a number of occasions, the choir had to stop Leo. If the choir did not 'Man talk, man fear' could go on singing endlessly. He loved Latin hymns but seemed to display some aversion to English hymns for reasons no one knew. His social life too seemed quite interesting. He smoked and was partial to a glass of wine. Above all, Leo loved the company of beautiful women even at age eighty four. It was to Pa Leo that I went to seek help for Bakassi native population.

"Good morning Pa Leo"

I greeted, my voice tinged with a hint of anxiety as a servant ushered me into Pa Leo's living room. It was a well-built, solid house, more than a century old, one of the few homes which had belonged to the white folks during the colonial era. Since Leo had not undertaken any kind of renovation of it, the house still maintained that antique look of homes of the era. From it Pa Leo operated his little provisions store and off- licence bar. From there he attended to both the basic needs of the native population and fishermen communities.

"They call me 'man talk, man fear' around here."

He began, paused for a moment as one who was uncertain of what next to say and then continued.

"I don't really care you know. I think I even love it that way. By the way, I do not recall ever seeing your face around here. Any way, what can I do for you?" he said almost counting his words.

I introduced myself and presented Pa Leo with a bottle of gin. Before intimating him about my mission I requested to speak to him in confidence. Pa Leo quietly ushered me into an inner room and offered me a seat next to him. After a brief exchange of pleasantries I went straight into my mission.

"I am here to seek your help for Usakedet people" I told pa Leo, paused a few seconds and continued.

"As you may be aware, Nigeria has landed troops on a number of fishing settlements in the Bakassi Peninsula. This, I believe is a welcome development. It seems to me that Nigeria's action may be the lead up towards bringing back Bakassi peninsula to Nigeria. When this happens, I want our people to remain customary owners of the Bakassi Peninsula. But this is looking increasingly difficult to guarantee because fishermen communities are now also claiming ownership of the peninsula and I have no evidence to prove that the peninsula belongs to Usakedet people. Can you help find some evidence to support Usakedet claim?"

Pa Leo took a deep look at me for a while and then burst out excited.

"You have come to the right place my son. I will gladly give you all the help you need but you know we cannot discuss such matters here. It is too risky. We will have to go elsewhere. I have heard of the landing and it is the greatest thing that will ever happen to the Bakassi Peninsula. You know our people are going through a lot of trouble. I was born here and I have been living in this enclave since I returned from Europe many years ago. I can tell you the difference between life in this place today and life here several years ago. Nothing would make me happier than to see our people and this land return to our kith and kin in Nigeria."

I took Pa Leo's advice and we discontinued our discussion on Bakassi Peninsula and talked generally about his well-being before I took my leave. We would continue our discussion when "man talk, man fear" came to Calabar ostensibly for medical check up. Excited, I offered to make arrangements for the journey, bear his transport and accommodation cost in Calabar for as long as was necessary. Our Calabar rendezvous took place as planned. For two days in a quiet off the way hotel pa Leo and I worked long hours in search of evidence to prove Usakedet ownership of the Bakassi Peninsula.

"Did you say fishermen communities are now laying claim over the Bakassi Peninsula?" Pa Leo asked.

"Yes" I replied almost instinctively.

"That is not possible." Pa Leo cut in "Fishermen communities have lived with us in peace and harmony for centuries. They would do no such thing. They come to see me daily. I cannot imagine anyone of them making such silly claims. That can only be the handiwork of some powerful politicians who, behaving like little tin gods want to exploit the vacuum in the Bakassi Peninsula to make quick money. In that case, I do not think there is much you and I can do against an onslaught of powerful and influential politicians or what do you think?"

I remained silent for a while pondering over what Leo had just said. The picture Leo just painted terrified me. Leo was right. The threat was not being posed by fishermen communities per se but by unscrupulous politicians claiming to represent fishermen communities. That notwithstanding, I was not going to give up that easily. I was determined to give anyone falsely claiming ownership of Bakassi peninsula a run for their money regardless of how powerful and influential they might be. Leo had spoken of nothing he and I could do but Leo had probably not thought of what Usakedet people working together could do. Besides, I did not consider these unscrupulous politicians as powerful and influential as Leo believed them to be. If only I could find some evidence!

"Pa Leo," I ventured quite unsure of what exactly to say "You and I may not be able to do much but Usakedet people working together could move mountains. I have strong faith in our people. If only we could find some evidence, some documentary evidence to prove that Usakedet people actually own the Bakassi Peninsula."

"Abundant evidence you shall have my son," Pa Leo cut in. "I have my fear though" Leo sounded really anxious.

"Fears, what fears?" I enquired

"Yes, fears, fears about Nigeria. Take a look at the genesis of this problem, for example. You'll find that the problem would never have existed if Nigeria had seized all the opportunities she has had to deal with this problem," Leo snapped and quickly resumed.

"As you may be aware, the Bakassi Peninsula was part of Old Calabar in the Southern Protectorate of Nigeria until Great Britain; a tiny island nation whose seafaring abilities, world wide colonisation enterprise and economic domination brought her great fame and reputation gave the Bakassi Peninsula out to Germany; a nation renowned for her order, discipline and hard work in 1913. Since then the Bakassi Peninsula has swung from Nigeria to Britain to Germany to Cameroon to Britain to Nigeria to Cameroon and now, hopefully back to Nigeria. We pray that this may be the last movement the Bakassi Peninsula would make. You are of course aware that the Bakassi Peninsula was part of Southern Cameroons that was administered as part of Nigeria up to 1959. You will also recall that in 1961 the United Nations conducted a plebiscite in the territory to enable the people to determine whether they wished to remain in the Federation of Nigeria or to join the French Republic of Cameroun. You must also be aware that Southern Cameroonians rejected Nigeria and voted to join the French Republic of Cameroun. We lost. Had the plebiscite in Southern Cameroons favoured Nigeria like the plebiscite in Northern Cameroons did, the Bakassi Peninsula crisis would never have happened. The Bakassi Peninsula including the entire Southern Cameroons; today Southern and North Western Regions of the Republic of Cameroon would have been part of the Federation of Nigeria today."

"So why did Nigeria lose?" I questioned.

"Geo-political rivalries; geo-political rivalries in Nigeria my son, coupled with the lack of foresight and the inexperience of the political class can be said to have been responsible. According to wild-eyed conspiracy theories, prominent politicians from various parts of Nigeria appear to have been involved in a conspiracy to ensure that Southern Cameroons never became part of the Federation of Nigeria after they had earlier ensured that Northern Cameroons voted to join Nigeria."

"Strange isn't it? How could politicians do such a cruel thing to their own country?" I asked naively.

"Selfish geo-politics my son, you would find it difficult to believe but a little scrutiny will bring home the logic behind this seemingly senseless reasoning," Leo replied and continued

"You see, if Northern Cameroons became part of Nigeria, it would become part of the Northern Region. It would enlarge the region and increase its resource base and population. Northern politicians toiled endlessly to ensure that they added Northern Cameroons; today's Adamawa and Taraba states of Nigeria to the Northern Region. If Southern Cameroons on the other hand that included the Bakassi Peninsula became part of Nigeria, it would become part of the Eastern Region. It would equally enlarge the Eastern Region and increase its resource base and population. Given the enormous resources in the Bakassi Peninsula, such a merger could dramatically alter the political and economic landscape and tilt the balance heavily in favour of the Eastern Region, both in terms of population and resources. Such an outcome, it was believed, would be a threat to the Northern and Western Regions and shockingly too, the Eastern Region. The Northern and Western Regions are said to have succeeded in making leaders of the Eastern Region believe that if the Southern Cameroons were allowed to join the Eastern Region, they that is, the Southern Cameroons were likely to join forces with the Calabar, Ogoja and Rivers Provinces to strengthen the already existing agitation in these provinces for the creation of another region from the Eastern Region since Southern Cameroons was contiguous to these provinces. The Eastern Region leadership is said to have bought this propaganda and thus did nothing to bring Southern Cameroons into Nigeria."

"Does this mean politicians from these regions worked against Southern Cameroons becoming part of Nigeria?" I asked.

"Those politicians were said to have done a little more than that my son. It was a tri-partite conspiracy that was said to have been masterminded by the North, supported by the West and endorsed by the East. Nigeria has always been renowned for the constant competition and rivalry among its constituent regions; not for cooperation. This strange cooperation in effect shot Nigeria in the foot."

"Why?" I cried..

"Politics, politics, politics," Leo bellowed, pausing momentarily before continuing.

"That however does not appear to be the only conspiracy theory regarding why Nigeria lost Southern Cameroon. Speak to some Cameroonians today and they will tell you they hold Nigerian traders who dominated both the public and the commercial sectors in Southern Cameroons during British colonial rule responsible for the failure of Southern Cameroonians to vote for union with Nigeria during the 1961 United Nations plebiscite. A Cameroonian once told me that his kinsmen still nurse unpleasant memories of how Nigerian traders in Cameroon used sharp business practices and highly questionable tactics to impose high prices on naïve Cameroonian clients. As a result, unsuspecting clients often fell victim to this under hand market strategies by paying much higher prices for commodities that were sometimes worthless or worth much less. If the buyer tried to protest, seek a better deal or remonstrate in any way, the buyer risked being beaten up. Quite often these intolerant traders would threaten their clients and literally force them to pay arbitrary prices. This high handedness did little to endear Nigeria to Southern Cameroonians. Thus, when the time came for Southern Cameroonians to decide their fate, they voted not with their heads but with their hearts, not for the devil they knew but for the angel they did not know. Nigerians once again shot Nigeria in the foot."

I listened with rapt attention as Leo resumed his narrative this time reading from some printed material he had just pulled out of his briefcase.

"Political analysts also believe that the loss of Southern Cameroons might not have been unconnected with the crisis in the Eastern Region's House of Assembly where nine out of the thirteen members of that Assembly from Southern Cameroons pulled out of the National Congress of Nigeria and Cameroon Citizens; (NCNC) the party on whose platform they had been elected to the Assembly on the grounds that they were not Nigerians. The inability of the leadership of the Eastern House of Assembly to successfully deal with the crisis would lead to the dismissal of the only Southern Cameroonian in the Region's Executive Council and trigger a change of the party's name. Tension in the Assembly would deteriorate to the point where Southern Cameroons would demand the unconditional withdrawal of her members from the Eastern Region's House of Assembly. Great Britain, the colonial master would oblige and turn Southern Cameroons into a semi-autonomous Region with its own House of Assembly and Executive Council within the Federation of Nigeria. It does not seem unlikely that the experience of Southern Cameroonians in the Eastern Region's House of Assembly may have significantly contributed to Southern Cameroon's rejection of Nigeria during the U. N. Plebiscite in 1961." (1)

Leo paused; looking extremely tired but surprisingly tried to continue. I could not let him continue seeing how tired he looked. I cut in.

"Pa Leo, trying to unravel the veracity of this complex pot of wild-eyed conspiracy theories would be like trying to understand the numerous mysteries of Christianity. You were bound to come face to face with a mountain of contradictions and unverifiable theories and hypotheses. It would be a pure waste of time and energy and would serve no useful purpose. The truth about these conspiracy theories may never be known. It does however appear safe to say that Nigeria lost Southern Cameroons and the Bakassi Peninsula with it as a result of conflicting self-interests; regional, personal, ethnic and political rivalries as well as manipulations and conspiracies in Nigeria. It also seems safe to conclude that Southern Cameroons failed to become part of Nigeria because Nigeria wanted it to be so. Nigeria's reaction to the outcome of that plebiscite tends to give credence to such a conclusion. While the Republic of Cameroun reacted angrily to the loss of Northern Cameroons and even threatened to take Nigeria to the International Court of Justice, no tear was shed in Nigeria for the loss of Southern Cameroons."

Whether these conspiracies theories are true or not we may never know but sitting down there listening to Pa Leo's narrative made me sick. I however felt that if the deed had been done it served no useful purpose dwelling on the past. What had been done, if it had been done, had been done. What mattered now was evidence to prove that Usakedet people own the Bakassi Peninsula. But Pa Leo seemed visibly exhausted and I thought it would be wise to discontinue the session. It was obvious Pa Leo needed to rest. So I suggested we called it a date and continue the next day and Pa Leo agreed.

Our meeting the following day kicked off as agreed. Pa Leo, now refreshed and energized went straight to business after a few drinks and pleasantries.

"Today we will concentrate on evidence in support of Usakedet ownership of the Bakassi Peninsula. For this reason, I have brought with me a report that shows how this ownership controversy was dealt with in the colonial era. I am sure by the time we go through this report we will have a clear idea about how the dispute was resolved in colonial times."

As he spoke Pa Leo brought out two reports from his briefcase. The first report was entitled *Isangele Community*; an Intelligence Report on the Usakedet people, by Mr. H. O. Anderson; a British citizen who worked in the Bakassi Peninsula as an Assistant District Officer during British colonial rule. The second was a publication entitled *Ekpe in the Rio Del Rey*, by Dr. Keith Nicklin. Leo began to read directly from Anderson's Report.

> "This volume embraces the Isangele (Usakedet) kindred comprising the four village groups of Efik ancestry and one village group of Balondo heritage. The sixth village group used to be a settlement of members of the family of Prince Archibong of Calabar that became known as Archibong town. The whole community is formed of fishermen who are almost as at home in their canoes than on land." (2)

Pa Leo took a deep breath and continued,

> "The people inhabiting this area are virile and comparatively healthy as should be expected from the life they lead. They all have small farms, but the soil, which is almost purely sand is not fertile and sufficient food cannot be grown. Fish is sold and exchanged for food at Ikang and Calabar. The housing conditions are a great improvement on the rest of the division. (Kumba division) Houses are well-built and often have very well made lattice-work verandas. A number of houses have zinc-roofs and the walls are of mud instead of tree bark or mats as is usual in this division." (3)

"Go on Pa Leo" I urged seemingly elated.

"Christianity is quite general in the area. The English language is generally spoken in all the villages. Although almost the whole population is formed of fishing people yet the social progress is greater in this area than anywhere else in the division. Through marketing their fish in Ikang and Calabar in Nigeria, they come into contact with more progressive and better educated people and have thus been influenced. Both men and women in Isangele (Usakedet) dress quite well and their manners are good. The people of Archibong town are stubborn, take no notice of Native Court judgements and often evade arrest by escaping to Calabar and resisting court messengers but those of the other village groups are much more law abiding and tractable." (4)

"Amazing" I interjected compelling Leo to pause for a moment before resuming.

"The unit under report is small, but apart from the village group of Balondo origin the remaining villages in the area have no relationship with the peoples of Cameroon. The area occupied by Isangele (Usakedet) people is difficult to estimate as in the northern part the boundary lies in almost uninhabited bush and is not properly known, while in the south the boundary is with the fishermen who have settled in the mangrove creeks, some of whose land is claimed by Usakedet people. It is estimated that the area of the mainland owned by Usakedet people is about eight miles square or 64 square miles."(5)

Turning to *Ekpe in Rio Del Rey* Pa Leo read a short passage on the social structure of the Usakedet people.

"The social structure of the people of cross river and Rio Del Rey is dominated by the segmented lineage principle. Political organisation is a cephalous and the function of the village chief is largely ritual or ceremonial. Political authority is vested in a council of village elders and individual elders enhance their prestige and wield what limited power they have largely by virtue of their membership of non-kin-based associations, connected with activities such as warfare, hunting, moral instruction of the young, social control and recreation. Women have equivalent institutions which are generally perceived to be less prestigious." (6)

"Let me add, that personal achievement confers a degree of power and recognition to individuals in the Bakassi Peninsula. Membership of the 'Leopard Spirit Cult'; 'EKPE' for example is recognized as a mark of success and honour. The head of that cult; the IYAMBA, wields a lot more power than the village head. Membership of certain female associations also confers a degree of importance to women in our land. More importantly, women, not men guarantee the defence of the land in times of war. Men go to war and women guarantee victory. I hope you do understand?"

I certainly did not understand that bit but this was no time to interrupt Pa Leo. I did nevertheless realise that Leo was trying to introduce a new dimension into our discussion. Whatever it was, I was sure I could find out from my mother the real import of that reference to women guaranteeing victory later. Luckily, I still had one living. So, I nodded in the affirmative and Pa Leo continued.

"The history of Bakassi Peninsula and Usakedet people is well remembered and documented. It goes as far back as the fifteenth century when Usakedet people were said to have first settled in

Uruan, like all other peoples of Efik ancestry. From Uruan Usakedet people moved southwards because while they were still around Uruan, news came that White men had been sited on the coast. By this time, no European had ever been seen or heard of by Usakedet people. Curious to meet the White men, Usakedet people decided to sail down the Cross River to the coast. On getting to Bonny, they were said to have been fascinated by the guns, tobacco, salt, gin and clothes brought by Europeans. In their excitement they tried to persuade the Europeans to sail up the Cross River to Uruan but were disappointed that Europeans could not go to Uruan because there was not enough wind to take their boats up the Cross River."

"So Usakedet people decided to go after the Whiteman?" I asked.

"Not exactly", Leo replied and resumed reading from his intelligence report.

"Usakedet people were so impressed by what they had seen that they decided to move closer to the coast in order to get closer to Europeans. The entire people set off down the Cross River and founded a new settlement at Udah that was relatively close to the coast. From Udah they could easily reach the coast and trade with the Whiteman. But they found already settled in Udah two different groups of people; the Udahs and the Ewangs. Shortly after settling in Udah, war broke out between the Udahs and the Ewangs. Hostilities continued for a prolonged period with none of the belligerents getting the upper hand until Usakedet people decided to throw their weight behind the Udah by introducing them to the use of guns Usakedet people had acquired from Europeans. With such superior firepower the Ewangs were easily subdued and compelled to make peace. But the Ewangs soon found out who had been responsible for their defeat and humiliation and decided to pay Usakedet people in their own coins by attacking them. The plan leaked and before the Ewangs could get to the Whiteman to obtain similar or superior weapons to teach Usakedet people a lesson, a terrified Usakedet people decided to take to their heels and flee from Udah in the middle of the night in search of a more peaceful home unmindful of the English adage 'he who fights and runs away stands to fight another day.' No one at the time believed that they would someday face a crisis they would be unable to run away from in their new home. The land Usakedet people left behind in Udah remains to date unoccupied, perhaps awaiting their return.

This new movement would lead Usakedet people into the Bakassi Peninsula where they first settled at a place called NDO. However, on arrival at NDO, it was discovered that some of their boats had not made the journey to NDO. These boats apparently had gone missing during the night crossing of the Calabar channel. It has been widely speculated that some of the missing boats might have taken the wrong direction and landed around Creek town and its environs. The names of people living around Creek town bear striking resemblance to names Usakedet people bear. But Usakedet people's sojourn in NDO was strikingly also very short. The absence of potable water would soon force the entire population to once again be on the move in search of potable water and a more dependable permanent home. That search came to its definitive end at the head of Rio Del Rey where the villages of Odon, Amoto, Efut Inwang (Bateka), Aqua and Archibong town are located. Wherever Usakedet people sojourned, they left behind easily identifiable footprints and historical relics that are characteristic of Usakedet way of life. From the present mainland location, Usakedet people have been able to exercise control over the entire waters of the Bakassi Peninsula and its environs without serious challenge from anywhere or anybody for centuries."

"Eh em em" I tried to say something but Leo butt in an emphatic "hold it" manner.

I do not know what I was thinking not to notice that we had been talking for more than five hours from nine in the morning. In spite of Pa Leo's enthusiasm to carry on, he was visibly tired and I felt so sorry that I did not realise in time that Leo was showing signs of fatigue. I was so carried away that all I wanted was for Leo to continue his narrative. We had been talking for more that five hours already and it should have been obvious to me that Leo would need a rest or even call it a day. So, I suggested we called it a day but Leo refused. He wanted to have it done with. Then I suggested we went for lunch and resume thereafter. That worked but by the time we were through with lunch Pa Leo suggested we should have a little nap and resume at night. I had a two-hour nap and Pa Leo slept for four. When he got up a few minutes past eight at night he looked refreshed and energized. I was glad to see him so refreshed.

"You wanted to ask me a question before we went for lunch?"

"Yes Pa Leo," I replied and went on, "You said that Usakedet people have from the present location administered the entire Bakassi Peninsula without serious challenges from any individual or group. How did they with such a small population manage to control such a large territory and its huge population?"

"I expected that question," Leo cut in and immediately continued.

"For centuries Usakedet people have been associated with strange and mysterious powers. News of their extraordinary prowess is said to have reached the four corners of the earth. An air of awe and mystery surrounds the homeland; Bakassi Peninsula. Among Efik speaking people, Usakedet people are known to possess some of the most sophisticated and awesome witchcraft that ever existed. There is profuse reference to this outrageous reputation in Efik oral and written literature. This dreadful reputation has tended to terrify and unduly instil fear in people who have to do business with the Usakedet people especially when it has to do with the use of supernatural powers. This awesome reputation for extra-ordinary and mysterious powers continues to date to attract seekers of supernatural powers to the Bakassi Peninsula. Hardly a month passes by without people of diverse socio-economic and political status sneaking into the Bakassi Peninsula in search of one form of power or the other. People of all walks of life, including "men-of-god" come to Bakassi peninsula in search of spiritual intervention in their lives. Some come to have a work-place problem taken care off, and others come in search of political power, love, wealth and good fortune." Leo affirmed.

"Does that mean Usakedet people can bring this awesome reputation to bear on any situation?" I asked not instinctively but in the secret hope of using such traditional powers to achieve our dream.

Leo nodded in agreement apparently sensing what was on my mind and quickly resumed.

"You must not forget that Usakedet people are not just renowned for their awesome reputation for mysterious powers, Usakedet people are more significantly renowned and universally acknowledged as custodians of the secrets of the 'Leopard Spirit Cult' called *Ekpe* in Efik language. *Ekpe* is the most prestigious socio-political association in the Efik world and beyond. Usakedet people are universally recognized as the custodians of the secrets of this 'Leopard Spirit Cult'. Because of *Ekpe* Usakedet is regarded in Thompson's *Flash of the Spirit* among some Afro-Cubans ... as a holy city where the first secrets of God were revealed by the banks of the River Ndian creek (Abakua: River Odan,) imaginatively further creolised by Christians as the River Jordan.

Usakedet people have made enormous contribution to Efik tradition and culture. As founders and custodians of the secrets of *Ekpe*, Usakedet people gave the Efik nation its most significant symbol. Today, *Ekpe* all over the world derive their authority from the Usakedet people. No *Ekpe*, *anywhere* in the world, is superior to *Ekpe* in the Bakassi Peninsula. No one initiated into the 'Leopard Spirit Cult' "Ekpe" outside the Bakassi Peninsula; the homeland of the Usakedet people can, regardless of the level they might have attained in the society elsewhere, occupy certain seats in the *Ekpe* shrine in Usakedet. Such persons are often not permitted to participate in certain ceremonies in Usakedet *Ekpe*. To do so, they may be required to perform rites that could tantamount to a re-initiation."

Hearing this, I recalled an incident I witnessed several years earlier during the funeral rites of a prominent Bakassi native. The deceased children, grand children and friends; all prominent persons had come to Usakedet (Isangele) from Calabar to attend the funeral but were not allowed to remain in the *Ekpe* shrine to witness the initiation of new members, despite the fact that they were all senior members of *Ekpe* in Calabar. The reason I would learn was that they had not been initiated into Usakedet *Ekpe* and so could not witness or take part in certain *Ekpe* ceremonies. The deceased children and their mother felt so embarrassed and humiliated that they immediately packed their bag and baggage and returned to Calabar before the funeral rites of their grand father could be concluded.

Pa Leo simply smiled and resumed his narrative.

"Usakedet people have for centuries been Lords and Masters of the Bakassi Peninsula. During the many centuries of their existence in the Bakassi Peninsula, there has never been any serious challenge to Usakedet hegemony over the Bakassi Peninsula. Anderson's Report clearly shows that Usakedet people first settled in the Bakassi Peninsula in the early fifteenth century when the Portuguese first arrived in the peninsula. Eventually, their Efiat cousins came to join them and gradually other ethnic groups across Nigeria and beyond have come to fish in the peninsula. Usakedet rule over the fishermen population has always been generous, benevolent and most enlightened. And throughout the centuries, there has never been any serious challenge to Usakedet hegemony in the Bakassi Peninsula.

The fishermen population has always paid homage to Usakedet people whom they have always recognized as customary owners of the peninsula. Fishermen communities and Usakedet people have always forged fraternal relations that were indicative of the common bond existing between them. Whenever disputes arose within fishermen communities, such disputes were brought to Usakedet people for settlement. Fishermen communities brought their disputes to Usakedet people because they recognized Usakedet people as landlords of the Bakassi Peninsula. And on such occasions whatever decision the Usakedet people reached was respected by the fishermen."

To reinforce this last point, Pa Leo handed over to me a copy of a letter written in 1988 by fishermen from "Ine Atayo" fishing settlement calling on Usakedet people to urgently intervene in a dispute between them and other fishermen communities.

"This letter," Pa Leo said "is a clear testimony of the landlord-tenant relationship that has always subsisted between Usakedet people and the teeming fishermen population in the Bakassi Peninsula. From what you are telling me it appears unscrupulous politicians want to wave aside such incontrovertible evidence and lay spurious ownership claims over the Bakassi Peninsula. You must not let them get away with it."

I assured Pa Leo that I would do everything within my powers to ensure that no stranger took control of Usakedet land and Pa Leo continued.

"Also note that whenever the fishing season went bad and the catch was poor, as occasionally did happen, fishermen communities often came running to Usakedet people begging them to perform traditional sacrifices to sea deities for improvement in the catch and for a generally better fishing season because only customary owners of the peninsula could perform such elaborate traditional rites. Usakedet people would oblige and carry out sophisticated traditional rites and ceremonies after fishermen communities had met substantial demands required for such ceremonies. Such collaboration often left everyone happy and helped to sustain the harmonious and peaceful co-existence that was characteristic of life in the territory before the advent of Cameroon."

As Leo spoke, I recalled how my mother; Mma Obot Antigha Oku would dress colourfully before taking her place as priestess of "Ate Ering Ata", one of the principal sea deities of the Bakassi Peninsula in the boat conveying people to sea to offer sacrifice to "Ate Ering Ata" and wondered how these same fishermen could turn around to contest ownership of that same Bakassi Peninsula. It seemed a strange way to show gratitude. I was still buried in these thoughts when Pa Leo resumed.

"The outbreak of hostilities between Nigeria and Cameroon over the ownership of Bakassi Peninsula is however not the first time fishermen communities would try to claim ownership of the Bakassi Peninsula. Centuries earlier, some fishermen led by one Eket man, Abana Ntuen Umoh; founder of Abana fishing settlement made unsuccessful attempts to claim ownership of some fishing settlements in the Bakassi Peninsula. The crisis was resolved only after Abana Ntuen Umoh had taken an oath never to try to claim ownership of any piece of Bakassi peninsula again. More recently, between 1886 and 1900, renegade Prince Archibong Edem of Calabar whose temperament was a source of deep concern for the Efik world, woefully failed in his misguided effort to subdue the Usakedet people and forcefully settle in what today is known as Archibong Town. His ill-conceived expedition to forcefully settle in that location ended in disaster as he met a formidable Usakedet force that not only humiliated him but forced him to make peace with Usakedet people before he was allowed to settle in present day Archibong Town."

I was all ears as Pa Leo went on.

"After the First World War, fishermen communities who had rendered significant support to the British in the war against Germany sought to take control of portions of the Bakassi Peninsula as compensation for the support they gave British colonial administration. Usakedet people vehemently challenged and resisted any attempt to transfer or make outright concession of any part of Bakassi peninsula to any other peoples."

Again, Pa Leo read from Anderson's Report.

> "The reason for this was probably that they; Isangele (Usakedet) people feared that their own fishing rights would be disturbed by such a transfer and the fact that they had some fishing camps themselves among the fish towns which they naturally did not wish to lose made the situation more difficult." (7)

Managing the fishermen population had also never been easy. Colonial reports speak of the stubbornness of members of fishermen communities who when summoned to testify on the ownership of the Bakassi Peninsula controversy would;

> "During the intelligence enquiries the village heads of some of these fish towns would return to their homes and

never show up at the peninsula until they were sure colonial officers had returned to their base. When asked to come and see the intelligence officer, they sent ready excuses. The council would neither deny nor confirm the story in the absence of the village head. Nonetheless, a member of a fishermen community admitted before all present that Usakedet people owned the land and that they the fishermen were settlers stressing that Isangele (Usakedet) people performed the annual sacrifice to sea deities for heavy catch as owners of the land." (8)

To prove that fishermen communities were not permanent residents of the Bakassi Peninsula as they claimed pa Leo read out the following passage;

"My information about the fishing settlements, I fear is so vague as to be valueless, but pending further on the spot investigation, I believe the fishing settlements to be recently formed, temporary and heterogeneous settlements of various clans from Nigeria... I shall endeavour to find out here whether the respective clans are in the habit of operating from one fishing port every year or whether they use different bases as the spirit of the season moves on" (9)

The report recommends;

"It follows that provided Isangele (Usakedet) people and the fish town area remain in the same province the present harmony of fishing rights will continue. Should the two be separated there is every chance of a protracted inter-communal dispute in which the decision could not be made effective unless the fish town area was under close control." (10)

Finally, after an on-the-spot investigation had been conducted, colonial authorities arrived at the following conclusion;

> "The conclusion on the facts of settlement and fishing rights appears to be that the original Isangele (Usakedet) people were the first to settle and fish in the area but planted only two settlements and these temporarily... Isangele people have lived for generations on fishing and gradually their relatives from Efiat were allowed to settle temporarily at the beginning of each fishing season and that these settlers gave gifts of bags of fish to Isangele (Usakedet) people." (11)

"There" pa Leo told me "is the evidence you will need to defend this land and your people. Go and do not look back"

I thanked pa Leo immensely and made arrangements for his return to the Bakassi Peninsula the next day. Before taking my leave I gave him my word that I will not relent until Bakassi peninsula was free. Pa Leo had been of incalculable help. It was now left to me to make judicious use of the knowledge I had just acquired. The various sessions I had with Leo had clearly showed the landlord-tenant relationship that had always subsisted in Bakassi peninsula between fishermen communities and Usakedet people. That *modus vivendi* had also served everyone well. Going by the incontrovertible evidence presented by Pa Leo, the question of ownership of Bakassi peninsula among the various clans of Efik extraction had been settled centuries ago. Unscrupulous politicians would exploit the vacuum created by the Bakassi crisis to reopen a wound that had long healed.

These opportunistic politicians would take their claim to annoying heights. Engineers, doctors, nurses, messengers and persons of undistinguishable careers would turn historians overnight and make amazing efforts to rewrite the history of Bakassi peninsula. Some would claim that around 1883 Bakassi peninsula was 'stormed and brought into conformity' and that the military action led to the signing of some capitulation agreement between the Usakedet people and the Efik nation. That is fiction not history. Usakedet people have never signed any agreement with any people regarding the ownership of the Bakassi Peninsula. Even when these writers are compelled to admit that Usakedet people sacked their Efik cousins around 1886 in the Bakassi peninsula, they must add that Usakedet people did it with the help of some colonial power. Thank God! At least they admitted. This admission appears to be reference to the defeat of Prince Archibong Edem which we have already alluded to above. Although Efik writers claim that the fish settlements in Bakassi peninsula were not within the jurisdiction of the Usakedet people they nevertheless admit that Usakedet people were often called upon to perform annual traditional rites to appease sea deities in the Bakassi Peninsula. They however would like to play down the significance of such traditional rites in Efik tradition and culture by trying to make their reader believe that Usakedet people were mere adepts in black magic; indeed magicians who were invited to perform such significant traditional rites on someone else's land. How strange!

Efik writers and politicians even tried to conjure a meaning for the word 'Bakassi'. In their effort to trace the origin of the word 'Bakassi' they came out with meanings that revealed a rich and very creative imagination. They claimed that the word 'Bakassi' originates from the Efik expression "Akai Abasi Eke" roughly translated 'the forest of Abasi Eke'. According to this hypothesis the Whiteman simply could not pronounce 'Akai Abasi Eke'. So the Whiteman simply called it Bakassi. This is nonsense. In the first place "Akai Abasi Eke" and "Bakassi" do not rhyme. The truth about the matter is that 'Bakassi' simply means 'Go back home' that is 'Go back to where you came from' in both ancient and contemporary Usakedet dialect. Although research is still on going to find out why the peninsula became known as Bakassi Peninsula, it does not appear one might need a very high sense of imagination to guess what probably might have led Europeans to call that territory Bakassi Peninsula. The fact too that the other two peninsulas "Jock" and "Erong" in the area and most prominent waterways in Bakassi peninsula such as Ofa, Andonkot, urufian etc derive their names from the Usakedet dialect seems to reinforce the claim that Bakassi Peninsula derives its name from the Usakedet word 'baka-asi' 'go back home' thus also reaffirming the claim that the Bakassi Peninsula belongs to the Usakedet (Isangele) people. Fishing settlements in the Peninsula and throughout the Gulf of Guinea are named after individuals or groups that establish them as a mark of honour and recognition. Names of fishing settlements do not imply ownership of the locations where these fishing settlements are established. If it were so, Nigeria would own the entire Gulf of Guinea coastline because Nigerian fishing settlements litter the entire coastline.

Armed with this history, I went into battle. I would spare no effort and leave no stone unturned in my effort to try to publicize the history of the Bakassi Peninsula and to stress Usakedet ownership of the territory. It turned out to be an up-hill task; an extremely difficult mission. My message ran against the interest and ambition of many whose sole desire was to draw the wool over the eyes of the world and claim ownership of the Bakassi Peninsula. Opposition notwithstanding I devoted as much time as I possibly could to tell Usakedet story to friends and foes alike. I needed to check the spread of the false claim that Bakassi peninsula belonged to fishermen communities or that Bakassi peninsula was a no man's land; a *'terra nullius'* from gaining ground. I however had one huge constraint. Although I needed to counter these false claims, I could not go public with my history.

Firstly, being a civil servant, I could not grant press interviews or openly comment on sensitive national issues. Bakassi peninsula crisis was one truly sensitive national issue. Besides such constraints, one could find oneself unintentionally providing information that could serve the interest of the adversary. Because of such considerations, I had to be extremely circumspect. I never granted interviews, never wrote or commented on articles about the Bakassi crisis in magazine or the dailies and never even joined my colleagues in the FORUM where Bakassi crisis was a daily subject of discussion for our Foreign Service Officers. Let me confess here however, that I found some of the contributions of my colleagues in the Forum quite enlightening. Indeed, some of those contributions were simply brilliant. Others however chose to follow their hearts not their heads and provided the FORUM readership with mere expressions of sentiments and old fashioned and outdated notions of patriotism. For those colleagues who might have felt disappointed that I made no contributions to the debate knowing I come from Bakassi, I hope they now understand why I had to disappoint them.

Due to such constraints I had to reduce my duty to that of a petitioner; a reputation I strongly detest but had to bear. My campaign thus became confined to quietly drawing attention and writing memoranda and petitions. I would draw attention to policies I felt did not serve the interest of my people or could be detrimental to Nigeria's interest in the Bakassi Peninsula. Even that would put me on the collision path with fishermen communities and desperate politicians who were bent on expropriating the enormous resources of the peninsula. To them, I was an enemy; a traitor and an unpatriotic Nigerian. These people would have wished that I turned a tolerant eye and allow them expropriate the land and resources of my motherland. Most reacted with determined opposition and sometimes outright hostility whenever they saw me or where ever my name was mentioned. Some even tried to destroy my career. As far as I was concerned all that meant little or nothing to me. I was prepared to pay any price in defence of my motherland. Thus, I carried the history of Bakassi peninsula everywhere infuriating fishermen communities and unscrupulous politicians.

In the beginning, it seemed so difficult to understand why the Efik nation itself seemed not to share similar ideas with me on Bakassi crisis, Indeed, I could not understand why everyone seemed so unsympathetic to Usakedet cause. I simply could not understand why anyone could have any other interest other than the return of the Bakassi Peninsula to Nigeria. It was only much later that it began to dawn on me that someone could be nursing expansionist ambition in Bakassi peninsula. Even so, the last people I expected to nurse such feelings were Efik people on whom the Usakedet people were counting on in their struggle for Bakassi peninsula. As the crisis evolved, it gradually began to dawn on me that the Efik nation could have other ideas. When it came to Bakassi peninsula, some politicians of Efik heritage behaved with arrogance and abrasiveness and without regard to the propriety of their actions. It was simply sad that at a time when every hand needed to be on deck, unscrupulous politicians and others of uncertain professions and origin would dissipate energy engaging in a totally fruitless struggle for ownership of the Bakassi Peninsula, completely ignoring the potential inherent in such situations to derail the principal goal of the struggle.

Nigeria's refusal to listen to Usakedet concerns would encourage and embolden fishermen communities and unscrupulous individuals and groups who saw the outbreak of hostilities in the Bakassi Peninsula as an opportunity to make money. They would turn a liberation struggle into a viable commercial venture. This sad turn of events would take steam out of the struggle for the Bakassi Peninsula and open up a new front on the wings of the crisis between Nigeria and Cameroon over the ownership of Bakassi peninsula. This tragic turn of events would complicate matters for me who hardly knew how to go about achieving my life's ambition and dream to bring my motherland back to my fatherland. The struggle for Bakassi peninsula between different clans of Efik extraction and others of uncertain heritage would throw a spanner into the wheels of my dream and become one huge distraction that Nigeria would have been better off without in her attempt to regain sovereignty over the Bakassi Peninsula.

CHAPTER THREE
Providence Sets the Agenda.

"Go and do not look back." These were Pa Leo's last words to me. For me these were powerful words indeed. These words were more like an injunction, a mandate or a commission. For someone who had embarked on a self-appointed mission, purely from a personal conviction, without any mandate from his people, these words would become a great source of inspiration. Henceforth, at moments of deep frustration and seemingly insurmountable difficulties, these words would ring in my ears and hope would again be rekindled in my mission.

Before now it had been different. Some twenty-three years before the outbreak of the Bakassi Peninsula crisis in 1993 when I embarked on the mission to get Usakedet people and the Bakassi Peninsula back to Nigeria, I had no such mandate. Now, I had the great feeling that I had been given a clear mandate and that boosted my ego and confidence. For a young man who only became aware that Nigeria and Cameroon were contesting ownership of the Bakassi Peninsula in his early twenties by accident, it was indeed a feeling that made me feel good. I only become aware of this fact when I returned to the Bakassi Peninsula after some fifteen years or so of absence from the territory. That home-coming, occurring at the end of the secessionist war in Nigeria brought me face to face with the misery and hopelessness that life had become in the peninsula. Life in the Bakassi Peninsula had become intolerable as a result of the sad experiences of Bakassi inhabitants during and in the aftermath of the Nigerian civil war. Subtle pressure and acts of indignity by the new authorities in the peninsula would further complicate the life of fishermen communities and Bakassi natives.

Bakassi natives and fishermen communities saw hell during and in the immediate aftermath of the Nigerian civil war when the Bakassi Peninsula was transformed into a safe haven for renegade soldiers, sea pirates and armed robbers. From their hide-outs in the maze of creeks and islands in the peninsula, these criminals carried out all sorts of nefarious activities. They invaded and rampaged through villages, stealing, harassing the innocent, brutalizing men and raping women. Occasionally, they killed their victims. From their hide outs in the maze of the mangrove swamp forests, sea pirates pounced on innocent traders commuting between Nigeria and Cameroon through the Bakassi Peninsula dispossessing them of their goods and valuables.

These invasions reached their crescendo in the early seventies when on a number of occasions, persons believed to be renegade soldiers raided villages in the Bakassi Peninsula, looting homes, raping young women, beating up chiefs and elders they suspected of sympathy or collaboration with the 'enemy' and occasionally killing innocent people. On one such occasion, the activities of these unwelcomed visitors led to the death of the most prominent Bakassi son; Chief Henry Anjeh Usim, paramount ruler-elect of the Bakassi Peninsula in December 1971. On another occasion, these renegade soldiers shot and killed a prominent Bakassi native woman leader; Madam Oku Efa. On yet another occasion, these invaders stabbed a seven-month pregnant woman; Madam Adiaha Dan to death because she resisted being raped. Usakedet people often brought these horrendous crimes to the attention of authorities in Nigerian and Cameroon. On one such occasion they brought their death to Nigerian authorities in Ikang and were advised to take their death and complaints to Cameroon. In Cameroon they were told to take their death and complaints to Nigeria.

It is impossible to convey the horror experienced by Usakedet people and fishermen communities during and in the aftermath of the Nigerian civil war in just a few words. That experience would fill volumes. Suffice it to say that the experience of Bakassi inhabitants during that period increased the fixation I already had to get Bakassi peninsula out of Cameroon. My one-year stopover in Abana and Atabong fishing settlements from September 1970 to September 1971 would bolster my determination to finding a solution to the troubles of my people. That sojourn in Abana and Atabong would make me particularly alive to the terrible dilemma of a people living as neither bat nor bird. That one year of living among fishermen communities in a mix of sand and muddy make-shift structures would turn out to be one instructive year that would awaken my consciousness and set the stage for me to embark on a journey that I had not the slightest idea where it would end.

September 14, 1970 marked the beginning of that tortuous journey on an extremely long and lonesome road. I had barely landed at the Abana fishing settlement to take up appointment as a teacher in a school that had been built through communal effort to carter for the educational needs of children of fishermen communities long before the outbreak of the separatist war in Nigeria. Nigeria had troops stationed in Abana fishing settlement during that fratricidal war. Nigeria pulled out her troops at the end of the war and Cameroon quickly moved in a company of its armed forces and a civil administration into the Bakassi Peninsula as soon as Nigeria moved out.

To continue to run the school, Cameroon needed Efik speaking teachers to facilitate communication with the largely Efik speaking population and pupils. I happened to be available for the job. But the events of September 14th 1970 would terrify me. That fateful day September 14th would mark my first encounter with death. The time was about four o'clock in the evening, barely an hour or two after I disembarked on the sandy beach of Abana fishing port. That was the first time I would be stepping on that sandy beach again after some fifteen years or so of absence. The feeling was clearly that of nostalgia. As I approached the fishermen population on disembarking I recalled with delight that a significant part of my childhood had been spent on that same sandy beach in the company of my beautiful aunt Mma Oyo. I had no foreboding that I would be having a rendezvous with death on that day. Yet, I would witnessed one of the most tragic and totally avoidable waste of human life, and my own life would be put in terrible jeopardy as a result of the reckless and senseless action of Cameroonian soldiers stationed at Abana fishing settlement.

Although the details of the tragic events of that fateful day remain rooted in my memory, it would serve no useful purpose recounting details of the horror of that fateful day here. Suffice it to say that I accompanied Cameroonian soldiers stationed at Abana to Akpankanya; a neighbouring fishing settlement to urge the population to send their children to school because a teacher had arrived. It turned out that the soldiers who were taking me on what to me was a simple familiarisation tour had other ideas. They would use the occasion to harass and molest the fishermen population. On our way back to Abana we had a boat mishap in which an innocent baby girl lost her life. Her crime; her father proved smarter than soldiers. The girl's father had slipped through the back entrance of his hut and disappeared into the mangrove swamp to avoid payment of outrageous levies soldiers had arbitrarily imposed on him. When the soldiers realised that they had been outwitted, they simply took the man's wife and baby girl hostage and added them to their other captives that included human beings, goats, fish and bags of crayfish. Our overloaded boat would capsize on the return voyage to Abana fishing port. Within the few seconds I found myself completely submerged in the Atlantic Ocean, the only thought that came to mind was to bid my mother adieu. I recall vividly saying to her "Oh my mother, so today is my last day." But it was not to be. I had no rendezvous with death. I managed to secure a firm grip of the capsized boat and clung to it until rescue came. This regrettable incident would further give impetus to my passion, indeed obsession to bring the Bakassi Peninsula back to Nigeria.

My stay in Bakassi fishing settlements lasted exactly one year and although I felt extremely happy to go, my heart continued to bleed for the hapless kinsmen I was leaving behind. My one year stay in Bakassi Peninsula did not only make me alive to the need to get the Bakassi Peninsula out of Cameroon, it brought me face to face with the horror of life in the peninsula. Increasingly, the idea of getting the Bakassi Peninsula and the Usakedet people; the only people of Efik extraction located outside the Federation of Nigeria out of Cameroon was becoming an obsession. The more I pondered over it, the more I felt the urgency to get it done with. In spite of my passion, I had not the slightest idea what needed to be done to achieve that goal. Somehow, I believed that something could be done. Hardly did I imagine or even dream that providence would one day bring the Bakassi peninsula under the spotlight and even provide a role for me to play. Hardly did I imagine that that day would come much sooner than I ever could imagine.

Before that could happen trying to influence events that would bring about the desired change would prove more daunting than imagined. In the first place I had no idea how to go about achieving my dream. Besides, I needed to go to higher school and to university.

When it seemed like I had found a leeway, it often turned out to be a mirage, a trip on a lonely and lonesome path. Besides such handicap, I had no real idea about the magnitude of the problem I was about to embark upon. Nonetheless, I seemed sufficiently motivated to carry on. The opportunity came while I was in higher school. As I groped along in what seemed like a wilderness in search of a way forward, I would come to learn of a certain Dr. Ajato Amos who later became known as Professor Amos Gundunu. Professor Gundunu at the time was carrying out some research work on the Bakassi Peninsula. I would learn that the professor had already paid several visits to the peninsula to conduct his research. On one of such visits he had taken a Bakassi native boy along with him to Lagos. I imagined Professor Amos Gundunu could be of help and felt a strong urge to meet him. I would abandon higher school and proceed to Lagos to pursue my dream.

In Lagos, I was delighted and overjoyed to meet Professor Amos Gundunu who equally seemed quite delighted to meet me. What was abundantly clear to me on that day was that I had come to the right place to pursue my dream. I would soon discover that Professor Gundunu not only shared similar ideas with me about the Bakassi peninsula, he was indeed an authority on Bakassi peninsula. His doctoral thesis was said to have been on the history, people, culture and language of the peninsula. Professor Gundunu himself spoke fluent Efik; a condition that made it possible for me to discuss Bakassi peninsula with him even in the market place without bothering about eavesdroppers. My interaction with Professor Gundunu clearly helped advance the cause of my Bakassi dream.

With Etim Anke and Etim Ekpe; the other Bakassi natives I was working with, we did the little we could to advance the Professor's research and promote our dream on Bakassi peninsula throughout the 70s and early 80s. Professor Gundunu on his part did all he could to assist us in every way possible. He gave us both material assistance and the psychological and academic orientation that immensely helped move our dream project forward. It was largely thanks to Professor Gundunu that an indigent student like me managed to sail through university. Now, with hind side, it seems pretty obvious that the undergraduate scholarship I obtained may have been fixed by Professor Gundunu. Without Professor Gundunu's support and orientation, our feeble efforts would have been meaningless. His inspirational role greatly helped boost my knowledge and confidence. Although Professor Gundunu would inexplicably eventually disappear from the scene, Professor Gundunu remains the veritable pioneer and father of the struggle for the Bakassi Peninsula. It is sad that no one thought of bringing Professor Gundunu on board during the Bakassi crisis.

The disappearance of Professor Gundunu from the scene deprived us of his valuable contribution, support and orientation. We now became like veritable sheep without a shepherd. Without Professor Gundunu, my little group's enthusiasm also began to wane. It was clear that we needed someone like Professor Gundunu to continue to motivate and orient us. Unfortunately we could not find one devoted man like Professor Gundunu. Most people I tried to reach out to seemed to want to exploit the situation for their personal gains. The unpredictable political environment in Nigeria resulting from constant military interventions in the polity did not also help the situation. Rather, it made our dream quite difficult and cumbersome to achieve. Each new regime brought with it new actors who quite often had little sympathy or understanding of the Bakassi situation. Under such circumstances, achieving our dream became a real nightmare. As a result our little group collapsed.

I refused to give up the dream. I went on, hoping to secure the support of the Efik world. But the Efik nation I hoped to count on seemed unprepared for my mission. The Efik nation at the time hardly seemed to understand the problem. I recall time and time when I tried to approach the Efik throne to present the Bakassi peninsula situation without success. The protocol was not only expensive; it was time wasting and cumbersome. As an undergraduate who was managing to stay in school by skipping meals here and there, I hardly could foot such bills. At a point I felt like giving up my dream out of frustration. If the Efik nation, I said to myself whose territory the Bakassi Peninsula was said to be, could care less, why should I bother? At such moments, I would feel deeply depressed but would soon remind myself that getting the Bakassi Peninsula out of Cameroon was a personal mission not an assignment imposed on me.

Thus, in spite of moments of frustration, I continued to pursue my dream in a cautious and steady manner. Since I was never actually in control of anything, I could not set an agenda for myself. Providence often set one for me. And that was exactly what happened when five Nigerian soldiers were ambushed and killed in the Bakassi Peninsula by Cameroonian soldiers in May 1981. The incident brought the Bakassi Peninsula into renewed focus and rekindled hope in my mission. I saw this tragedy as a real opportunity for Nigeria to settle the Bakassi Peninsula irritant once and for all.

The killings steered up national emotions and whipped up sentiments that nearly brought Nigeria and Cameroon to the precipice. Nigeria claimed the soldiers were killed within her territorial waters. Cameroon countered that the incident took place deep inside Cameroonian territory. Not a few Nigerians would have wished Nigeria to go to war with Cameroon over the incident. The political leadership of both countries however thought otherwise and opted for a peaceful resolution of the crisis. Cameroon was said to have tendered an apology and paid compensation and the matter was put to rest. But the controversy over ownership of the Bakassi Peninsula to my greatest delight continued to linger on.

Even before Nigeria and Cameroon had time to consider appropriate responses to the crisis, I swung into action. I saw the crisis as a momentous event, the kind of opportunity I had been waiting for and swiftly moved into action. For me, the time had come. Thus, while Nigeria and Cameroon were still contemplating how to respond to the killings in the peninsula, I seized the momentum to send out two quick memoranda to the National Assembly and to President Shehu Shagari.

My memorandum to parliament retraced the history of the Bakassi Peninsula before embarking on an elaborate evocation of life in the peninsula from colonial times to date. In the memorandum I lamented the fate of Usakedet people whom I stated had been truncated from the rest of their Efik kinsmen and forced into union with people they shared nothing in common. I drew attention to the constant harassment of the fishermen population and expressed disappointment at the lukewarm attitude with which Nigeria had tended to deal with the situation, noting that Nigeria's reaction had been confined to watching events in the Bakassi Peninsula while Cameroon went about implanting her administrative machinery in the territory. My memorandum accused Nigerian leaders of selling the Bakassi Peninsula to Cameroon.

I regretted that Usakedet people were being falsely accused of collaboration with Cameroon in their constant harassment and maltreatment of the fishermen population and noted that that perception was generating strong negative sentiments towards Usakedet people who, in reality, were the real victims of the high handedness of Cameroonian officials in the Bakassi Peninsula. I regretted that such a perception was compounding the dilemma of the Usakedet people who, captured as they seemed in the Bakassi Peninsula, had no option but to do as they were told. It was time Nigeria had a better understanding of the situation in the Bakassi

Peninsula and acted accordingly. The memorandum finally lamented the lack of capacity of the Usakedet people to independently deal with the Bakassi situation and called on Nigeria to rise to the occasion and save the Bakassi Peninsula and its peoples from further torment.

Parliament quickly reacted to my memorandum and wrote back advising the people to stay calm and assuring that the matter was receiving due attention. I was excited. It was refreshing and heart warming to receive such reassurance from Parliament. In spite of the satisfaction the reaction of Parliament gave me, I still felt I should take the case of the Bakassi Peninsula and its people one step higher; to the highest authority in the land. So I sent a "Save Our Souls" to President Shagari.

In my 'Save Our Souls', I intimated the President about living conditions in the Bakassi Peninsula and lamented how, for years government had ignored the cries and warnings of the people of the peninsula. I talked about how tension in the peninsula was giving Bakassi inhabitants serious concerns and how their lives had become worthless and unbearable. I told the President that although he could not be held responsible for the situation which was as a result of years of neglect and nonchalance by past administrations, the responsibility for finding lasting solution to the situation in the Bakassi Peninsula rested squarely on the President's shoulders.

I painted a disturbing picture of life in the Bakassi Peninsula, highlighting its contradictions and blaming unprincipled individuals and past administrations for a situation where Usakedet people had completely been cut off from their kith and kin in Nigeria. I told the President that the situation had led to the severance of family ties and had raised the ugly spectre of one family belonging to two nations. I noted that Usakedet people who had insisted on maintaining contact with their brothers on different sides of the border were being viewed with suspicion on both sides stressing that something needed to be done to change that perception.

My memorandum told President Shagari that Usakedet people were a people who had made significant contributions to Efik tradition and culture and expressed fear for the survival of that culture in the Bakassi Peninsula. I further informed the President of how Cameroon was renaming fishing settlements in the peninsula, putting undue pressure on Bakassi natives and compelling them to stop giving their new born babies names of Nigerian origin. Acknowledging that mistakes had been done, I told the President time was propitious for those mistakes to be corrected and expressed confidence in the President's ability to do so.

My 'Save Our Souls' expressed happiness that the matter was to be looked into by an international arbitration tribunal and expressed the hope that the Usakedet people would be given the chance to testify at the tribunal. I noted that the Usakedet people were better positioned to provide clarifications that could help throw some light and help find durable solutions to the conflict. My SOS tried to correct the erroneous impression that the Bakassi Peninsula only comprised mangrove swamp forest that was inhabited by migrant fishermen and informed the President that the peninsula had a mainland that was inhabited by an indigenous population that was the customary owners of the Bakassi Peninsula. I noted that the mangrove swamp forest where itinerant fishermen built their temporary abodes belonged to the Usakedet people and expressed fear that this lack of knowledge could be embarrassing and called for the inclusion of someone knowledgeable about the Bakassi Peninsula and its people on Nigeria's team on the territory. I warned that Nigeria would be millions of miles away from achieving a permanent solution to the Bakassi Peninsula crisis if any Usakedet people were separated from their legitimate possession in the Bakassi peninsula. Finally, I warned that Usakedet people remained inseparably attached to their land stressing that any settlement that did not take cognizance of this fundamental truth would be deficient and doomed to failure.

My 'Save Our Souls' did not appear to have had any impact whatsoever. The President never reacted to the SOS. It remains unclear whether the 'Save Our Souls' even got to the President. In spite of my efforts, Nigeria dashed my hope by failing to use the opportunity provided by the tragic killing of five Nigerian soldiers in the Bakassi Peninsula to settle the ownership dispute once and for all. Before long the euphoria that had accompanied the killings died down and enthusiasm for war waned. Bakassi peninsula once again became a forgotten issue until Nigeria landed troops in the peninsula on December 23rd 1993.

What perplexed me most from that initial effort was how copies of my memoranda found their way into Cameroonian hands. These individuals who were born and raised in the Bakassi Peninsula accused me of embarking on a mission for which I did not have my people's mandate. These my childhood acquaintances using fake names went to the extent of publishing articles in Cameroonian newspapers accusing me of selling the Bakassi Peninsula to Nigeria. They equally made ignorant assertions of the circumstances of my birth. That was to be expected. Much later during the crisis, I would ironically also be accused in Nigeria of being some kind of spy for Cameroon. Since no one made any effort to bring such serious allegations to my notice and although I noticed a certain change in attitude towards me in certain circles, I let people believe what they wanted to believe. I had a job to do and I needed to give something back to the people that gave me life.

My critics were however right about one thing. I had no mandate from the Usakedet people to take them and the Bakassi Peninsula;

their homeland back to Nigeria. It was all my idea. Until I went to the peninsula to seek evidence to prove Usakedet ownership of the Bakassi Peninsula, I had never held a meeting to discuss my plans about the Bakassi Peninsula with the Usakedet people. My meetings with a few elders and Pa Leo on that occasion had been extremely discreet. I never consulted nor summoned town hall meetings to discuss my dream for the the Usakedet people and Bakassi Peninsula.

Looking back, I cannot even today sincerely tell myself what attraction the mission held for me. I have no idea why I felt so motivated to embark on a mission the magnitude of which I could not imagine. Not even my one-year sojourn in Abana fishing settlement or my anger over what Cameroon was doing to Usakedet people seems sufficient justification for what I went into. And it does not seem as if I wanted to gratify myself; become some kind of hero. None of these silly ideas ever crossed my mind. Yet, as unexposed and totally unequipped for a mission as complex as adjusting international boundaries, I went ahead without looking back and never for one moment sat back to think about the consequences of my action. Something, I cannot tell seemed to urge me on; something that made my mission seem so natural a thing to do kept urging me on.

Perhaps the fact that I happened to be the first home-grown Bakassi native university graduate at the time made me feel that it naturally behoved on me to provide leadership and chart the course of the destiny of my people. May be the knowledge too that Usakedet people were a people of Nigerian extraction who left the territory now known as Nigeria to occupy Bakassi peninsula centuries ago and the fact too that the land they left behind remains unoccupied in Nigeria to date, perhaps awaiting their return played an important part in my judgement. Again, I cannot tell. Although I seemed unperturbed by my critics, I learnt a number of useful lessons and became alive to the dangers inherent in my mission. From that moment on, I would be on my guard. I would exercise more caution although I remained conscious of the fact that being too careful could stifle initiative.

However, I had from the outset, by mere intuition, felt the need to protect the Usakedet people by not getting them overtly involved with efforts to bring the Bakassi Peninsula back to Nigeria while Cameroon remained in charge in the peninsula. As long as the Bakassi Peninsula remained under Cameroonian rule as was the case before the landing of troops in 1993, keeping the Usakedet people ignorant and uninvolved seemed in their best interest. This way, I could ensure the secret nature of my mission and also ensure their protection. Any blunder in this regard could be extremely expensive. And as was observed during the crisis, as soon as Nigeria regained control of any section of the Bakassi Peninsula, the switch in allegiance was automatic.

It is also largely for this same reason to protect my people that I have had to play down some of the outstanding contributions of my Usakedet kinsmen to the struggle for the Bakassi Peninsula. It is also for this same reason that I can justify my excessive use of the personal pronoun 'I' in this book. This way I can also provide protection for those who played double game; for those who showed little or no enthusiasm for the struggle; for those who actually worked for the enemy and for those who simply sat on the side lines and only surfaced to reap where they did not sow. I hold nothing particular against them. In the confused state of affairs that the Bakassi Peninsula had become and might probably remain in the foreseeable future, theirs may have been a wise choice.

CHAPTER FOUR

January 1994;
Battle Ground Shifts to Lagos

Efforts to bring the Bakassi Peninsula to the front burner and get Nigeria interested in the wretched plight of customary owners of the Bakassi Peninsula seemed like a wild goose chase. It did not take long before the tragic incident of the killing of five Nigerian soldiers by Cameroon gendarmes in the Bakassi Peninsula was forgotten. Getting the territory out of Cameroon essentially remained a solitary struggle on a lonesome and tortuous road. But providence would again smile on me. General Sani Abacha would come to power in Nigeria in November 1993. Barely one month after his accession to the throne of the most populous black nation Bakassi Peninsula crisis would break out in December 1993.

I was delighted. Attention once again became refocused on the Bakassi Peninsula. The development rekindled hope and gave me further strength and inspiration to pursue my dream. Destiny had again shone bright on the Bakassi Peninsula. I would seize the momentum and advance the cause of my Usakedet people. I would not let the opportunity slip pass me again. I saw the crisis as divine intervention; a god-sent chance to settle once and for all the dilemma confronting my people. Earlier efforts to get this matter resolved had yielded no fruits. But Nigeria's initial reaction to the crisis would give me real cause for concern. In spite of the many decades of dealing with this border problem, initial response to the outbreak of hostilities was rather clumsy, belying the long decades Nigeria had had to deal with the problem.

Press statements on the crisis for example generally lacked depth revealing a certain lack of knowledge about the Bakassi Peninsula. Names of places in the Bakassi Peninsula were for example mixed up and used confusedly. Abana and Jabane for example, were presented as two different places. So too were Atabong and Idabato; Idombi and Bamusso presented as separate places. Names that had recently been given to fishing settlements by Cameroonian authorities were commonly used in Nigeria instead of sticking to the original Efik names of these fishing settlements. Even places that were nowhere near the Bakassi Peninsula were said to be in the peninsula. It was obvious the writers of these statements lacked adequate knowledge of what they were dealing with. Such gaffe tended to give tacit recognition to Cameroon's claim over Bakassi peninsula. These mix-ups were not only embarrassing; they could be detrimental to Nigeria's interest in the Bakassi Peninsula. Such a situation, it was obvious, could cause Nigeria the Bakassi Peninsula.

I often reacted swiftly by drawing government attention to such blunders and by calling for the inclusion of a Bakassi native or someone knowledgeable about the territory in Nigeria's team on the Bakassi Peninsula. My call apparently fell on deaf ears as no true Bakassi indigene to my knowledge was ever injected into Nigeria's team on the Bakassi Peninsula. No one appeared to pay heed to that kind of advice. No native of Bakassi peninsula was ever included in Nigeria's team. Rather, I watched bewildered as persons who knew nothing about the Bakassi Peninsula made the team. Such persons would in the cover of darkness, crawl to Bakassi natives for documents and briefings on the Bakassi Peninsula. Why Nigeria refused to include Bakassi indigenes in her team to the end remains a puzzle. It surely would have made Nigeria's job much easier. As a result of this handicap, Bakassi peninsula affairs remained to the very end bedevilled by an unacceptable level of gross, monumental ignorance. Yet, this was one handicap Nigeria should never have experienced.

Even in the Cross River State where the Bakassi Peninsula was now said to belong after the landing of troops, Usakedet people had to mount pressure on government to get recognition. Without such pressure customary owners of the peninsula would simply have been ignored. Without pressure they would not be invited to meetings convened to discuss the future of the Bakassi Peninsula; their homeland. They hardly were consulted on critical matters affecting the Bakassi Peninsula and even when they happened to be consulted, their opinion hardly counted. Regrettably, while Bakassi overlords were being treated with contempt and scorn, fishermen communities were being promoted and made to believe that they owned the Bakassi Peninsula. I knew that Usakedet people would never surrender an inch of the Bakassi Peninsula to any one and I made that known to the authorities. For the Usakedet people such an idea was unthinkable. There was an area in which there could be no compromise.

Despite all Usakedet efforts, the Cross River State Government would in January 1994, send a delegation to Lagos to discuss the Bakassi Peninsula without the inclusion of representatives of customary owners of the peninsula in the state delegation. Instead, the state delegation comprised members of the fishermen communities and members of the state civil service. That the Cross River State Government would send a delegation to Lagos to discuss the Bakassi Peninsula without the participation of the owners of the territory made one truly begin to doubt Nigeria's real intention in the Bakassi Peninsula. Could Nigeria want to take back the Bakassi Peninsula and abandon customary owners of the territory like Great Britain had done? It was too early to say but things were beginning to point in that direction and making me feel truly uncomfortable. In my mind the Bakassi Peninsula was beginning to catch fire, little by little.

In spite of my apprehension, I refused to let the thought linger too long on my mind. If I did, I could easily be distracted from my mission. The answer to these seeming treats was not to sit back and brood over them. The solution was to fight back and fight back I was prepared to do. Besides it was too early to draw conclusions. All that was important at the time was to ensure that customary owners of the Bakassi Peninsula took part in a meeting where their future and the future of their territory could be determined. I would take the bull by the horns. The meeting in Lagos was an opportunity for Usakedet people's voice to be heard and I was determined to make that voice heard. That Lagos meeting was an opportunity I could not miss.

Before now, the struggle to bring the Bakassi Peninsula back to Nigeria had been a lonely battle fought largely by me. Before now, I had not succeeded in finding Bakassi indigenes of significant political stature to join me in the struggle for the Bakassi Peninsula. The struggle too, had largely been fought-behind-the-scenes and on the side lines. Now that the crisis had come to the open, there was need not just for the involvement of a larger number of Usakedet people, but for a political platform from where we could launch an offensive.

Happily for me, I did not have to search too far or for too long at the inception of the Bakassi crisis. Usakedet people in Calabar, unlike their ancestors who centuries ago had simply abandoned the Bakassi Peninsula and melted into the wider Efik world, had prior to the outbreak of the Bakassi crisis began to show some interest in the ancestral homeland their parents had abandoned centuries earlier. The outbreak of the Bakassi crisis would heighten that interest. In their anxiety to re-assert their Usakedet identity they had formed an association called *'Mbono Ndito Usakedet.'* It seemed only natural that I should exploit this new found passion and make Usakedet people in Calabar provide not just the badly missing political platform but also assume the leadership of the struggle for the Bakassi Peninsula. I would continue to stay in the shadows to provide guidance and logistic support.

It was thus to Chief Dr. Archibong Edem Young; president of *Mbono Ndito Usakedet* that I would go to discuss the exclusion of Usakedet people from the Cross River State delegation. After carefully explaining the implication of Usakedet exclusion from the state's delegation to him, Young expressed outrage at the news and immediately accepted to accompany me to Lagos to confront the state delegation. Young saw the inclusion of representatives of fishermen communities in the delegation as a conspiracy that had to be stopped. I further impressed upon Young the need for his *Mbono Ndito Usakedet* to provide the political platform for the struggle for the Bakassi Peninsula as well as the need for Usakedet people to play the leading role in the struggle for Bakassi peninsula. I did not need to persuade Young. My thoughts were in line with his thinking. Young, without hesitation immediately agreed to get *Mbono Ndito Usakedet* totally involved with the struggle for the Bakassi Peninsula. Young was not one who needed persuasion when it came to service to his people. He was prepared to leave for Lagos immediately but neither he nor the association he led had funds to foot the bill for such a mission. I picked up the bill for our three days trip to Lagos.

Unknown to me, the news I had just conveyed to Young had so infuriated him that he was in no mood for compromise. I only realised this when we were about to begin our meeting with members of the state delegation in Lagos. Had members of the state delegation too been aware of Young's state of mind, they probably would have been more tactful in dealing with us when we met. Young and I had departed Calabar a day ahead of the delegation to give us time to prepare a position paper on the crisis on behalf of our Usakedet people. On arrival in Lagos, we spent the entire night putting together a "PETITION TO THE MILITARY ADMINISTRATOR OF THE CROSS RIVER STATE ON THE NIGERIA-CAMEROON BORDER DISPUTE". By this time, I had become a bit more familiar with the issues involved. So I did the writing and Young provided back-up services like "suya" and beer that kept us both awake throughout the night. Armed with my collection of books, newspaper cuttings, maps and other documents on the Bakassi Peninsula, I managed to complete the writing of the memorandum that would become the first position paper of the "Obong of Calabar"; Paramount Ruler of the Efiks on Bakassi crisis by seven o'clock the next morning.

We requested to meet the Cross River State delegation later that evening determined to have the voice of Usakedet people heard. Nothing in Young's demeanour gave me the slightest impression that he was still raving with anger over the exclusion of customary owners of the peninsula in the state's delegation on the Bakassi Peninsula. Thus, while I was trying to see how best to approach the delegation, to harmonize our views with that of the delegation, Young mostly remained silent, hardly saying more than a few words. I thought of what would happen if the delegation proved to be unfriendly, hostile or refused to give us audience. Unsure of what reception awaited us I counselled we approach the delegation with tact and caution. Young replied with a cynical smile.

Young may have been right. The delegation showed little or no enthusiasm to receive us. They nearly could have succeeded had it not been for Young's 'can't take no for an answer' posture. Young insisted so much that after much foot-dragging the delegation had to bend and grant us audience. Our meeting would eventually kick-off on a terribly bad note. The poisoned atmosphere resulting from the delegation's initial reluctance to grant us audience would further infuriate Young who was still boiling with anger over the exclusion of customary owners of the peninsula from the state delegation. Young's anger might even have subsided but the composition of the state delegation would make his anger boil several times over. Besides one senior technocrat; a surveyor-general, the state delegation we met comprised low level civil servants and a few chiefs from Akpabuyo Local Government Council who although had nothing to do with the Bakassi Peninsula were being paraded as Bakassi natives and customary owners of the Bakassi Peninsula. The delegation also included a representative of the "Obong of Calabar" Chief Jacob Duke and a representative of the fishermen community; Chief Okokon Ibok; head of Abana fishing settlement. The only people missing in a state delegation set up to discuss the future of the Bakassi Peninsula were customary owners of the peninsula.

That would not be the only shock awaiting us. While Young and I had spent the previous night working on a memorandum we hoped to present at the meeting, the delegation had come to the meeting empty handed, seemingly unprepared. Besides the representative of the "Obong of Calabar" who had come to the meeting with a copy of *'Anterra Duke's Diary'* a book containing the itinerary of a prominent Efik merchant in Bakassi peninsula during the colonial era, and the state surveyor- general who came to the meeting with a map that put the Bakassi Peninsula clearly outside Nigeria, no other member of the delegation appeared to have made any kind of preparation for the meeting.

The anger generated by the exclusion of customary owners of the Bakassi Peninsula in the state delegation, the composition of the delegation, the surveyor-general's blunder and the general lack of preparation all combined to make Young and me mad. Young would mince no words when his time came to speak to fiercely castigate whoever had put up such a delegation. He, in his characteristic fiery manner launched the first tirade lambasting members of the delegation for the non-inclusion of Usakedet people in the delegation and for all the blunders that had been observed. The delegation visibly caught unaware would not take it lying down. Its members responded even with greater venom; forcefully and abrasively. Before you knew what was happening, everyone began to argue vociferously throwing abuses at each other. For some fifteen minutes or more, pandemonium reigned supreme in the meeting venue. You could feel the roof vibrating, the walls trembling and unless you were made of iron, you probably would have thought the roof was about to collapse on you. For a brief moment, I thought hell had been let loose in the Cross River State liaison office where our meeting was being held.

In the confusion, I began to feel quite uneasy, worried that the purpose of our coming to Lagos could be defeated if nothing was done to restore calm. I began to wonder how a meeting convened to discuss the destiny of the Bakassi peninsula and its peoples that obviously included the teeming fishermen population could so easily turn into an undeclared verbal war where everyone freely hauled insults and abuses at each other. The situation was beginning to get out of hand and the attacks were getting too personal. It seemed a few individuals in the room had scores to settle with each other and were using the occasion to try to do just that. It was to avoid a situation like this that I had at the beginning felt the need to be cautious and tactful in dealing with the delegation. Now, everyone appeared to have thrown tact and caution to the dogs. The situation was increasingly becoming truly menacing making me become genuinely disturbed. The confusion had the potential to derail my dream. Something had to be done to bring the situation under immediate control. In the heat of the arguments and insults, I stole out of the room and sought help.

The quick intervention of officers of the liaison office would restore order and bring me some relief.

Our meeting eventually kick-off on that sour note. My frustration would however further deepen when at close scrutiny of the surveyor-general's map I discovered that all of mainland Bakassi Peninsula where customary owners of the territory live had been placed outside Nigeria. The surveyor-general's map only featured fishing settlements. All mainland villages; Aqua, Amoto, Odon and Efut Inwang including Archibong town were conspicuously missing from the surveyor-general's map of Nigeria. Asked why these villages were not featured the surveyor-general explained that he had found no evidence to support the inclusion of those places on the map of Nigeria. Asked what evidence he had found to justify the inclusion of the fishing settlements on his map of Nigeria, he had nothing convincing to say. Not even Archibong town that the Efik nation was heavily relying upon to sustain its claim of the Bakassi peninsula was featured in the map of Nigeria. That was a fundamental blunder.

The only thing these omissions would succeed in doing would be to increase Usakedet (Isangele) doubts about Nigeria's motives and real intention in Bakassi peninsula. Too many negative things seemed to be happening too frequently to Usakedet people. I was beginning to find it difficult to accept all these negative events as mere co-incidences. Nonetheless, Young and I expressed strong objection to the omissions and called for the immediate inclusion of the missing villages in Nigeria's map of the Bakassi Peninsula. The delegation agreed and I then seized the relative calm that had been established to brief the delegation and present the memorandum we had prepared the night before to the delegation.

Our memorandum drew attention to earlier communications I had made on behalf of customary owners of the peninsula. It made particular reference to my memorandum to the National Assembly and to the 'Save Our Souls' to President Shehu Shagari. It again drew attention to the fact that although the Bakassi Peninsula and its inhabitants were Nigerians, the territory had for decades been ruled by Cameroon. The petition attributed this bizarre situation to negligence, nonchalance, complacency and complicity on the part of various administrations in Nigeria. It reiterated that Bakassi peninsula had been part of Old Calabar not merely because the inhabitants were of Efik ancestry but also by virtue of the fact that Great Britain and the Chiefs and Kings of Old Calabar had entered into an agreement in which Great Britain had pledged to 'extend Her Majesty's 'gracious protection and favour' to Efik people. The memorandum wondered how Great Britain could in 1913 renege on her treaty obligation and transfer the Bakassi Peninsula that did not belong to her to Germany without the consent of the Chiefs and Kings of Old Calabar.

Before going into the discussion of the March 11, 1913 Anglo-German treaty our petition took a quick overview of other treaties signed between Great Britain and Germany that supported Nigeria's claim over Bakassi peninsula. It cited the 1885 Anglo-German agreement where both colonial powers had 'engaged not to make acquisition of territory, accept protectorate or interfere with the extension of influence in the territories each other controlled.' It equally drew attention to the 1890 and 1893 agreement between Great Britain and German that made further adjustments on their common borders and the 1906 agreement that provided for equal fishing and navigation rights on river boundaries as well as ensured the freedom of indigenes who occupied land, due to be transferred to the other power, to choose which side of the boundary they wished to reside. The 1906 treaty equally gave local representatives of the two colonial powers the discretion to vary the line by mutual agreement, if local circumstances so demanded.

All but one of the above mentioned treaties, our memorandum stressed, strongly supported Nigeria's claim over the Bakassi Peninsula. The contentious Anglo-German treaty of March 11, 1913 however, remained the principal source of conflict between Nigeria and Cameroon. Although the treaty envisaged the demarcation of the boundary, that physical demarcation, it appeared was never undertaken before World War 1 broke out and put an end to Germany's colonial empire. That Anglo-German treaty of March 11, 1913 was the treaty that was purported to have transferred the Bakassi Peninsula from Nigeria to Cameroon. The petition further noted that although Nigeria had complicated matters by entering into other agreements with Cameroon that appeared to rely on the validity of the 1913 Anglo-German agreement, the 1913 Anglo-German agreement had remained the greatest source of conflict between Nigeria and Cameroon.

Presenting legal opinions on the controversy, our memorandum drew attention to the fact that legal opinion was divided with regard to the validity of the 1913 Anglo-German Agreement. Jurists who believed the 1913 Agreement was binding argued that it was binding in accordance with customary international law as reflected in Article 11 of the Vienna Convention on state succession. They also cited the 1964 OAU Declaration on the inviolability of colonial boundaries and dismissed the 1884 treaty between Great Britain and the Chiefs and Kings of Old Calabar as an unequal treaty. They noted that Great Britain had entered into some 360 such treaties with native communities and drew particular attention to the treaty with King Dosumu of Lagos in which the Dosumu family gave Lagos and its environs to the Queen of England and her heirs 'for ever and ever.' Had such treaties been valid, Lagos and some 360 communities in Nigeria would probably never have been part of Nigeria.

Jurists who rejected the validity of the 1913 Anglo-German Agreement based their arguments on the fact that the 1964 Cairo

Declaration of the Organisation of African Unity had no effect as Africa had witnessed the emergence of new states like Eritrea that had been carved out of Ethiopia. They also drew attention to the fact that since the collapse of the Soviet Union the world had undergone significant boundary adjustments resulting in the emergence of new states. They accordingly found nothing wrong with redrawing the Nigeria and Cameroon boundary in the Bakassi Peninsula area. Exponents of this view noted particularly that in 1884 Great Britain had entered into agreement with the Kings and Chiefs of Old Calabar to extend to them and their territory Her Majesty's "gracious protection and favour" that included the Bakassi Peninsula. They argued that Great Britain violated her agreement with the Kings and Chiefs of Old Calabar by giving the Bakassi Peninsula to Germany. They opined that by virtue of the 1884 treaty with the Kings and Chiefs of Old Calabar, Great Britain held the land in trust for Efik people. They had no right to transfer Efik land to a third party without the consent of the Kings and Chiefs of Old Calabar. That consent was never sought nor given. These jurists further argued that the 1913 treaty was never registered with the League of Nations. Neither was it registered with the United Nations. Furthermore, neither Great Britain nor Germany ever ratified the treaty stressing that at independence the 1913 treaty was not handed over to Nigeria. They insisted that because the Maroua Declaration between Nigeria and Cameroon was not ratified by Nigeria's parliament, the Declaration was not binding.

We concluded our memorandum by stating that none of the agreements Nigeria had entered into on the Bakassi peninsula, including the 1913 Anglo-German treaty imposed any serious incontestable obligations on Nigeria and maintained that the rather woefully disappointing result obtained in dealing with the Bakassi Peninsula problem was a reflection of the lack of resolve on the part of Nigeria to vigorously tackle the problem and expressed the hope that Nigeria would go the extra mile to finding a lasting solution to the Bakassi Peninsula border conflict.

Most members of the delegation gave our memorandum enthusiastic welcome. A few however remained unimpressed sceptical, perhaps still brooding over the rowdy and acrimonious session that had marked the beginning of the session. That was to be expected. The vicious attacks and insults that had preceded our meeting were bound to leave wounds that would need time to heal. The representative of the Obong of Calabar who seemed particularly impressed with our effort requested that the memorandum be adopted as the position paper of the Obong of Calabar; Paramount Ruler of the Efiks.

I was more than pleased with the request. I buzzed with excitement as I now reasoned that from that moment on my struggle would become the struggle of the entire Efik nation strongly believing that the involvement of the Efik nation would mark a real turning point in the struggle for the Bakassi Peninsula. That would give the Usakedet people an additional platform to articulate theirs views. I conferred with Young and we immediately handed copies of our memorandum to the representative of the Obong of Calabar. That sudden interest by the Efik nation contrasted sharply with the indifference manifested by Efik leadership in the early 70s when I tried to enlist Efik support for the struggle for the Bakassi Peninsula. Efik nation had at the time shown little or no interest in the Bakassi Peninsula. For the first time since I embarked on the mission to bring the Bakassi Peninsula out of Cameroon, I had real hope that the era of fighting a lonely battle was over. I was convinced that from that moment on, a hitherto reluctant and seemingly unwilling Efik nation would no longer sit on the fence and watch but would throw its full weight behind the Usakedet people and the struggle for the Bakassi Peninsula. Subsequent events would cast serious doubts on my conviction.

Meanwhile, members of the delegation who seemed truly impressed with our memorandum wanted Young and me to integrate the delegation. That was not an idea I found particularly attractive. As a public servant I needed permission to attend such meetings. That permission I did not and could not have. Besides, I truly found no reason to want to be present at a meeting where the position I had been canvassing for was to be articulated by no less a personality than the Obong of Calabar. The words that would flow out of the mouth of the Obong of Calabar would be my words. As far as I was concerned there could be nothing more satisfying than hearing my words flow from the mouth of the Obong of Calabar. I gave Young reasons why I could not and did not want to attend and asked him to attend if he so desired and be witness, but Young declined and decided we both stay back.

To say Young and I were overjoyed by the success we had achieved would be to miss the point completely. I in particular was over the moon already dreaming of the liberation of Bakassi peninsula. Yet, in spite of feeling so elated, a number of questions continued to bother me. The delegation had come to Lagos with the impression that the Lagos meeting would involve delegations from Nigeria and Cameroon. Based on that assumption it was essential to ensure that the map the delegation brought was not presented at such a meeting because of the obvious defects it contained. We needed to have guarantees that that map would not surface at the meeting. Thus, before our meeting rose, Young and I requested to have audience with the Military Administrator of Cross River State, Air Commodore Ibrahim Kefas who was to lead the state delegation. The delegation quickly offered to secure the audience for us the following morning and we returned to our hotel that evening to celebrate.

Young and I returned to the liaison office the next morning optimistic and ready for the promised audience with the military administrator only to discover that no arrangement had been made for us to see the head of the delegation. Our celebration the previous night had been premature. Something seemed to have gone terribly wrong between the time we left the previous evening and that morning. The jubilant atmosphere in which we had bid each other goodnight the previous evening seemed to have evaporated. No one would confirm or deny that the audience had been sought, granted or denied. Young and I were however aware that the head of the delegation was still in the premises and that he had been briefed about our meeting of the previous evening. With such assurances we decided to wait in the lobby knowing too well that the building had no other exit. We waited, waited and waited. Thirty minutes past by and nothing happened One hour, an hour and a half, an hour forty-five minutes; nothing happened. Young was beginning to feel angry and betrayed. I too was beginning to lose patience. No one seemed willing or anxious to speak to us despite the assurances we had received the night before.

No member of the delegation seemed to want to come close to Young and me. They just kept milling around in silence. We seemed like a bunch of nuisance. That piercing silence began to make me very uncomfortable. I began to wonder what could be responsible for the sudden change of attitude. Could it be as a result of the acrimonious session of the previous night? But we had made peace and the delegation had promised. Now it seemed we were too naïve to expect the psychological scars and wounds inflicted on the egos of members of the delegation the previous evening to easily get healed and be forgotten. Now it seemed what we had the night before had been a temporary truce. The war it appeared was not over. The atmosphere was still very poisoned. Though Young and I had discussed the possibility of our request for audience falling through and had worked out a plan "B" we never imagined it would take this twist.

Meanwhile, the waiting game continued. We waited and were prepared to wait as long as it would take when suddenly members of the delegation began to move out into vehicles stationed in the premises ready to convey them to the meeting venue. They trooped past us without a word as if we were total strangers. Surely, the delegation was up to no good, I told myself, as we watched astonished as the delegation walked past us. The events of the previous evening were still vey fresh in my memory and I felt nothing in the world would justify a repeat of such ugly scenes. We needed to avoid the kind of emotional outburst that nearly ruined our meeting the previous evening. We needed to be calm and mature in dealing with the Head of delegation. But before I had time to transmit my thoughts to Young, the head of delegation accompanied by his Aides made their way into the lobby and began to head straight for the exit. Before I knew what was happening, Young, to my utter shock and bewilderment literally threw himself between the head of delegation and the exit, thus preventing Air Commodore Ibrahim Kefas from stepping out of the state liaison office.

You can not imagine a more tumultuous and chaotic scene. For the second time in less than twenty-four hours, hell was once again let loose in the Cross River State Liaison Office in Lagos. There, in front of a seemingly bemused head of delegation, Young and I and members of the state delegation re-enacted the shameful acrimonious trading of insults, accusations and counter-accusations that had preceded our meeting the previous evening. Members of the state delegation who were already in cars on hearing the commotion quickly jumped out of their cars and rushed back in to join in the commotion. And with security agents joining in the foray whether on the side of the delegation or to protect the Military Administrator I could hardly say, the confusion seemed even greater than the previous day's. Our plan "B" did not envisage such an outcome. This was exactly the kind of situation I had been anxious to avoid. Now, it seemed too late. We had unwittingly walked into a dangerous path in which our people may have to pay a heavy price. If the Head of delegation refused to listen to us, Usakedet struggle could suffer. The gains we had made the previous night could be in jeopardy. I could never forgive myself for such an outcome.

For a brief moment, the head of delegation just stood there watching his delegation and security men put up some disgraceful show with Young and I. Should he continue to watch as we freely traded verbal blows and insults or should he take charge of the situation? The Head of delegation opted for the latter, quickly took control of the situation and restored calm and order. Calm and order restored, the head of delegation wanted to know what the trouble was. Young quickly seized the occasion to introduce himself and me before filling in the Head of delegation on our previous night encounter with the delegation He admonished the delegation for their failure to live up to their promise to secure audience for us with the Head of delegation and concluded by representing our request for audience. The Head of delegation, seeing the desperation in our action had no option than to grant us quick audience right there in the lobby of the state liaison office.

Young, again thanked the head of delegation before expressing indignation over the non-inclusion of the Usakedet people; customary owners of Bakassi peninsula in a delegation set up to discuss the future of their territory. Young wondered how a delegation composed of strangers intended to discuss the future and destiny of a territory they knew nothing about. The delegation, Young noted had not only failed to include customary owners of the territory, it had come empty-handed and unprepared for such a meeting of utmost importance to the people of the Bakassi Peninsula. To make matters worse, the delegation had come to the meeting with a map that clearly put core Bakassi Peninsula villages outside Nigeria. Young insisted that the map of the Bakassi Peninsula the delegation had come to Lagos with be brought before the head of delegation.

As the Cross River State Surveyor-General spread out his map of Bakassi peninsula on the floor before the Head of delegation, I kindly requested the Surveyor-General to indicate where Archibong town was located on his map. The Surveyor- General was completely taken aback. There was no Archibong Town on his map of the Bakassi Peninsula. Yet, the delegation included descendants of Archibong Edem's Family whom the Efik nation hoped to use to justify its claim over the Bakassi Peninsula. It was on the strength of such claims that they made the state delegation. The absence of Archibong Town on the map of Nigeria was therefore unimaginable because it made nonsense of Nigeria's claim over the Bakassi Peninsula. Efik nation's claim over the Bakassi Peninsula was predicated on the assumption that because Prince Archibong Edem had sojourned briefly in what became known as Archibong Town in Bakassi Peninsula during his exile years Archibong Edem had established Efik ownership of Bakassi Peninsula. Now Archibong Town that seemed so critical to Efik claim over the Bakassi Peninsula was missing from Nigeria's map of the Bakassi peninsula. This was not just embarrassing; it could be detrimental to Nigeria's claim over the Bakassi peninsula.

Archibong Town could indeed be critical to Nigeria's claim over the Bakassi Peninsula. Prince Archibong Edem had spent his exile years in the Bakassi peninsula after he lost the fight for the Efik throne in the early 20th century. Now that important piece of Efik history was missing from the surveyor-general's map of the Bakassi peninsula. Not only was Archibong Town that was so crucial to Nigeria's claim over the Bakassi Peninsula missing from the map of Nigeria, none of the other villages that are occupied by the native population of Bakassi peninsula was featured in the Surveyor-General's map of the peninsula. The surveyor-general's map merely featured fishing settlements; heterogeneous and temporary settlements in the Bakassi Peninsula. Nevertheless, anxious not to disappoint his boss, the Surveyor-General took out a pencil from his pocket and after fiddling with it a few moments, made a pencil mark right in the middle of River Akpayefe as if to say this is Archibong Town.

That was a grievous mistake. I immediately pounced on the error and gave Air Commodore Ibrahim Kefas a clearer picture of the true location of Archibong Town across River Akpayefe. I then made the head of delegation know that not only was Archibong Town missing from the map, all villages inhabited by the Usakedet people; customary owners of the peninsula were equally not featured in the Surveyor-General's map of the Bakassi Peninsula. I told the head of delegation that not featuring these places on the map of Nigeria could have grave consequences for Nigeria and called on the head of delegation to take immediate steps to ensure that the Usakedet villages of Aqua, Amoto, Odon, Efut Inwang and Archibong Town were not only featured on the map of the peninsula but to also ensure that Nigeria took immediate steps to have a presence in the area. At the time Nigeria had no such presence. The delegation thereafter departed for their meeting leaving Young and I to return to our hotel to relish our victory.

I chose to attack the absence of Archibong Town on the Surveyor-General's map because I knew that the Efik nation was trying to project Archibong Town as the customary owners of the Bakassi Peninsula. Although I was totally opposed to that idea, I saw in it a window of opportunity. I knew that Archibong Town and all the other Usakedet villages had always featured on maps as part of Cameroon. If Archibong Town were now to feature on the map of Nigeria, it would make the case for the inclusion of all the other Usakedet villages in Nigeria much easier. The continued absence of these villages on maps of Nigeria weakened Nigeria's case for the

Bakassi Peninsula. Their inclusion on the other hand would have the reverse effect and boost Usakedet chances of a quick return to Nigeria.

Although I could not say whether the omissions were mistakes or deliberate acts, too many negative things had already happened to customary owners of the peninsula for one to take any thing for granted. Firstly, Usakedet people were not being consulted. Secondly, they were not being included in teams set up to discuss the future of their homeland and finally they did not even feature on maps of their homeland. These curious happenings increasingly made me apprehensive. It no longer made sense to assume these events to be mere accidents or coincidences. I had to find a way to bring all Usakedet people into Nigeria. Ensuring the inclusion of Archibong Town on the map of the Bakassi Peninsula would hasten the achievement of that objective. Fortunately, I would not have to push too hard to achieve this goal. The battle Young and I fought in Lagos began to yield fruits. Soon after our Lagos encounters, Archibong Town and all Usakedet villages would feature on the map of Nigeria for the first time since 1913. Nigeria would also a few weeks after the Lagos meeting make her presence felt in Archibong Town, Aqua and the surrounding farmlands leaving Amoto, Odon and Efut Inwang (Bateka) under Cameroon control.

These were small but extremely significant achievements even though significant portions of the Bakassi Peninsula, including the above mentioned core Usakedet villages remained outside Nigeria's control and stayed so until the end of the Bakassi Peninsula crisis. In spite of the acrimony it engendered, the Lagos encounter was a critical breakthrough for me. For the first time in nearly a hundred years, all Usakedet villages would feature on the map of Nigeria. Usakedet people would, for the first time since 1913 feel like Nigerians again. Usakedet people in the liberated areas would again formally be reunited with their kith and kin in the rest of the Efik world. From whatever angle I looked at it, the Lagos encounter was a resounding success and a critical turning point in the struggle for the Bakassi Peninsula.

That Lagos meeting also had its negative side. It was remarkable for the damage it did to old time friends and allies. The mutual exchange of harsh and unfriendly words created a hostile environment that was not conducive and would prove unhelpful in creating the kind of collaborative atmosphere that was necessary to successfully prosecute the struggle for the Bakassi Peninsula. The heated encounters did offend delicate sensitivities. Young and I had put people laying false claims on Bakassi peninsula on notice. If any one had hoped to run away with the enormous resources of the Bakassi Peninsula without a fight, they now had an idea of the battle ahead. They were now certain that Usakedet people would not fold their hands and watch them make away with their resources and ancestral homeland. The heated sessions left indelible scars on some members of the delegation, making any form of reconciliation impossible. In many cases yesterday's friends became bitter enemies for life. The poisoned atmosphere engendered at the Lagos meeting would continue to dominate Bakassi peninsula domestic politics to the end. Members of the delegation and Young and I would repeat the shameful exchange of abuses at the Lagos airport as we boarded the flight back to Calabar. Tempers would again rise uncontrollably when we met to brief traditional rulers about the outcome of the Lagos meeting at Ikot Nakanda, headquarters of Akpabuyo Local Government Area. That meeting would end in another shouting match.

Perhaps, the most unexpected fallout of our Lagos meeting was that it shot me into lime-light. Despite some twenty-four years of work behind-the-scenes on the Bakassi Peninsula, I had always remained in the shadows; a relatively unknown quantity. The Lagos meeting would shoot me into prominence. The Obong of Calabar would confer on me the prestigious Efik traditional title of *'Ada Idaha K'Efik Eburutu'* in recognition of my work on the Bakassi Peninsula. I received the title with mixed feelings. Firstly, I felt flattered and humbled to be considered worthy to receive such a prestigious Efik title. Secondly, I hardly could say whether the award was truly in recognition of my contribution to the struggle for the Bakassi Peninsula or a Trojan gift designed to secure my silence when unscrupulous politicians began to claim ownership of the peninsula and expropriate its resources. Such scepticism would cast a pall on the only traditional recognition I had ever received.

CHAPTER FIVE

Unscrupulous Politicians Hijack Bakassi Peninsula

That Lagos encounter was a real eye-opener. Virtually every lingering doubt about the direction Nigeria was heading was beginning to be beyond doubt. The lessons learnt from our Lagos encounters would remain instructive to the end of the crisis. Although the Lagos meeting provided a good number of answers, a few questions remained unclear. I still could not say whether Nigeria did recognize the Usakedet people as customary owners of the Bakassi Peninsula. Given the kind of pressure fishermen communities and unprincipled politicians were mounting on government, I knew it would be a hard decision to make. I was equally uncertain what Nigeria would do if she had the choice to take part of the Bakassi Peninsula and abandon the part occupied by the Usakedet people. I also hardly could say whether Nigeria even considered the land occupied by the Usakedet people as part of the Bakassi Peninsula. We had put up a strong fight in Lagos to ensure our people were not abandoned but you never could be sure what Government would do. Nigeria had made her presence felt in Archibong Town and Aqua, weeks after our Lagos meeting. Our expectation was that Nigeria would quickly move and occupy the remaining Usakedet villages of Odon, Amoto and Efut Inwang (Bateka) that are about seven kilometres from Aqua and Archibong Town. As children we took less than an hour thirty minutes to cover that distance through bush paths. Today, with a newly constructed road linking the two communities, the journey takes some fifteen minutes by car. I could not understand why Nigeria did not make that move at a time when these villages were practically undefended. Questions like this kept bugging me.

Before now the struggle for Bakassi peninsula had largely been a one-man-clandestine-struggle on a lonesome and tortuous road. I had confined my actions to keeping relevant authorities informed about the situation in the Bakassi Peninsula and occasionally intervening like I did at the Lagos meeting. All along the twenty-three years I had been on this mission, it had largely been my struggle. But the struggle could no longer be my struggle alone. The Lagos momentum had to be sustained. I needed to get the Usakedet people engaged in the fight for their homeland. If Usakedet people must assert their claim over Bakassi peninsula, they had to assume primary responsibility for the struggle for that homeland. They had to take active part in the fight and be actively involved in decisions that would shape that homeland; Bakassi peninsula.

To achieve that objective I had nowhere else to go than to turn to the association of Usakedet people in Calabar; *Mbono Ndito Usakedet* that was being headed by the very Chief Dr. Archibong Edem Young who had accompanied me to the Lagos meeting. Turning *Mbono Ndito Usakedet* into a viable political platform and arrow head for the struggle for the Bakassi Peninsula proved to be no easy task. The association was young, still in its formative years and as a matter of fact not established for the kind of role it now had to play. There was therefore need to reorient its members and build capacity. More importantly, the association operated on a critically slim purse that negatively affected its ability to function as an effective association. In spite of these handicaps, *Mbono Ndito Usakedet* held out hope and promise for Usakedet people. Unlike their ancestors who centuries earlier had simply abandoned the Bakassi Peninsula and returned to Nigeria to found new settlements or simply melt into the wider Efik world, this generation of Usakedet people appeared to have found renewed interest in their roots and ancestral homeland. At the outbreak of hostilities in the Bakassi Peninsula, it only seemed natural that they should take over the baton from me and lead the struggle for their ancestral homeland.

Mbono Ndito Usakedet did not disappoint. Under the leadership of Young and the support of prominent members like Muri Benjamin Effiong Edet, Chief Ekpo Eyo, Madam Iquo Effiom and Chief Boko Asuquo, the association became transformed into a virile socio-political organization that would play vital roles in the struggle for the Bakassi Peninsula. Under the leadership of Young, the association assumed this new role with pride and confidence. *Mbono Ndito Usakedet* provided the badly needed political platform that the struggle had for years, so badly longed for. Besides the provision of a political platform, the association made available to the struggle for the Bakassi Peninsula a generation of Bakassi natives, young and old, of diverse experience and knowledge that would play key roles in the struggle for the Bakassi Peninsula. Usakedet people would serve as resource persons on a number of occasions. Some would become arrow heads in the fight against unscrupulous politicians bent on expropriating Bakassi peninsula and its rich marine and hydrocarbon resources. Many would, in the course of the struggle pay the supreme price. They gave their lives for the Bakassi Peninsula.

It was therefore no surprise that *Mbono Ndito Usakedet* became synonymous with the struggle for the Bakassi Peninsula. *Mbono Ndito Usakedet* greatly inspired and tremendously boosted the struggle for the Bakassi Peninsula. For a reasonable length of time, the association remained the only authentic and dominant voice for Bakassi people. *Mbono Ndito Usakedet* grew in strides and bounds. And as the association grew, it began to attract the attention of members of the fishermen communities who began to troop to the association in droves in search of membership. We reasoned that enlarging the association would not only improve the association's purse but would also bolster the struggle for the Bakassi Peninsula but we decided not to open the doors of the association to strangers because that would defeat the purpose of its founding fathers. Members of the fishermen communities and others of uncertain heritage who tried to infiltrate the association meetings were unceremoniously walked out. The association needed to retain its identity as an association established exclusively for Bakassi natives. In spite of such caution, a few camels managed to pass through the eye of the needle and people who had no blood ties whatsoever in the Bakassi Peninsula slipped through our net and gained admission into *Mbono Ndito Usakedet*. They would eventually be responsible for bringing down the association.

Before that could happen *Mbono Ndito Usakedet* had so evolved that anyone who had any kind of ambition in Bakassi peninsula simply felt they had to identify with the association. *Mbono Ndito Usakedet* became the place where everyone who wanted to play any kind of role in the Bakassi Peninsula had to be. Individuals and groups of Efik extraction kept trooping to the association in search of recognition and legitimacy. Number Seven Saint Mary's Street, Calabar; my residence soon assumed the role of the association's secretariat and became a regular meeting spot for Bakassi natives and members of fishermen communities. They flocked to Seven St. Mary's as pilgrims flock to holy lands. They flocked to Seven Saint Mary's during the day; they flocked to Seven Saint Mary's at night. Seven Saint Mary's became synonymous with the struggle for the Bakassi Peninsula. When I was home, Seven Saint Mary's seemed a veritable beehive of activities for Bakassi natives and fishermen communities alike. During my often prolonged absence from home my wife, Christy so effectively held fort that she became affectionately known as 'First Lady'. It did not matter whether I was home or away from home, people simply would not stop trooping to Seven Saint Mary's to identify with the struggle for the Bakassi Peninsula. Multitudes gathered at Number Seven Saint Mary's Street to celebrate or to empathize depending on the circumstances. Soon Seven Saint Mary's became transformed into a symbol of the struggle for the Bakassi Peninsula. Most of today's self-styled princes and princesses of Bakassi and Bakassi politicians are largely products of Number Seven Saint Mary's Street. They all had their initiation into Bakassi politics at Number Seven Saint Mary's Street. Never mind that today they all seem to have forgotten how and where it all started.

I was particularly impressed with this swarming on Seven Saint Mary's and as a matter of fact did what I could to encourage it. The presence at Seven Saint Mary's; residence of an Usakedet man of a large number of members of fishermen communities and their politicians was a clear indication of the primordial role Usakedet people had always played and continued to play as customary owners of the Bakassi Peninsula. The presence at Seven Saint Mary's of large numbers of members of the fishermen population and their politicians was a clear affirmation and an eloquent testimony of Usakedet ownership of the Bakassi Peninsula. The situation made me happy but it was a feeling that would not last. Trouble would begin when these people began to present the Bakassi Peninsula as the place of birth and ancestral homeland of Ijaws, Ilajes, Okobos, Efiats, Orons, Ibibios, Efiks, Igbos and Yorubas who make up the overwhelming fishermen population in the Bakassi Peninsula. A single ancestral homeland for such diverse ethnic groups!!! certainly not in the Bakassi Peninsula.

But Abuja would make matters worse by recognizing fishermen communities and their politicians as landlords and customary owners of the Bakassi Peninsula. Nigeria would go ahead to transform heterogeneous fishermen communities in the Bakassi Peninsula into homogeneous clans and fishing settlements into villages and towns. These policies would alarm Bakassi natives and make them more determined to defend their ancestral homeland. If they did nothing to challenge these policies they risked being dispossessed of their land and resources for ever. I found such policies clearly unacceptable and often made every effort to draw the attention of relevant authorities to such obnoxious policies but was often ignored. No one lifted a finger against whatever fishermen communities and their politicians did. Government simply turned a blind eye or looked the other way. Any one who dared challenge these politicians was simply said to be unpatriotic. When it came to the Bakassi Peninsula, people seemed unable to make a distinction between truth and falsehood, right and wrong. Bakassi peninsula seemed to be engulfed in a veritable integrity crisis. The situation not only alarmed Bakassi indigenes it would constitute the greatest threat ever posed to Usakedet people's hegemony over their homeland. It is hard to understand how a Nigeria that has made unassailable mark in her support for the freedom and independence of African states; sacrificed so much in the defence of the inalienable rights of indigenous people throughout Africa and demonstrated total commitment towards the complete eradication of Apartheid and colonisation on the African continent could so easily abandon such time-honoured stance to succumb to the whims and caprices of overzealous politicians.

Under pressure from politicians and fishermen communities, *Mbono Ndito Usakedet* could hardly find room to breathe or manoeuvre. Its fortunes would soon decline. But as the fortunes of *Mbono Ndito Usakedet* were declining that of another association; *Bakassi Welfare Union* was on the rise. Founded by Senator Florence Ita-Giwa; a lady of considerable personal charm and beauty, *Bakassi Welfare Union* seemed well positioned to cater for the wellbeing of Bakassi people. Ita-Giwa had demonstrated enough political sense and succeeded in carving out a fine niche for herself in the political landscape of

Nigeria. Very strong willed and uncompromisingly hard, this one of a kind woman politician had succeeded in getting doors opened on a number of occasions. It was hoped Ita-Giwa would do same for Bakassi people. Collaborating with Ita-Giwa in the struggle for the Bakassi Peninsula seemed a logical and wise move that would bolster the struggle for the Bakassi Peninsula.

That was not to be. *Bakassi Welfare Union* would become a veritable commercial and political enterprise whose sole objective it appeared would be to foster the political and economic wellbeing of its leadership. One of its very first engagements would be to collaborate with unscrupulous public servants in the compulsory deduction of funds from the salaries of miserably remunerated civil servants in the state in the name of a "Bakassi lottery" ostensibly to raise funds for Bakassi people and contribute to win the war effort. Although millions of naira was believed to have been realized through the scheme, no millionaires were known to have been created. *Bakassi Welfare Union* would transform itself into a Bakassi Peninsula overlord and take charge of everything Bakassi.

Although the leadership of *Bakassi Welfare Union* had never been resident in the Bakassi Peninsula and as a matter of fact largely had no blood ties whatsoever in the territory, *Bakassi Welfare Union* would turn the Bakassi Peninsula into its private estate and hijack the politics and economy of the peninsula. *Bakassi Welfare Union* would transform the struggle for the Bakassi Peninsula into a veritable money-guzzling and self-promotion enterprise. Attention would become focused on how to share political positions and oil revenues. The accumulation of wealth and political power now seemed the main aim of the struggle for the Bakassi Peninsula. That goal not only ran against the objectives of our struggle; it also ran against the interests and ambitions of the largely unskilled and amateur politician membership of *Bakassi Welfare Union.* The resultant conflict would put a virtual end to the *Bakassi Welfare Union* but not an end to a leadership that would continue to exploit the Bakassi situation even after the territory had been lost. In the end, *Bakassi Welfare Union* would add nothing to the struggle for the Bakassi Peninsula. Bakassi peninsula would not be liberated. Nigeria would lose the Bakassi Peninsula but the leadership of *Bakassi Welfare Union*; comprising largely of non natives of the Bakassi Peninsula would ride on the back of the misery of Bakassi native population to secure their political and economic well-being.

The desire to break *Bakassi Welfare Union's* monopoly of Bakassi politics and economy would lead to the creation of the *Bakassi Native Assembly*; an amalgamation of Bakassi natives and fishermen communities' politicians. *Bakassi Native Assembly* as a matter of fact was born at the famous Number Seven Saint Mary's Street with an initial subvention from me. In the beginning the association seemed poised to fill in the gaps and provide the much needed leadership for the continuation of the struggle for the Bakassi Peninsula. The young men and women who constituted the association appeared to have great potential and passion to embark on a vigorous struggle. The association contained elements that seemed to have the requisite experience and a clear vision of the onerous task ahead. It was hoped that given the calibre of persons involved, the association would inject new blood and ideas into the struggle for the Bakassi Peninsula. Subsequent events would prove me wrong.

Bakassi Native Assembly too, would sadly also suffer from the same disease that had crippled its predecessor; *Bakassi Welfare Union*. It too, would be overrun by a cabal of ambitious individuals whose sole desire it seemed, was to secure juicy political and economic advantages in the Bakassi Peninsula. They would transform themselves too into a new set of Shahs and colonial masters for the Bakassi Peninsula. The leadership of *Bakassi Native Assembly* would equally get enmeshed in a tawdry tussle for control of the enormous marine and petroleum resources in the peninsula instead of seeking ways to liberate the territory. Fishermen communities and unscrupulous politicians would use all sorts of strange and highly questionable tactics to try to gain control of the Bakassi Peninsula and its enormous resources. Individuals and groups would try to manipulate everything and everyone in a bid to secure top traditional or political positions. In the end, winning the struggle for the Bakassi Peninsula would simply take the back seat; indeed, winning the Bakassi Peninsula would be relegated to the background.

Once again I was dejected. My over trusting naïveté had again failed me. I had for reasons I cannot tell, seen the birth of the *Bakassi Native Assembly* as an event that would signal the end of the solitary struggle that essentially the struggle for the Bakassi Peninsula had been before *Mbono Ndito Usakedet* came into the picture. *Bakassi Native Assembly* had been born in my residence with a little take off grant from me. Seeing so many talented young men join in a fight that for decades had been a lonesome and lonely battle had given me real hope. In the euphoria of the moment, I failed to see through the smoke screen. Instead, I had the disingenuous feeling that my prayers had finally been answered. How it took me so long to realise that anyone that came rushing to identify with the struggle for the Bakassi Peninsula had a hidden agenda remains a puzzle. It was so frustrating to realise that the only reason why these non-Bakassi natives came to join the struggle for the Bakassi Peninsula was to help them get recognition and expropriate the peninsula and its enormous resources.

In my frustration, I tried without success to create another exclusive association for Bakassi natives. Bakassi natives had lost their vanguard role in the struggle to strangers and inadvertently accelerated their own demise. Unscrupulous politicians would step in fully, drown the voices of Bakassi natives and hijack Bakassi peninsula affairs. Bakassi natives themselves had become so compromised that they could no longer unite and speak with one voice. Dodgy politicians fully exploited the situation as they took deliberate steps to further weaken Bakassi natives. They played off one against the other and fomented unhealthy rivalries among Bakassi natives. Where such strategies failed to work, ruthless politicians took steps to purchase the friendship of Bakassi natives. They gave Bakassi natives presents, sponsored the election of amenable Bakassi natives into the Bakassi Local Government Council, fuelled crisis among Bakassi natives and financed opposition within the Bakassi native community. Occasionally they intervened in the most subversive way in the affairs of Bakassi natives. And whenever Bakassi natives proved too stubborn, difficult or unwilling to do their wish, they did not mind the use of cheap blackmail and other devious strategies against Bakassi natives.

Once Nigeria had allowed fishermen communities and unscrupulous politicians; strangers in the Bakassi Peninsula to claim ownership of the peninsula and take advantage of Bakassi indigenes' rights and entitlements, including its enormous oil wealth, Nigeria dangerously veered off the road, threw a spanner into the works and lost a vital ally in the struggle to regain sovereignty over the Bakassi Peninsula. The tragic happenings of December 12, 1999 as we would later see remain a puzzle. It does however appear that the events of that fateful day might have been a brutal intervention by Bakassi natives on the side of the adversary. If that suspicions were ascertained, it would be a regrettable reaction of a desperate people to policies that seemed designed to dispossess them of their homeland and resources; their only source of livelihood. If the sad events of December 12, 1999 turn out to be what they seemed, it would mean that Nigeria lost the case for Bakassi peninsula on December 12, 1999 and not on October 10th 2002 when the International Court of Justice laid down its judgement. Perhaps those at the various fronts; military, diplomatic and legal of the struggle might want to tell how their fronts faired after December 12, 1999.

The only people who could have turned things around and put an end to all this confusion were the Efik people. This Efik people who the Whiteman said "if their countenance did not speak of their character, their dress proclaimed their importance" were the only people who could have brought sanity to Bakassi peninsula affairs. And Efik people of old made sure they lived up to that noble reputation by the way they conducted themselves. Honesty and integrity were synonymous with Efik nature. Efik nobility of character made Efik people stand out quite distinctly from the crowd. It was therefore hardly surprising that Efik people were deservedly admired and remained the envy of their countrymen and everyone who came in contact with the Efik world.

Efik nature detests ignoble acts. *"Afia ebot imaha indek."* In the past you hardly could find an Efik man willingly engaging in any criminal activity. The reason was simple. If an Efik man or woman were accused of any criminal act, it was their entire family that stood so accused. If they happened to be convicted, it was equally their entire families that were so convicted. Every member of the family suffered the pain and ostracism. Marriages into such families were often prohibited. For such reasons the Efik man and woman so valued their name and jealously guarded it against anything that would tarnish their image or bring it to disrepute. This extraordinary character coupled with a great passion for a highly evolved tradition and culture made Efik people exhibit a strong sense of superiority towards all they came into contact with. Efik people did not just feel superior; they lived up to that reputation by the way they carried themselves and related to others.

Little wonder the city of Calabar; (OBIO) home of all Efik people became the first capital of Nigeria, became Nigeria's first centre of learning, trained Nigeria's first indigenous president, produced Nigeria's first indigenous Inspector General of Police and produced

Nigeria's first professor. This same Calabar would be where the first competitive football, hockey and cricket matches would be played in Nigeria and the Efik language would be the first Nigerian language that the Bible would be translated into. Efik people had every reason to be proud.

No more. All that noble quality now seems to have gone with the wind. The Bakassi Peninsula crisis brought out the ignoble in the Efik nation. For reasons extremely difficult to fathom, Efik people seemed to have relegated Efik glorious past and fascinating history to the archives of history during the Bakassi Peninsula crisis. Times seemed to have changed and Efik people appeared to have changed with it. Bakassi crisis threw the Efik nation off balance, into confusion and disarray. For a people who had the most credible claim to the Bakassi Peninsula, Efik response to the Bakassi crisis left too much to be desired. The Efik just seemed unable or unwilling to play the role destiny had bestowed on it in the territory. Bakassi peninsula crisis would overwhelm the Efik nation and bring out the ignoble and absurd in a nation in decline.

As far as the Bakassi crisis was concerned, the Efik nation appeared to have broken away from its noble and glorious past; away from its rich tradition and culture to something that defied description. The result was that noble qualities such as honesty and integrity that are recognized integral parts of Efik nature were simply thrown overboard in the name of politics. When it came Bakassi peninsula affairs, even Efik people would join unscrupulous groups and individuals in behaving with little or no care for the propriety of their actions in the name of politics. Everything became justifiable in the name of politics. It is hard to understand how a people with the kind of amazing glorious past and impressive pedigree like the Efik people could descend to the level of near irrelevance that was witnessed during the Bakassi Peninsula crisis.

And since its seeming departure from its noble and glorious past, the Efik nation has remained divided and in endemic crisis. While most Nigerian nationalities have an inclusive policy that strives to bring all their peoples into one fold regardless of dialectic differences that sometimes make understanding each other difficult, the Efik nation has a restrictive and discriminatory attitude that turns to alienate its very own people. As a result, ethnic groups or clans like the Ibibios, Annangs, Orons, Okobos, Efiats, etc that do not even have significant distinctive dialectic differences with the Efik language, are discriminated against when they should all have constituted a strong and powerful CALABAR NATION. The problem has further been aggravated by the political fragmentation of OLD CALABAR along linguistic, dialectic, clan and tribal lines which has impaired the crystallization of a collective CALABAR national identity. It is strange that although Nigerians everywhere recognized a group of people as CALABAR PEOPLE, there is no CALABAR NATION.

While other Nigerian ethic groups go beyond their regions to other states and even to other African nations to claim people they recognize as theirs or of their ancestry, Efik people close their doors against their very own because of simple dialectic or cultural differences. As a result of this restrictive and discriminatory attitude, the Efik nation has shrunk so dangerously that Efik people today can rightly be said to be endangered species. Consequently, while most ethnic nationalities in Nigeria continue to increase and expand, the Efik nation continues to shrink and decline. Thus, instead of seeing the Bakassi Peninsula and its people as one of its own, the Efik nations appears to have seen the territory as one of its lost colonies that was about to be returned to its colonial master; the Efik nation and Bakassi natives probably perceived as Efik subjects. This arrogant perception would constitute a major stumbling block to Nigeria's ambition in the Bakassi Peninsula.

The Efik situation has further been compounded by the fact that the Efik throne has been bedevilled by a seemingly intractable succession crisis that has in no small way helped cripple the Efik nation. Contemporary Efik Monarchs; The Obong of Calabar; Grand Patriarch and Paramount Ruler of the Efiks have often found themselves isolated and spending useful time, energy and resources struggling to make peace with rebellious and recalcitrant councils that often are in no mood to make concessions or compromise. As a result, contemporary Efik Monarchs have found themselves unable to wield much power and influence over their subjects and territory. This inability to find solutions to internal crisis has quite often led to more crises. Contemporary Efik Monarchs have often reacted to such crisis by dismissing their councils and replacing them with more amenable councils. But the break up of one council has often led to the creation of factions; one for the Monarch, the other, die-hard opponents. This approach, as would be expected has only led to interminable wrangling and conflicts that have often crippled the reign of contemporary Efik Monarchs. As a result, contemporary Efik Monarchs have often failed to wield enough power to influence events and add value to the Efik nation.

This happened to be the sad state the Efik nation found itself at the outbreak of the Bakassi Peninsula crisis. For a people that had the most credible claim to the Bakassi Peninsula, Efik nation's reaction to the crisis was embarrassingly lame and baffling. Although it was obvious that the Efik nation could not directly intervene at The Hague because it is not a sovereign state, one expected the Efik nation to wield sufficient power at home to take charge of the domestic front and lead Nigeria's preparation of the case. That did not happen. Rather than seize the initiative and take charge of the situation at home, the Efik nation allowed Bakassi crisis to slip out of its hands; making it possible for a clique of unscrupulous individuals, corrupt politicians, racketeers, and fraudsters to hijack the Bakassi peninsula. The Efik nation would be misled into the pursuit of a futile and senseless policy of territorial expansion in which she would be out-manoeuvred and overwhelmed. In the end, in spite of the Efik nation's claim over the Bakassi Peninsula, a non-Efik man would emerge traditional ruler of the Bakassi Peninsula.

Efik fiction and oral literature contain abundant references to the Usakedet people and the Bakassi Peninsula. For quite curious reason, even the Efik nation seemed to lack the courage or appeared simply unable or unwilling to speak the truth. The Efik nation simply abandoned the Usakedet people; customary owners of the Bakassi Peninsula. Bakassi Peninsula crisis would however not be the first time Usakedet people would feel let down by their Efik kith and kin. Efik nation's reaction to the crisis was reminiscent of Efik nation's response to Usakedet call for help when renegade soldiers wrecked havoc on the Bakassi Peninsula during, and in the aftermath of the Nigerian civil war.

This general negative stance of the Efik nation notwithstanding, I made spirited effort to reach out to prominent Efik sons and daughters to explain the situation of the Usakedet people and solicit support for Usakedet cause. Although my efforts generally came to naught, I continued to take the troubles of Bakassi natives to the doorsteps of prominent Efik people in search of help for Bakassi natives. I took Bakassi troubles on countless occasions to Edidem Boco Ene Mkpang Cohbam V; the Obong of Calabar, Grand Patriarch and Paramount Ruler of the Efiks who always gave me unfettered access to his palace. I pestered Governor Donald Duke as often as the occasion would permit. I made unscheduled visits to Ms. Nella Andem Ewa; Cross River State Attorney General and Commissioner for Justice. I harried Etubom Ukorebi Ukorebi Asuquo and Dr. Akpanika who both gave me particular attention, all in search of help for my motherland. Few Efik people held sway in Nigeria at the inception of the Bakassi crisis but there was one Efik man who appeared to rule the waves.

That man was Chief Tony Ani. Chief Ani was not just a proud holder of two important ministerial portfolios in an extremely competitive Nigeria, Chief Ani was said to have been given a carte blanche and a blank check so to speak to take care of Bakassi crisis as he deemed fit. Being a trusted member of cabinet, Ani had the President's ears and immense powers and could easily have turned things around for Bakassi people. It was thanks to the personal intervention of Chief Ani that Bakassi peninsula itself had become a local government council in the Cross River State because Akwa Ibom State had finalised plans to incorporate the territory into one of its local government areas. Chief Ani's timely intervention is said to have nipped the plan in the bud.

It was to an Efik man with such an impeccable credential and pedigree that I took the troubles of Bakassi natives to in 1994. But I will not forget in a hurry the day I took the troubles of Bakassi natives to the door steps of Chief Ani. I arrived at the Honourable minister's office as early as ten o'clock in the morning and had my presence and object of my visit duly announced. The Honourable Minister kept me waiting till seven o'clock in the evening when he left his office without granting me audience. That was the amazing treatment I got for travelling thousands of kilometres to bring the miserable plight of Bakassi natives to an Efik Minister. It was obvious from the Minister's reaction that he knew exactly who I was, where I came from and where I stood on the Bakassi crisis. The Minister's reaction seemed in line with a script that had been played over and over before my eyes. My problem was that I could not tell who had written the script. It was disappointing that Chief Ani did not deem it necessary to at least listen to whatever rubbish I had to tell him but his reaction summed up the general frustration I found in dealing with my Efik kith and kin. May be in the rubbish I would have said lay the solution to the Bakassi crisis. But the Honourable Minister did not give me a chance. He denied me audience and Bakassi natives lost a great opportunity.

In spite of the many disappointments, it would be unfair not to acknowledge the many contributions, support and personal sacrifices made by a good number of Efik people; too many to mention in the struggle for the Bakassi Peninsula. Although we could not achieve the desired goal, Bakassi natives remain grateful. It would equally be a disservice not to give recognition to the many Bakassi natives for their unequalled commitment to the struggle. Before the demise of the association of Bakassi natives; *Mbono Ndito Usakedet*, the association had provided the struggle for Bakassi peninsula with a generation of Bakassi natives; men and women: young and old, too many to mention whose commitment, loyalty and sacrifice to the struggle was unequalled. Some made the supreme sacrifice. The best we can do for them is to continue the struggle and to dedicate this book to them so that they die not in vain

Regrettably, not every Bakassi native can be said to have demonstrated that same level of commitment. As would be expected in similar circumstances, there were Bakassi natives whose attitude towards the struggle left much to be desired. There were those whose loyalty was suspect. They were those who played double game. There were those who stood and still stand on the side of the enemy. There were those who put their selfish interest far and above the interest of their people. There were those who simply sat on the side-lines and only emerged to reap where they did not sow and there were those who remained undecided to the end. It would be embarrassing to recall how some of these fellows behaved. Even so, we remain disinclined to judge them too severely, not to speak of denouncing or condemning them. These were hard times and the struggle for the Bakassi Peninsula had its own share of individuals who could not function under the kind of pressure that they were subjected to.

The situation would however degenerate into a silent but potentially dangerous conflict on the fringes of the struggle for ownership of the Bakassi Peninsula between Nigeria and Cameroon. I refused to be drawn into an open conflict with fishermen communities and unscrupulous politicians, convinced the time for that would come. I was equally confident that when that time came Bakassi natives would easily win the contest. Thanks to the help I had got from Pa Leo, I had a mountain of literature in favour of Bakassi natives' ownership of the Bakassi peninsula. But there were more compelling reasons not to open up a new front in the struggle for the Bakassi peninsula even though the battle could easily be won. The International Court of Justice was yet to determine the ownership claims between Nigeria and Cameroon. In the circumstance, it was unwise to take action that could distract attention from the principal goal of winning the Bakassi Peninsula. Pursuing any other option when the World Court had yet to give its judgement was equally fraught with danger. Such action could unintentionally turn into help for the adversary. It was a risk I could ill afford to take. Despite such caution, my critics continued to blame me for crying out against strangers trying to expropriate the Bakassi Peninsula. I refused to be intimidated, knowing too well that had Bakassi peninsula been their homeland and Bakassi natives their people, they would do a lot more than I could ever imagine.

Nonetheless, the situation needed one to tread with care caution. Caution then became the watchword but the more restraint one displayed the more strange things happened to one's people. The problem was not that Usakedet dominion over the Bakassi Peninsula had never been challenged. As we saw earlier there had been half-hearted and dispirited challenges to Usakedet (Isangele) hegemony of the Bakassi Peninsula. This time however, the threat was real. A non-indigene had been appointed paramount traditional ruler of the Bakassi Peninsula and a Bakassi Local Government Area had been created with strangers at the helm. Bakassi peninsula history was being rewritten without a finger being raised. Although Usakedet people had in the past successfully defended their territory against people like Prince Archibong Edem and others, I doubted the ability of Bakassi natives to repeat such feats in the face of the kind of onslaught politicians were subjecting them to. Whereas in the past, whenever the interest of Bakassi natives was in conflict with the interest of fishermen communities, the interest of Bakassi natives always prevailed, the reverse was now the case. The Bakassi Peninsula was being gradually hijacked by migrant fishermen communities and their politicians. Steadily, people of uncertain origins were all claiming to come from the Bakassi Peninsula. None of these persons had an ancestor lying in peace in the Bakassi Peninsula; had ever been resident in the territory or had a family home in the Bakassi Peninsula. However, buoyed by apparent support from a misguided government, these persons would turn themselves into neo-colonialists and tin-gods in the peninsula. The Bakassi Peninsula would remain to the very end of the crisis and beyond dominated by a pervasive and totally unacceptable level of gross, monumental falsehood that may have immensely contributed to the final outcome of the Bakassi Peninsula crisis.

This unexpected threat to Usakedet hegemony over its ancestral homeland would change the dynamics of the struggle for the Bakassi Peninsula and give it a new meaning. It would take steam out of the struggle for the Bakassi Peninsula between Nigeria and Cameroon and turn it into a struggle for the survival of the customary owners of the Bakassi peninsula. Now I had to fight on two fronts. I had to defend my maternal ancestral homeland against politicians with no scruples trying to expropriate and exploit that homeland as well as keep afloat my dream to bring the Bakassi Peninsula back to Nigeria. Although both objectives were not mutually self-exclusive, my attention would become consumed by strategies to ensure that Bakassi natives remained masters of their homeland and the enormous marine and hydrocarbon resources therein. That struggle appears to be on-going.

CHAPTER SIX
Mistakes upon Mistakes in an Incredible Rat Race

Meanwhile, in their anxieties to demonstrate they had effective control of the Bakassi Peninsula, both Nigeria and Cameroon would embark upon an incredible rat race in the Bakassi Peninsula. They competed with each other in their effort to provide social, economic and political structures in areas they each controlled. This was a novelty. Never, in the history of the Bakassi Peninsula had any government made any serious effort to bring development to the people. Now Nigeria and Cameroun were building schools where there were no pupils to attend. Bore holes were being sunk where practically no potable water could be obtained.

Never before had Bakassi inhabitants witnessed the kind of development that was being brought to their door steps by Nigeria and Cameroon. Nigeria in particular showered the territory with projects. Before the crisis, Nigeria had had no presence in Bakassi peninsula besides a brief stay during the Nigerian civil war. Cameroon on the other hand had moved into the peninsula immediately after the Nigerian civil war ended and had since 1974 turned the peninsula into what became known as Isangele (Usakedet) sub-division under the sovereignty of the Republic of Cameroon. Before the outbreak of hostilities in 1993, Cameroon had had a civil and military presence in the Bakassi Peninsula for over twenty years. Now Nigeria needed to overtake Cameroon but first she had some catching up to do. Cameroon would however, not allow herself to be outdone. She clearly had the advantage in this regard and did not want to loose it. This competition turned the Bakassi Peninsula into the most sought bride of the last century and plunged prospective suitors; Nigeria and Cameroon into a veritable rat race. Each suitor in their effort to impress the bride; Bakassi peninsula, went head over heels in the process and the racketeers had a field day.

Besides this lack of a presence in the Bakassi Peninsula prior to the crisis, Nigeria had another major handicap. Either by omission or commission, Nigeria allowed ambitious and deceitful groups and individuals to hijack the Bakassi peninsula. These persons would not only mislead government, they would succeed in foisting falsehood on the entire nation. In the circumstance, Nigeria had no option than to put political and economic structures on ground that would match the falsehood that had already been foisted on the nation. The alternative would have been a terrible disaster. It could have plunged Nigeria and indeed the Bakassi Peninsula from the very beginning into a terrible credibility crisis. Once a false foundation had knowingly or unwittingly been established, subsequent action had to be predicated on such foundation to sustain the logic. Behaving otherwise would have exposed the nation to ridicule and risked seeing Nigeria's claim over the Bakassi Peninsula collapse like a pack of cards upon itself from the very beginning. That was too great a risk for any nation to take. Thus, the greater the effort Nigeria made the more mistakes she accumulated and the slimmer her chances of regaining the Bakassi Peninsula.

In the very competitive environment that the Bakassi Peninsula had become, contestants had to base their action on a sound knowledge of the territory. The only way that could be achieved was for contestants; Nigeria and Cameroon to listen to owners of the territory and carry them along. It does not appear Nigeria paid much attention to this fact and it is hard to understand why she did not. Nigeria refused to engage customary owners of the Bakassi Peninsula and instead relied on the falsehood provided by unscrupulous individuals and groups who had nothing to do with the territory in the formulation of her Bakassi policy. That turned out to be a terrible mistake. This handicap would largely be responsible for much of the blunders that was witnessed in the Bakassi Peninsula

Nigeria turned the Bakassi Peninsula into a local council area in 1996. Cameroon swiftly responded in the same year by splitting Bakassi peninsula from the single 'Isangele sub-division' she had created in 1974 into four sub-divisions. The creation of Bakassi Local Government in Nigeria did not elicit much celebration. Bakassi natives, in particular had no illusions about what to expect from a local council in the Bakassi Peninsula that was going to be controlled by strangers. Besides, the customary owners of the peninsula had demanded that the council headquarters be sited on mainland Bakassi peninsula. Instead, Nigeria chose to site Bakassi local government headquarters in a fishing settlement in total disregard for the views of customary owners of the territory. Sitting the council headquarters at Abana; a fishing port was a painful slap on the face of Bakassi natives. Fishermen communities were used to travelling to Bakassi mainland to deal with government matters, pay allegiance and homage to the landlords as well as pay the necessary taxes to the owners of the land. Fishermen communities were used to going to Bakassi mainland to replenish their supplies, get fresh water and spend the off fishing season with loved ones, friends and families. Sitting the council headquarters in a fishing port meant that Bakassi natives now had to sail to the fishing ports to deal with government. That was not just a bad joke; it was an unacceptable reversal of fortunes. I made sure I did not set my foot at Abana as a sign of protest until the crisis came to an end.

As both nations hurried to provide schools, health care centres, social amenities, administrative set ups and political structures in the Bakassi Peninsula, the race for Nigeria that had had no real presence in the Bakassi Peninsula since 1914, was clearly a race against time. Besides establishing a sub division in the Bakassi Peninsula in 1974, Cameroon's presence in the Bakassi Peninsula too had largely been on paper. In Cameroon, the Bakassi Peninsula had largely been seen as an 'impenetrable marshland' occupied by Nigerians. It was only after the Bakassi Peninsula was known to harbour rich hydrocarbon deposits that Cameroon began to take keen interest in the territory. Even so, Cameroon found it more convenient to exploit these resources from bases in Douala and other Cameroonian cities instead of setting up bases in the peninsula. Bakassi crisis would change that perception. Cameroon would construct a road to link this 'impenetrable marshland' with mainland Cameroon during the Bakassi crisis. The race equally seemed a little easier for Cameroon not only because she had put a civil administration in place in the Bakassi Peninsula decades earlier but also because she had had a military presence in the peninsula since the early 1970s. Surely, Cameroon was undoubtedly more familiar with the Bakassi terrain. The outbreak of hostilities would witness the acceleration of these efforts both in degree and tempo.

Except for the overwhelming presence of Nigerians in the Bakassi peninsula, Nigeria had no sovereign presence in the peninsula prior to the outbreak of hostilities between Nigeria and Cameroon in 1993 over ownership of the territory. Nigeria needed strong evidence to convince the world that the Bakassi Peninsula truly belonged to her. For that to happen, Nigeria needed the support of the owners of the territory but Nigeria seemed to have closed that window. Nigeria did not appear to recognize the people who own the Bakassi Peninsula and as such never appeared to take steps to engage them in any kind of dialogue. Nigeria continued to act and adopt policies that clearly tended to alienate customary owners of the peninsula. It was clear that unless some of Nigeria's Bakassi decisions and policies were reversed, she would run into difficulties in the Bakassi peninsula. Nothing ever changed and Nigeria kept piling mistakes upon mistakes that ended up undermining her own efforts in the Bakassi Peninsula.

The creation of clans in the Bakassi Peninsula for example, was one policy that I would totally be opposed to. I could not be impressed by a policy that was going to transform heterogeneous fishing communities in the Bakassi Peninsula into homogeneous clans, especially at a time when the bona fide owners of the Bakassi Peninsula were not even liberated. I had advised that the plan be put on hold until the Bakassi Peninsula was fully liberated. That would have made it possible for Bakassi natives; customary owners of the peninsula to convey their views to Government on clan creation in their territory. Government failed to heed my advice and went ahead to create clans that had never existed in the Bakassi Peninsula. Government would end up appointing strangers chiefs, clan heads and paramount ruler both for the natural Bakassi clans and for the artificial clans it created to sustain its falsehood.

As feared, these clan creation and appointments would turn individuals of unknown origin and persons of little integrity and accomplishment into traditional rulers. Paupers would become 'royal highnesses' overnight. The policy would turn tenants and strangers into indigenes and landlords in the Bakassi Peninsula. Heterogeneous fishing settlements would be transformed into homogeneous villages. Soon, fishermen communities who come to Bakassi peninsula to seek an honest means of livelihood would begin to claim fishing settlements as their ancestral homeland. Never in the history of the Efik world had anyone ever claimed to come from a fishing settlement; to come from an 'Ine'; to come from a fishing port.

Bakassi peninsula crisis would change all that and even Efik people would claim to come from fishing settlements.

Bakassi peninsula would become a veritable circus where sons and daughters of circus dancers, gurus of coercive tactics, masters of dirty tricks and persons capable of all forms of perfidy would manoeuvre their way to positions of power. Not only would a man whose father was a common man and still living manipulate his way to become paramount ruler of the Bakassi Peninsula and thus assume the title of "His Royal Highness" the Bakassi Peninsula itself would have a paramount ruler and a traditional rulers' council that largely comprised of common men and non-Bakassi-natives. I hardly could understand what reason government had to permit such desecration of time-honoured traditional institutions. Not surprisingly, neither the Bakassi paramount ruler nor the Bakassi traditional rulers' council could perform simple traditional rites in the Bakassi peninsula. They could not offer libation to the ancestors because they had no ancestors to invoke in the peninsula. They equally could not offer sacrifice to Bakassi sea deities because Bakassi peninsula sea deities would not recognized them. In spite of such evident lack of legitimacy, these persons would be permitted to disinherit Bakassi natives and appropriate the Bakassi Peninsula. One lie would lead to another and before you knew it, Bakassi Local Government Council would become completely transformed into the greatest lie of the last century.

I felt extremely sad especially because I had earlier tried to convey my fears about clan creation before the Bakassi Peninsula was completely liberated. Since no one took notice I had to follow up with a despatch in which, in very simple terms, I tried to expose the complexity of traditional matters in the Bakassi Peninsula. My despatch noted that ordinarily the creation of clans and the appointment of clan heads would be a welcome event but Bakassi

Local Government Area I observed, could not be said to be ordinary. Bakassi Local Government Area, I noted, was the only local council area in Nigeria that had a huge chunk of its territory and people still under the control of some foreign nation. As a result of the situation, family members on one side of the Bakassi divide were having real difficulties visiting or communicating with those on the other side. The situation, I explained, had become so bad that fathers could not see their children; husbands could not see their wives; people could no longer give their dead befitting burials. To say life in Bakassi peninsula had become a dreadful nightmare for owners of the peninsula was to express their hardship mildly.

I expressed surprise that persons dealing with the Bakassi Peninsula appeared not to know Bakassi history and noted that it had taken tremendous effort and understanding for Bakassi indigenes to go along with some of the decisions that Nigeria had taken on the Bakassi Peninsula. I nevertheless gave the assurance that Bakassi natives would continue to demonstrate that high sense of responsibility in order not to derail from our primary objective of total liberation of the Bakassi Peninsula. I expressed surprise and anger that government could lump two clans; Amoto and Efut Inwang villages that were inhabited by people of different ethnic origins into a single clan while Archibong Town with barely a dozen houses or less and heterogeneous fishing settlements were being transformed into clans.

My despatch noted that as custodians of the tradition and culture of the people of the Bakassi Peninsula, the Usakedet people reserved the exclusive right to advise government on traditional matters in the Bakassi Peninsula and lamented their inability to effectively play that role because most of them were still largely on the Cameroonian controlled side of the peninsula. No Individual or group of individuals, I emphasized, could, regardless of their position in society, perform those traditional functions. I warned that it would be an exercise in self-delusion for any one residing outside the Bakassi Peninsula to think they could transform themselves into clan heads and paramount rulers in the Bakassi Peninsula. Such a culture was alien to the tradition and culture of Bakassi natives and was certain to be rejected by the people. I warned that because there was no such precedent in the Bakassi Peninsula, such policy could have unpleasant repercussions.

My despatch called on government to tread carefully, stressing that without the total liberation of the Bakassi Peninsula, it would be difficult to see a definitive resolution of traditional matters in the peninsula. I advised that in the light of the foregoing, efforts should be intensified to liberate the Bakassi Peninsula before embarking on any form of clan creation and appointment of clan heads. The environment, I insisted, was not conducive. Nigeria could end up appointing strangers as clan heads and traditional rulers for the Bakassi Peninsula particularly given the multiplicity of clan head aspirants whose real origins were unknown. That representation apparently fell on deaf ears. Its recommendations were completely ignored. Government went ahead to create clans in Bakassi peninsula in complete disregard for the views of customary owners of the territory.

Four years later, I would be compelled to send another memorandum to government on the same subject. This time, the battle would be over the appointment of a certain Edet Effiong Atire clan head of Amoto/Efut Inwang clan. When Usakedet people learnt that the state government had issued this non-native with a certificate as clan head of Amoto/Efut Inwang clan, Usakedet people quickly petitioned the state governor who promptly ordered that the certificate be withdrawn. Weeks later, Usakedet people would learn of renewed moves to re-issue the certificate to the same fellow. After spirited efforts, including a court injunction failed to stop the re-issuance of the clan head certificate to a fellow who had no blood ties whatsoever in the Bakassi Peninsula, I had no choice than to send a strongly worded petition to the Cross River State Governor on behalf of customary owners of Bakassi peninsula.

In that petition I reminded the governor of why the certificate had been withdrawn in the first instance. I recalled that besides protesting, Usakedet people had gone to court to challenge the appointment and noted with profound regret that while the Court had curiously not deemed it necessary to give such a sensitive case expedited hearing, the government it appeared, seemed set to re-issue the certificate. I lamented that it had been a frustrating tale of interminable adjournments, adjournment and adjournment every time the case was brought up for hearing and regretted that in spite of an earlier injunction the Court had placed on the fellow, the fellow had continued to parade himself as clan head of Amoto/Efut Inwang clan. Usakedet people had reliably been informed that government was making plans to re-issue the clan headship certificate to a total stranger.

Usakedet people, I said, were at a complete loss to know how the state could arrive at a decision on such a sensitive matter without consulting the people. That decision, if it ever came to stand would have damaging consequences on generations of Usakedet people. For the avoidance of doubt, I again categorically reiterated that the fellow had no blood lineage whatsoever in the Bakassi Peninsula and as such could not, under any circumstance, occupy a traditional stool in the Bakassi Peninsula. It might be of interest to note that three out of the four persons who stood as plaintiffs in the case passed away before the case was finally determined in favour of the defendant.

I took the occasion to recall other decisions and policies that had impacted negatively on customary owners of the peninsula and told the governor that the only reason why such decisions and policies had been tolerated had been to allow everyone concentrate their energy on the case with Cameroon. I assured the Governor that Usakedet people would continue to show restraint in the overall interest of the nation but warned that I could not guarantee that Usakedet people would permit the desecration and adulteration of their tradition and culture of which the clan headship stool constituted an undeniable integral part and concluded by calling on the governor to give urgent consideration to the matter to save our traditional institution from imminent defilement.

Nothing happened. My petition was simply ignored. The state made a mockery of the traditional institution and reappointed a stranger, clan head of Amoto/Efut Inwang clan. But the rape and desecration of Bakassi traditional institutions did not stop there. The state went ahead to create artificial clans and appoint strangers as clan heads to head these artificial clans. The State would crown her efforts with the appointment of a stranger whose father was an ordinary citizen and was still living, paramount ruler of the Bakassi Peninsula. The son would soon confer a chieftaincy title on the father. Such sacrilegious acts only helped reinforce the belief that Nigeria was indeed working towards passing title in the Bakassi Peninsula to fishermen communities.

Such violations of the rights of Bakassi natives were not confined to traditional matters alone. Having subdued Bakassi natives on the traditional front, unscrupulous politicians turned their attention to the political front. In their desire to take full control of Bakassi peninsula resources, they began to act without regard to the propriety of their action. They would no longer let Bakassi natives choose candidates who would represent them in the Bakassi Local Government Council. Unscrupulous politicians did the selection for Bakassi natives in a crude, abrasive, and unbridle display of strength and undisguised contempt for Bakassi natives. Unscrupulous politicians would sometimes choose their own people to represent Bakassi natives and by so doing appropriate positions intended for Bakassi natives. Where they found themselves obliged to choose Bakassi natives, they choose indigenes who happened to be persons who had shown little or no interest, played no role and made no contributions whatsoever towards the struggle for the Bakassi Peninsula. It was unimaginable, even in the pitiable circumstances that Bakassi natives had found themselves for such persons to represent the interest of Bakassi natives.

But Bakassi natives had become so used to being battered that they had to swallow every bitter pill that was forced down their throat. Fishermen communities and unprincipled politicians took deliberate steps to prevent Bakassi natives from participation in the political process in the Bakassi Peninsula by installing a systematic process of impoverishment and marginalisation of Bakassi natives opposed to their ambition. Usakedet indigenes could not fight back. Decimated as Bakassi natives had become, they were no longer in any position to fight back. They stood no chance of winning. Although I was convinced that protests had become a mere routine and waste of time, I continued to draw government attention to these concerns to put things on record and in their proper perspective.

It was against this backdrop that I sent another petition to the state government, vehemently denouncing the imposition of strangers to represent Bakassi natives in the Bakassi local government council elections. As usual I began by broaching the familiar irritant of Nigeria's refusal to recognise customary owners of the Bakassi Peninsula clarifying that unlike fishing settlements that were heterogeneous, temporary and relatively recent establishment, Usakedet villages in the Bakassi Peninsula were ancient settlements of a homogeneous people who had lived in the peninsula since the fifteenth century.

I told the governor that it was important for Bakassi natives to choose individuals who enjoyed the trust and confidence of their people to represent them in council. Such persons had also to be individuals who had demonstrated adequate commitment to the struggle for the Bakassi Peninsula in which Usakedet people had been engaged in for some three or four decades. Their representatives had to be natives who not only had the capacity to understand the complexity of the struggle; they had to be individuals who were prepared to make the necessary sacrifices for their people. To ignore such considerations could prove expensive. I told the governor that none of the candidates chosen by his party to represent the Usakedet people at the local council elections met any of those criteria. Under such circumstances it was not too difficult to imagine the kind of representation these candidates would bring to Bakassi natives. These candidates, I stressed, were simply unacceptable and noted that although such acts might seem beneficial to politicians, they were in the long-term, counter-productive and detrimental to the overall interest of the party and the nation.

I called on the governor to reconsider the decision to impose strangers on Bakassi natives in the interest of his party and threatened that unless government reconsidered its nominations for the position of councillors in the five Bakassi natives wards in Bakassi local Government Area, Bakassi natives would be in no position to guarantee the success of the party at council elections. I told the governor that it was a step Bakassi natives did not like to take and would not wish to take but until the party began to take steps to right the wrongs that were being committed against Bakassi natives, conventional wisdom, ordinary rules of prudence and common sense demanded that Bakassi natives reconsider their stay in the governor's party. The governor called my bluff and ignored my petition.

In spite of the existence of numerous local councils in Nigeria, many communities continue to clamour for the creation of more local government councils in their area. This is hardly surprising. Local government councils not only bring development closer to the people, they increase the people's participation in governance. Viewed from the surface, there seemed nothing strange or unusual when people began to agitate for the creation of a new local government council in the Bakassi Peninsula. A closer look at the demand however revealed that those behind the demand were members of the fishermen communities and their politicians. A few Bakassi natives had strangely also bought the idea.

Attractive and beneficial as the creation of local councils may be, the demand for the creation of any local council needs to emanate from the indigenous population of the area. The demand for the creation of a new local government council in the Bakassi Peninsula did not meet that critical criterion. The demand came from fishermen communities' politicians wanting to expropriate the Bakassi Peninsula. Realising that Bakassi native opposition may not let them take control of the enormous resources in the peninsula, fishermen communities and unscrupulous politicians; Bakassi neo-colonisers devised an ingenious plot to split the Bakassi peninsula into two local government councils in a desperate attempt to try to go round the problem. It was indeed a clever plan. Had the plan succeeded the Bakassi Peninsula would have been split into two councils namely a Bakassi North Local Government Council where customary owners of the peninsula live and a Bakassi South Local Government Council where the overwhelming majority of fishermen communities carry out their fishing activities. Since the enormous marine and petroleum resources of the Bakassi peninsula are largely found in the south, fishermen communities would naturally have claimed ownership of the abundant resources therein leaving Bakassi natives in the north with virtually no resource.

That was unacceptable. This diabolic plan would give me sleepless nights. It constituted a major challenge to Bakassi natives because it tried to cut off Bakassi natives from their abundant marine and petroleum resources. Since fishermen communities largely occupy the mangrove swamps in the south, they would naturally have considered themselves owners of the southern part of the Bakassi Peninsula. If that were allowed to happen, it would have legalised and formally transferred the territorial waters of Bakassi natives together with its enormous mineral, marine and hydrocarbon resources to fishermen communities; strangers in the Bakassi Peninsula. Bakassi natives would freely be ceding their territory and only source of livelihood to strangers. It was a dangerous conspiracy that could have had grave implication for generations of Bakassi natives. It was beginning to look as if Bakassi natives had embarked on the struggle to bring the Bakassi Peninsula back to Nigeria to hand over their land and resources to strangers. That would have made our struggle totally meaningless. A second council in Bakassi peninsula would have had devastating consequences and grave implications for Bakassi natives. The idea had to be killed. It had to be shot down at all costs.

I sent a petition to the State House of Assembly in which I called the attention of the Speaker to moves to split Bakassi peninsula into two local councils and expressed serious reservation about the proposal. The Bakassi Peninsula, I told the Speaker was a territory that comprised land and water. The land was occupied by the natives and overlords of the Bakassi Peninsula while the waters were occupied by itinerant fishermen communities from across Nigeria and beyond. What the proposal for the creation of a second local council in the Bakassi Peninsula was trying to achieve was to separate the land from the waters. In other words, separate the people from their territorial waters and natural resources; the sole source of their livelihood. Such a proposal I told the Assembly was not only unwise; it was unlikely to guarantee peace and harmony in the Bakassi Peninsula. It therefore could not be in the interest of the state or Nigeria.

I reminded the Speaker that the mangrove swamp forests on which fishermen communities constructed their temporary abodes was part and parcel of the territorial waters of Bakassi natives; customary owners of the Bakassi Peninsula. Bakassi natives, I told the Speaker, had no intention, their present circumstances notwithstanding, to cede any part of their territory to any one. I was aware I said that some Bakassi natives might have joined in making the demand for the creation of a new local council in the Bakassi Peninsula. If any Bakassi native happened to have been involved, I told the Assembly, they must have done so in error and advised the Assembly to disregard the demand.

My petition expressed surprise at the apparent willingness of the State House of Assembly to cede a section of its territory to non-indigenes of the state, wondering whether the Assembly was unaware that the overwhelmingly fishermen population in the Bakassi Peninsula was comprised of non-indigenes of the Cross River State. Fishermen communities, I told the Speaker had no right to demand for the creation of a local council in the Cross River State. If they so badly needed a local council, they should return to their states of origin to make such demands. I reminded the Speaker that the Bakassi Peninsula was facing serious problems of a unique nature and advised that while efforts were being made to find lasting solutions to the problems, it was unadvisable for anyone to take any action that could aggravate the situation and concluded that while everyone had a duty to help find lasting solutions to the crisis, the Cross River State Assembly had a special responsibility in that regard. I expressed hope that the Assembly would not allow the meagre resources of the state to be transferred to other states.

The House of Assembly did not react to my petition but I did not have to spend sleepless nights or endlessly work hard to remove this local council creation headache. Help came from unexpected quarters. The proposal never saw the light of day. Attempts in other states to create additional local councils had received no support from Abuja. In some cases, states that had insisted on creating more local councils had run into trouble with the centre. In extreme cases, Abuja had imposed painful sanctions. In such hostile environment, I was convinced that the House of Assembly of the peace-loving people of Cross River State would not rock the boat. The proposal was simply swept under the carpet.

Fishermen communities and unscrupulous politicians would however not give up. They soon devised a new plan. Having failed to carve out a local council in the Bakassi Peninsula they could call their own, they tried new tricks. This time they tried to exploit a proposal that was under consideration at certain quarters to bring Tom Shot Islands; the homeland of my Efiat people into the Bakassi Local Government Council. Tom Shot Islands are located on the west of the Calabar channel directly opposite the Bakassi Peninsula. Tom Shot Islands are in Mbo Local Government Area of Akwa Ibom State. Like the Bakassi peninsula, Tom Shot Islands are very rich in petroleum resources. In fact, Tom Shot Islands are host to the controversial seventy-six oil wells that nearly brought the Cross River State and Akwa Ibom State to the edge. Bringing Tom shot islands into Cross River State would have made the state much richer.

The problem was that these politicians did not just want Tom Shot Islands brought into Cross River State. They wanted Tom Shot Islands brought into Bakassi Local Government Area. That did not go down well with me as I thought such a development would overwhelm customary owners of Bakassi Peninsula. I was also concerned about my Efiat people whom I believe were comfortable in Mbo Local

Government in Akwa Ibom State. Efiat people are the main crayfish fishermen in the Bakassi Peninsula and beyond. Bringing Tom Shot Islands; Efiat homeland into Bakassi Local Government Area was an attempt to smuggle Efiat people out of Akwa Ibom State. That would probably have led to conflict between the Cross River State and Akwa Ibom State. I thought our hands were already full and we did not need to add more tension to what we already were going through. Besides, such a transfer was not going to facilitate in any way our struggle for the Bakassi Peninsula. It was therefore not in the interest of our struggle nor was it in Nigeria's interest. More importantly, I did not want to see myself dragged into a crisis that would have been narrowed down to a direct confrontation between my father and mother.

Bringing Tom Shot Islands into Bakassi Local Government Area would have brought Efiat people; my father's people into direct conflict with Usakedet people; my mother's people. You can imagine the dilemma I would have had to face if that were to happen. But just as I was trying to work out a plan to shoot down this latest headache, the plan fell through. Providence once again came to my rescue. As expected, Tom Shot Islands became caught up in an ownership controversy between Akwa Ibom State and Cross River State. The tussle would drag on for years and despite political and legal efforts to put the matter to rest, the status of Tom Shot Islands remained in dispute until the Bakassi crisis was over. In the circumstance, it no longer made sense to talk about bringing Tom Shot Islands that no one was certain where they belonged to Bakassi Local Government Area. The matter would rear its ugly head again years after the crisis in the ownership of seventy-six oil wells controversy between Cross River State and Akwa Ibom State.

CHAPTER SEVEN

Nigeria tries to Exclude Bakassi Natives from her Claim over the Bakassi Peninsula

Bakassi Peninsula affairs were never one of the best kept secrets. When it came to containing gossip, no wall in the world was as porous as that surrounding the Bakassi Peninsula. Information often filtered through the labyrinth of the mangrove swamp forest with incredible ease and speed. Sometimes it came through like bush fire. At other times, it would fly around leisurely. At most times, it was unconfirmed hot breaking news. Soon it would become common knowledge and in no time, would receive the official stamp.

It had been trickling through for months that Nigeria's claim over the Bakassi Peninsula did not include all customary owners of the Bakassi Peninsula. Individuals you never expected to know much surprisingly seemed pretty conversant with the goings on in the Bakassi Peninsula and seemed quite willing to proudly spread such news. Some would even claim to have or seen maps to confirm their story. You were made to understand that a delegation that went to Abuja to see the President had failed to secure the President's approval for the inclusion of the Usakedet villages of Odon, Amoto and Efut Inwang; bona fide Bakassi natives on the map of Nigeria. And when one considered the fact that the forward formation of the Nigerian army on mainland Bakassi peninsula was located midway between Aqua and Amoto village, you had to take these rumours seriously. As a matter of fact, you had to believe them.

I had heard a lot of rumours and gossips about Bakassi peninsula since the crisis began. I knew that war situations were fertile ground for hatching rumours and gossips. However, none of the rumours I had heard until then had so alarmed me. As a matter of fact, I was frightened stiff. The threat to exclude some Usakedet people from Nigeria was unimaginable. The rumour however appeared to be in tandem with the treatment being meted out to Usakedet people since the beginning of the crisis. The rumours confirmed fears that Nigeria might indeed be willing to cut off some Usakedet people from their land and resources; their only means of livelihood like Great Britain had tried to do early in the century. Such a situation would make the struggle for the Bakassi Peninsula meaningless.

Despite the logic of the situation, I preferred to treat the matter as mere rumour until I stumbled on a map that actually placed core Bakassi native villages outside Nigeria. I found this curious and extremely difficult to believe, especially given the battle Young and I had fought in Lagos. Only Archibong Town and Aqua featured on the map of Nigeria. Odon, Amoto and Efut Inwang were conspicuously missing. That customary owners of Bakassi peninsula; raison d'être of the struggle for the Bakassi Peninsula could still be missing from the map of Nigeria left me dumbfounded. Besides being harmful to the interests of Bakassi natives, the continued omission of these villages could cause considerable embarrassment to Nigerian. Unless the situation was immediately remedied it could trigger a crisis the outcome of which we could easily not anticipate. I felt the problem was too big for the Cross River State Government. So I decided to take the matter to the National Committee on Bakassi Peninsula in Abuja.

Getting to secure audience with the National Committee on Bakassi Peninsula was never going to be easy but with help from persons sympathetic to our cause I secured audience with the National Committee on Bakassi Peninsula in Abuja on May 5th 1999. Armed with a map of the Bakassi Peninsula I had specifically commissioned to help me get a clearer picture of the area in dispute, I headed for Abuja. My goal; ascertain the veracity of the rumour that Nigeria was indeed excluding some Bakassi natives; customary owners of the peninsula from her claim over the peninsula, take the occasion to do some advocacy for Bakassi natives and show reason why all Bakassi natives had to be re-absorbed into the Federation of Nigeria.

If I had taken the battle of Bakassi natives to the National Committee on Bakassi Peninsula in the hope of preventing them from being excluded from Nigeria, I would return a disappointed and frustrated man. My encounter with the Committee was in many ways reminiscent of previous painful encounters I had had in search of help for Bakassi natives. Firstly, I observed that the National Committee on Bakassi Peninsula visibly seemed to be in a terrible hurry. I would later learn their meeting that day was in preparation for a trip abroad. In the eyes of many there present, I might simply have been seen as an intruder who was interrupting a very important meeting. Whether that was sufficient reason to justify the seeming impatience and unfriendly reception I got, I hardly could say. My frustration would increase after I took a quick look of the Committee and found no Bakassi native or anyone with a sound knowledge of the Bakassi Peninsula and its peoples in the Committee.

The first thought that came to mind was to attack the Committee for the absence of Bakassi natives in a national committee set up to deal with the problem of Bakassi people like we had done in the Lagos meeting. Then, I quickly recalled the commotion that had followed and immediately dismissed the idea from my mind. In the visibly unwelcoming environment I found myself, someone would probably have thrown me out of the meeting if I had dared to challenge the Committee. Besides, that was not the reason for my wanting to see the National Committee on Bakassi Peninsula. Thus, within the four or five minutes I was permitted to interacted with the Committee, I tried to draw the attention of the Committee to the omission of core Bakassi native villages; customary owners of the Bakassi Peninsula from Nigeria's claim over the peninsula. I struggled during the brief encounter to impress upon a seemingly uninterested audience the need to include all Bakassi natives in Nigeria's claim over the Bakassi Peninsula.

I would feel very insulted when a young member of the committee tried to remind me that the Bakassi Peninsula question was a territorial dispute involving land, not people and proudly went ahead to draw analogy with the situation in Sokoto where quite a reasonable percentage of the subjects of the Sultan of Sokoto were citizens of other African nations. I could hardly believe my ears. What other evidence did I need? This young man had said it all. Every lingering doubt on my mind began to dissipate. It now seemed as if the only thing Nigeria wanted in the Bakassi Peninsula was the rich petroleum and marine resources. Bakassi natives would be devastated by the news.

I further felt a surge of anger and despair when the Committee Chairman, Chief Richard Akinjide, SAN, enquired to know whether I knew or had been to Archibong Town proudly claiming he had been to Archibong Town twice. 'Twice', I murmured to myself, shocked and terribly disappointed. That question almost reduced me to tears. I felt so belittled that I thought I should explode into some emotional outburst but restrained myself. Under normal circumstances, I would have reacted forcefully to such provocation. Only a National Committee on Bakassi Peninsula that was truly handicapped would ask any one born and raised in the Bakassi Peninsula whether they knew Archibong Town.

Prince Archibong Edem may have stayed briefly in Archibong Town; Archibong Town remains Bakassi native homeland. I could see that Chief Richard Akinjide's National Committee on Bakassi Peninsula clearly needed help. It was evident that the Committee did not have all the kind of information it needed to have at it disposal. Such handicap did not only pain me very much, it made very angry because there was no reason why that Committee should have been deficient on such matters. I could not however outwardly manifest what I felt deep inside. Nothing would have justified any public show of disrespect to a Committee that included not only learned jurists but influential and powerful bureaucrats. Any public outburst would not only be foolish, it would have deprived Bakassi natives of a great opportunity to have their voices heard. Bakassi natives needed all the sympathy they could get. The meeting with the National Committee on Bakassi Peninsula was a unique occasion for Bakassi natives' voices to be heard. I could not squander the chance.

Thus, in spite of the anger and frustration I felt deep inside; I played the fool and remained calm. But how could the Committee ask me if I knew Archibong Town or anywhere in the Bakassi Peninsula; my birthplace and ancestral homeland of my mother? For a man who was born and raised in the Bakassi Peninsula; a man who had roamed the maze of creeks in the Bakassi Peninsula as a child and teenager doing fishing; a man who had several members of his family still residing on both sides of the Bakassi Peninsula divide; a man whose sister was comfortably married to the clan head of Archibong Town, that question was a bit too much to bear. To ask me such a question at a time when I had just completed the installation, at my expense, of a satellite viewing centre at Archibong Town to help our men on the front line relax and ease tension as part of Bakassi natives' win the war effort, that question was to say the least a bit humiliating. I further felt insulted when the Committee chairman sarcastically thanked me for my "emotions" and advised me to convey my concerns to the National Committee on Bakassi Peninsula in writing.

My encounter with the National Committee on Bakassi Peninsula would remain instructive throughout the crisis. I did not achieve the desired objective but it opened my eyes extremely wide. It yielded no fruits but remained a memorable road sign for me in the struggle for the Bakassi Peninsula. It confirmed fears and fixed a stamp on that which until then had simply been regarded as gossip or mere rumour. I now became aware of the tragedy that awaited Bakassi natives if Nigeria were to have her way. That realisation made me change strategy and tactics. Henceforth, I would devote a lot more time and effort to ensuring that Bakassi natives were not separated from their homeland and abundant resources. As I left the meeting I wondered how Nigeria could possibly think of taking the Bakassi Peninsula and abandoning customary owners of the territory. That would never happen, I told myself.

I would however, be consoled by history. Great Britain had tried a similar thing in the last century and failed. Nigeria stood no chance of success, I again told myself. But how could Nigeria even think of such a thing? How could anyone claim a territory and disclaim the people that own the territory? The chances seemed bleak. Firstly, I was convinced Bakassi natives would never accept such an outcome. Besides, Bakassi natives had in the past shown that they were capable of defending their territory. They had done so through the ages. I was sure they could do so again. If matters came to the worst and they felt truly threatened, I had the weird feeling that Bakassi natives would bring the awesome reputation for which they were notorious and dreaded to bear on the situation. Yet, in spite of such convictions, I could not stop worrying about the tragedy that would loom over the heads of Bakassi natives if Nigeria went ahead to accept a boundary in the Bakassi Peninsula that did not take on board all peoples of Efik ancestry into the Federation of Nigeria.

For weeks I could not concentrate on any other thing. The thought of this impending tragedy kept flashing through my mind. The threat to separate Bakassi natives from their rich marine and petroleum resources; to exclude them from Nigeria loomed menacingly before me and dampened my spirit. I would however find solace in the last words Pa Leo had said to me. 'Go and do not look back'. As always I found strength and inspiration in those words. It was in that spirit that I decided to heed the advice of the chairman of the National Committee on Bakassi Peninsula and took the battle of Bakassi natives back to the National Committee on Bakassi Peninsula in a twenty-page petition in August 1999.

With the exclusion of Bakassi natives from the Federation of Nigeria menacingly looming over my head and Pa Leo's words persistently ringing in my ears, I took the battle of Bakassi natives back to the National Committee on Bakassi Peninsula in Abuja. In my petition, I reminded the Committee of my encounter with it on May 5th 1999 and recalled the little effort I made to try to convince the Committee of the need to ensure that all Bakassi natives were liberated and brought into Nigeria. I reminded the Committee of persistent rumours that Nigeria planned to abandon non liberated areas of the Bakassi Peninsula and core Bakassi native villages to Cameroon and warned of the danger inherent in such a plan.

I reminded the Committee that what came out of my first encounter in May was far from reassuring. On the contrary, what came out very clearly of that first encounter was the alarming confirmation of the rumour that Nigeria had indeed no intention to seek the complete liberation of the Bakassi Peninsula and its people. Words, I told the Committee were insufficient to convey the outrage and grave concern with which Bakassi natives; customary owners of the Bakassi Peninsula had received that piece of information. The object of my petition, I told the Committee was to adduce reason why that decision needed to be rescinded.

Bakassi natives, I observed would be doing themselves and indeed Nigeria a great disservice if they failed to draw the attention of the committee to manoeuvres that in the long run could prove prejudicial to the overall interest of Nigeria in the Bakassi Peninsula. It was against that background that I was seeking the indulgence of the National Committee to grant me the liberty not only to make a few comments about the committee's work but also to bother the committee a little with matters of a purely domestic nature.

In that regard, I considered the conspicuous absence of Bakassi natives in the committee a serious impediment. When I spoke about Bakassi natives I clarified, I did not refer to individuals who began to claim to be Bakassi natives following the outbreak of hostilities in Bakassi peninsula between Nigeria and Cameroon. When I spoke of Bakassi natives, I referred exclusively to Usakedet people who before the outbreak of the crisis were referred to as Cameroonians and who even as the crisis progressed were still quietly regarded as Cameroonians and merely tolerated in Nigeria. These people, I emphasized were the only Bakassi natives; not the teeming population of migrant fishermen and their political class who began to claim to be Bakassi natives only after the outbreak of hostilities between Nigeria and Cameroon. I told the committee that fishermen communities were not a people without land coming to a land; Bakassi peninsula, without a people. They all have villages in Nigeria.

I drew the attention of the committee to the fact that a large territory such as Bakassi peninsula could not exist without indigenous owners in the twentieth century stressing that judging from the way the Committee had been proceeding, that recognition had either eluded it or had been misplaced. The way Bakassi peninsula affairs had been conducted clearly suggested that Nigeria was treating Bakassi peninsula as a "terra nullius", a no man's land. That impression, I emphasized was incorrect. The goal, it seemed, was to dispossess Bakassi natives of their land and enormous resources and abandon them to Cameroon.

I told the committee that I was short of words to adequately describe the shock, pain, anguish, alarm and confusion that the plan to abandon a significant section of the Bakassi Peninsula and its people had engendered. Usakedet people viewed the plan with grave concern and prayed Nigeria to reconsider her stand on the matter. Bakassi natives could find no justification for such a decision. Bakassi natives could never understand a plan that was going to spell misery for Bakassi natives. I told the Committee that it would be a poor imitation of Hanoi/Saigon Vietnam; an East/West Berlin or a North and South Korea in the Bakassi Peninsula. The world, I reminded the Committee was aware of the political, economic and social upheavals that had accompanied those experiments. Bakassi natives did not wish such conditions for themselves. In none of these places had the experiments worked then, there were no guarantees that the experiments would work now. Nigeria, I said could not on the eve of the third millennium when nations were seeking solutions and ways of reuniting families torn apart by those dark events, opt for solutions that would surely lead to more misery and separation of families.

Bakassi natives, I told the committee, were convinced that it would be a tragic mistake for Nigeria to accept a border in the Bakassi Peninsula that did not take on board the entire territory and people of the peninsula. Such a situation would have serious implications. It would not eliminate the prevailing sense of insecurity and threat to life and property in the Bakassi Peninsula. On the contrary, it would fuel and increase tension and probably engender massive outpouring of anger, animosity and hatred towards the fishermen population and the Efik nation in particular whom Bakassi natives may probably hold responsible for such outcome. Most significantly, the plan would not provide Nigeria and Cameroon with secure borders along the Bakassi peninsula corridor. Such a situation could prolong the Bakassi Peninsula crisis. The need therefore to reconsider the plan and ensure that all Bakassi natives were brought under one umbrella within the Federation of Nigeria could not be over emphasized

My petition disagreed with those who relied solely on the colonial agreement signed between Great Britain and Efik Chiefs and Kings as sole evidence in support of Nigeria's claim over the Bakassi Peninsula. It also strongly disagreed with those who saw the Bakassi Peninsula crisis purely as a territorial dispute where human beings were of no consequence and drew the committee's attention to the nationality principle which in recent times had been responsible for the emergence of several new states in Africa and Europe and urged Nigeria to exploit the nationality principle.

I informed the committee that in my opinion there was no incontrovertible evidence that Germany had full control of Bakassi peninsula. If that had been the case, Germany would not have buried Arthur Biernatzski, a German national who died in Bakassi peninsula on June 17, 1911 in the mangrove swamp forest at Rio del Rey. Germany would surely have followed the example of Great Britain and given Arthur a befitting burial on solid ground on mainland Bakassi peninsula like Great Britain did to her nationals who perished in the Bakassi Peninsula around the same period. My memorandum went ahead to provide the committee information relating to the location of tombstones where these British nationals, Alfred Foreman and John Abend were buried in Odon Ambai Ekpa village in the Bakassi Peninsula in 1902 and 1904, respectively.

I argued that with that kind of evidence it was mind- boggling for Nigeria to exclude any part of the Bakassi Peninsula from her claim and noted that Usakedet people; customary owners of the Bakassi Peninsula would see such a decision as a tragic betrayal. I wondered whether the decision was due to ignorance of the existence of these facts or because the committee did not agree that such historic relics constituted concrete and incontrovertible proof in support of Nigeria's claim. I advised that if the committee could not base its case on the nationality principle, it should at least do so on the strength of existing evidence. I told the committee that Bakassi natives were of the opinion that such evidence had deliberately been kept away to justify their exclusion from the Federation of Nigeria and suggested that the plan might have been hatched by fishermen communities and unscrupulous individuals of Efik extraction intent on taking possession of the enormous resources of the Bakassi Peninsula.

My petition took time to give the committee a little more insight into the domestic politics of the peninsula. It expressed fear that Bakassi domestic politics may not only have crept into the work of the committee, it might as a matter of fact been responsible for decisions that were causing much damage to the interest of Bakassi natives. Contrary to the impression that had been created, I told the committee, the Bakassi Peninsula was not a "terra nullius." Bakassi peninsula was not a no man's land. Usakedet people own Bakassi peninsula. Bakassi peninsula, I stressed was not a no-man's land and its ownership had never been truly challenge. Although Usakedet people had witnessed dispirited challenges to their hegemony over the territory in the past, the challengers had always ended up recognizing Usakedet people as customary owners of the Bakassi Peninsula.

I informed the committee that the teeming population of fishermen in the Bakassi Peninsula came from across Nigeria and beyond to fish in the peninsula during fishing seasons. They always returned to their various states in Nigeria after every fishing season. These people were not permanent residents of the peninsula. These Ijaw, Okobo, Efiat, Ibibio, Hausa, Igbo, Yoruba, Ilaje and Oron fishermen have for centuries lived in peace and harmony with Usakedet people whom they have always recognized as customary owners of Bakassi peninsula. I noted that even as the crisis raged, most fishermen communities remained loyal to Usakedet people. I however noted that politicians of Efik heritage who had no residence, no landed property, no family compound and no parent or ancestor in the Bakassi Peninsula were taking advantage of the confusion and vacuum created by the crisis to behave as if the Bakassi Peninsula had just been discovered. My petition held the group responsible for the outrageous attempt to abandon Bakassi natives as that seemed the only way they could walk away with the enormous resources of the Bakassi Peninsula. I reminded the committee that the scramble for Africa ended in 1885.

Bakassi natives, I told the committee had a proud history. Bakassi natives were not just customary owners of the peninsula; they were most significantly, recognized as custodians of the great 'Leopard Spirit Cult'; EKPE, the greatest socio-political and cultural organisation of the Efik nation. Bakassi natives gave the Efik world its most significant symbol. I lamented that since the eruption of Bakassi peninsula crisis, unscrupulous individuals and groups of Efik ancestry had been trying to misrepresent the truth by presenting Bakassi peninsula as a no man's land. This, I insisted, was not only fraudulent but mischievous.

My memorandum noted that the existence of a large population of strangers in the Bakassi Peninsula was a mark of the level and degree of hospitality of the Bakassi natives. Usakedet people should not suffer for being generous. The presence of a large population of strangers in the territory was not unique to the Bakassi Peninsula. All over Nigeria and indeed throughout the entire west and central

Africa coastline, indigenous communities were playing host to lots of non-indigenes. Europe, the Middle East and the Gulf States were home to millions of economic migrants from across the world. There, these persons were seeking better means of livelihood and decent living conditions without meddling in the local politics or trying to appropriate the resources of the people providing them refuge and a decent means of livelihood. In Lagos, indigenes of Lagos continue to play host to millions of people from across the nation and beyond. In spite of their small population, indigenes of Lagos remain owners of Lagos. No stranger sits on the traditional stool of Lagos. No stranger sits in the traditional council of Lagos. There is no such precedent anywhere in Nigeria. The only exception was to be found in the Bakassi Peninsula where strangers not only sat in the traditional council but actually constituted the traditional council. Clearly, the existence of a large number of strangers in the peninsula had become an encumbrance on customary owners of the territory.

My petition equally noted that while settlers were being treated with gloves in hand, customary owners of the peninsula were being subjected to all forms of blackmail and deprivation. I lamented that even as Nigeria was claiming the Bakassi Peninsula, official attitude towards Bakassi natives remained at best tolerable. Nigeria continued to adopt policies that clearly favoured non-indigenes of the peninsula at the expense and peril of the native population and customary owners of the territory. Clans and clan heads had been created with total disregard for the views of the owners of the territory. Strangers had been made chairmen of the local council in flagrant violations of the spirit and principle of laws establishing local government areas in the Federation. My memorandum wondered for how much longer Bakassi natives would have to endure such unfair treatment.

I told the committee on Bakassi Peninsula that Usakedet people had exercised absolute jurisdiction over the peninsula for centuries. Before the outbreak of hostilities in the Bakassi Peninsula, Usakedet people granted permission to fishermen to establish fishing settlements in the territory. Usakedet people settled disputes between the different fishermen communities. Usakedet people performed traditional rites in the Bakassi Peninsula. Before the outbreak of crisis in the Bakassi Peninsula, fishermen communities paid allegiance to the Usakedet people. The crisis had so dramatically changed the situation that fishermen communities had become the ones collecting oil royalties on Bakassi native soil. That, I told the committee, was unacceptable.

These events I told the committee were causing Bakassi natives considerable pain. Usakedet people did not seek to liberate their homeland so as to hand it over to strangers on their land. Usakedet people could never accept such a situation. It was time, I stressed, for Nigeria to face the truth and dismantle the falsehood in the Bakassi Peninsula. I told the committee that it made sense for Bakassi natives not to raise these issues earlier because Bakassi natives believed that all hands needed to be on deck to confront the adversary. Although that goal was yet to be attained, the activities of unscrupulous politicians purporting to represent fishermen communities was harming the interest of Bakassi natives and making that good sense of judgement difficult to sustain. I told the committee that it no longer made sense for Bakassi natives to sit back and watch strangers who for centuries Bakassi natives had provided with a decent means of livelihood cart away their land and resources and called on Nigeria to take urgent steps to remedy the situation.

The National Committee on the Bakassi Peninsula did not even care to acknowledge my memorandum. Nothing was done to address the issues raised in the petition but the Cross River State Government however did take steps to bring all Bakassi native villages into the map of the state and by so doing brought all Bakassi natives though not all Usakedet territory into the Federation of Nigeria. For the first time since 1913 Bakassi natives would once again be Nigerians officially. Nothing however, was done to sustain this momentum. Nigeria continued to recognize strangers as customary owners of the Bakassi Peninsula. No Bakassi native was ever injected into the National Committee on Bakassi Peninsula to assist the committee. And this was not due to any shortage or lack of Bakassi native who could effectively perform such functions. Nigeria put the final nail on the coffin during the Oral Hearings at the World Court. Although Nigeria took an exceptionally large delegation for that exercise, no Bakassi native was included in Nigeria's delegation to The Hague. Bakassi natives got the message.

CHAPTER EIGHT
Ominous Signs

Meanwhile, as fishermen communities and unscrupulous politicians were dissipating energy scheming to take possession of the Bakassi peninsula and its enormous resources, living conditions in the territory were plummeting especially for people on the Cameroonian side of the Bakassi divide. Most had to flee to neighbouring villages and towns in Cameroon because of the difficulties and danger involved in coming over to Nigeria. To flee to Nigeria, Bakassi natives had to traverse two front lines. That was an extremely difficult and hazardous enterprise. Thus, in spite of discreet efforts aimed at encouraging Bakassi natives to run towards Nigeria during the crisis, people escaping from the war in the Bakassi Peninsula ran to places where the risk was minimal. And as living conditions continued to deteriorate we began to observe cracks in people's resolve to remain steadfast in their support for the struggle. Many, alarmed by the direction events were heading began to lose faith in the struggle. Although I had not consulted the people before embarking on my mission to bring mother's homeland back to Nigeria, I knew that the success of my mission would largely depend on the support of my people. As a matter of fact, I always knew that Bakassi natives held the key to success in the struggle for the Bakassi Peninsula. Because their support was critical, I had to do all I could to keep their hopes alive.

Sustaining the hopes of a people who, besieged on all sides by heavily armed soldiers were living in perpetual fear proved to be no easy task. Life for these people had become a terrible nightmare. Those who tried to find their way to Nigeria, to get to the market, to meet their loved ones and families or to escape from war had to face untold difficulties. Besides having to cross two front lines, they had to travel for days through thick and dangerous forest, across fast flowing and treacherous rivers and over hills and mountains to get to Nigeria. Only the young and physically fit could embark on such a journey. The weak and elderly were condemned to remain in the Bakassi Peninsula and await their fate. Before the outbreak of the crisis the journey to the market in Ikang or Calabar that Usakedet people undertake on a daily basis took less than one or two hours.

Anyone with a keen eye on the incongruities of war may also not have failed to observe that life for Bakassi natives had further been made difficult by restrictions and other impositions the military on both sides of the divide had placed on the population. There were and still are no-go areas in the Bakassi peninsula making it impossible for the population to fish, farm or even stroll around these restricted areas. Violations could have fatal consequences. But having imposed stiff restrictions on land and at sea; it was not uncommon to find soldiers take up the economic activities of the people. Soldiers engaged in fishing, farming or hunting. And since only soldiers could penetrate deep into the forest and far into the sea in pursuit of the enemy, soldiers nearly always brought home the biggest harvest and the largest catch which, in most cases they ended up selling back to the population. And, whenever such courageous efforts failed to yield enough, they helped themselves with the meagre harvest and catch of Bakassi inhabitants.

Bakassi natives' frustration would further be aggravated by the realisation that they were gradually losing control of their homeland and the enormous resources therein. As a matter of fact, everything they owned or possessed appeared to rapidly be slipping out of their hands as a result of the threat being posed to their homeland by fishermen communities and unscrupulous politicians. Gradually, Bakassi natives were beginning to feel like outcast and victims in their homeland. Many would begin to question the rationale behind a struggle that so far had only brought them hardship, death, political alienation, economic deprivation and a ruthless degradation of their environment.

That was not completely true though. The picture was not as gloomy as it seemed. Bakassi natives living on the Nigerian side of the Bakassi divide were enjoying a degree of political and economic freedom hitherto never imagined or dreamt of. In spite of the hardship, Bakassi natives had something to cheer about. There was reason to be hopeful. For the first time in the history of the peninsula, Bakassi natives were taking some part, albeit in very small degrees in the governance of their territory. In spite of moves by fishermen communities and unscrupulous politicians to alienate them, Bakassi natives, especially in the early part of the crisis had representatives in the Local Government Council, State House of Assembly and the State Executive Council. These were small but significant achievements for a people who had never before ever been recognized by any government.

Many Bakassi natives however remained unimpressed arguing that whatever gains had been made had come at an outrageous price. They argued that what was said to be gains had come with a new set of problems and challenges that were compounding a seemingly hopeless situation. Nigeria's refusal to recognize Bakassi natives as customary owners of the peninsula remained a major irritant. Nigeria's policy was depriving Bakassi natives of their legitimate rights in the Bakassi Peninsula and encouraging settlers to lay fraudulent claims over their territory. Unless that threat was removed, Bakassi natives ran the terrible risk of completely losing their homeland and its enormous resources to strangers.

Even more disturbing was the suspicion that Nigeria planned to abandon significant portions and people of the Bakassi Peninsula to Cameroon. My visit to the National Committee on Bakassi peninsula had confirmed that much. From available information Nigeria's claim over the Bakassi Peninsula did not include all Bakassi territory and people. That was going to have grave consequences for Bakassi natives who once again could be separated from their territory and kinsmen in Nigeria. Again, Bakassi natives would lose their land and its enormous resources to fishermen communities and unscrupulous politicians. That would make their struggle meaningless. The plan had to be resisted. It was obvious that any partition of the Bakassi Peninsula in the manner that was being contemplated was going to deepen the economic hardship and increase the political alienation of Bakassi natives.

But Bakassi natives would have more headaches to worry about. As the crisis evolved government policies and threats from fishermen communities and unscrupulous politicians no longer seemed the only source of worry and frustration for Bakassi natives. In addition to threats to the corporate existence of Bakassi natives as a people in the Federation of Nigeria and the deteriorating living conditions due to the economic hardship, Bakassi natives had to deal with series of other forms of tragedies that began to hit the people at an alarming rate. Bakassi natives began to die prematurely as a result of the war and harsh economic conditions. Women and children lost their lives at sea trying to run away from war in extremely pitiable circumstances. Many pioneers of the struggle never made it to the end.

Atim, never drank alcohol but had promised to gulp down the entire content of a bottle of beer the day the Bakassi Peninsula would be fully liberated. That day never came and Atim died without having that bottle of beer. Madam Iquo Effiom, woman leader, pillar of the struggle for the Bakassi Peninsula and pain-in-the-neck for fishermen communities and unscrupulous politicians struggling to appropriate the Bakassi Peninsula also never made it to the end. These persons and many others too many to mention all gave up their lives for the Bakassi Peninsula. Their demise deprived the struggle of key comrades in arms. Many could not be accorded befitting burials rites because it was too hazardous to try to take their remains to the Bakassi Peninsula; their ancestral homeland. As a result, not every child or loved one witnessed the last funeral rites of their parents or loved ones. People had to be laid to rest where it was most convenient, not where they would have wished to call their final resting places.

Even more worrisome were the constant deaths at sea. Bakassi natives believe that being a seafaring people they can not die at sea, especially when such waters like Bakassi peninsula waters is theirs. Every death of a Bakassi native at sea is seen as unnatural and believed to be the handiwork of some malevolent individual or group. Yet, Adim, a young Bakassi native woman, in her early thirties drowned along with her three children in the full view of a seemingly helpless crowd that watched the tragedy from the river bank at Ikang, unable to come to their rescue. Adim and her three kids perished at sea trying to run away from war. Effiong Okon Ntekim, my own brother would disappear at sea and the sea, would to date refuse to give up his body for burial. The deaths at sea of so many Bakassi natives would become a matter of serious concern but while efforts were being made to try to see how to unravel the mystery behind these sad occurrences, Bakassi natives were struck by two new tragedies at sea on December 12th 1999. These latest calamities caused considerable alarm and aroused strong feelings of suspicion against certain quarters. These deaths truly shocked the community. For the first time since the eruption of the Bakassi Peninsula crisis, one had the strange feeling that the struggle for the Bakassi Peninsula could be moving closer to tipping point.

My thoughts did not linger close to anything sinister when the telephone shrilled that fateful December morning and shot me out of bed. My eyes swollen and longing for more sleep, I tried to shake off the cobwebs of the sleep and reluctantly picked up the receiver.

"Good morning, who is on the line?"

A hesitant and apparently trembling female voice mumbled something inaudible at the other end.

"I can't hear a thing, can you be more audible?" I insisted. She again hesitated and then seemed to summon courage and said,

"Let me tell you, after all you are a man."

At this point I felt something terrible had happened and realizing who was on the line abrasively interjected

"Whatever the matter is, please go straight to the point."

"There is bad news from Bakassi peninsula"

The voice finally summoned courage and said,

"There has been a boat mishap. One of the boats that conveyed people to Abana for Bakassi Day celebrations capsized last night on its way back. Your sister's son, Cyril and one of Young's daughters were in the boat but have not been found. The search is continuing this morning." For a moment I remained tongue-tied; not knowing exactly what to say. Then instinctively replied,

"Thank you."

I dropped the phone and sank into a seat by the phone too depressed to walk back to bed, too depressed even to think. My wife was still in bed. I dared not go back to bed with a strange look on my face, else I betrayed my emotion. My wife would not bear the thought of losing Cyril, fondly called Akpong. I decided I would not immediately let her know about the tragedy. Sitting there confused, my head capped in my palms, I had all sorts of thoughts and ideas running through my mind. I even tried to convince myself that what I had just heard did not happen. How could Cyril, barely 19 or thereabout die at sea. That was not possible. Usakedet people have a great reputation as a seafaring people. We do not die at sea, especially when such waters happen to be Usakedet territorial waters. The waters of the Bakassi Peninsula are clearly Usakedet territorial waters.

In line with Bakassi native tradition and world view, someone had to be responsible for the tragedy and that someone had to be a blood relation of the victim. Who then could be responsible for the death of Akpong and for what reason? In these matters, silence is the golden rule. No one is ever willing to speak. Bakassi natives are generally not a sabre-rattling or muscle-flexing people. They tend to be rather contemplative and uncommunicative in these circumstances. This is not to say they would not take action that could becloud reason and sanity in other circumstances. This sad news made me begin to wonder whether we had not arrived at one of such occasions of insanity. The circumstances surrounding this tragedy made me begin to wonder whether some Bakassi natives had not on the eve of the twenty-first century re-enacted an outrageous and barbaric tradition for which they had in the past been so dreaded. The way those deaths were said to have occurred was quintessentially Bakassi native in character.

I returned from my reverie, regained my self-presence, picked myself up and made a few calls to confirm this terrible tragedy. Then I made my way back to the bedroom where I found my wife, awaken by the ringing of the telephone, anxiously waiting to know who had been on the line that early morning and what the call had been all about. I hardly knew how to break the terrible news but I had to. Cyril, my baby sister's first son had been one of my wife's favourite kids and she loved him. My wife and I shared Cyril's dreams of becoming a medical doctor; perhaps the first Bakassi natives would produce. That had been Cyril's ambition and he had earnestly been working towards that goal. This terrible tragedy had come to snatch Cyril away from his dream and shatter the hope of many.

As details of this ugly tragedy began to emerge, it became known that the second victim was Miss Ukpong, aged 16, daughter of the same Chief Dr. Archibong Edem Young who had accompanied me to the Lagos meeting. When it became clear that Ukpong and Cyril had gone to Abana to celebrate Bakassi Day, I nearly broke down in tears. I felt a deep sense of terrible loss. What made that feeling even more painful was the circumstance in which these kids lost their lives. Eye witness report said Ukpong and Cyril who were the youngest passengers in the boat were indeed the very first passengers to be rescued. They had indeed already secured firm and comfortable grip of the capsized boat while efforts were still being made to rescue the remaining passengers. Ukpong who was travelling with her mother was heard calling for help for her mother who was still submerged and hardly knew how to swim. There were a number of elderly women in the boat, few of whom could swim. Although the passengers attributed the disaster to the boatman's recklessness, the boatman and his assistant were said to have displayed outstanding bravery and courage when the disaster occurred and succeeded to bring all the passengers to a firm grip of the capsized boat. What happened next cannot be rationally explained. How a huge wave suddenly emerged and struck the boat taking away only Ukpong and Akpong remains a mystery. No one has been able to explain how these teenagers who were full of life and promise, knew how to swim and who already had secured firm grips of that boat lost that grip and disappeared into the sea for ever while others held on until help came.

In spite of my origins, I am by nature or perhaps by my education and orientation or by some stubborn application of character, what one would call a free-thinker. Consequently, I have always had a rather dismissive attitude towards everything superstitious. The circumstances surrounding that boat mishap would however shake the very foundation of my beliefs. It would make me begin to doubt myself and fear things I previously would dismiss with a wave of the hand. The tragic deaths of Ukpong and Akpong would make me want to probe the dark and mysterious world of Bakassi natives. I could not however summon courage to embark upon a mission everyone believed was dangerous. I surely was unqualified and unprepared for such a mission. The result; that is if one came out with one's life, might just have been some over simplification or inconclusive analysis of what is obviously a complex and intricate tradition. I probably may just have ended up adding more confusion to the community. I decided that the dark and mysterious world of my Bakassi natives was better left alone and decided to raise a foundation in the name of Ukpong and Akpong to keep the memories of these kids alive.

All deaths are painful. One death that pulled the carpet under the feet of the struggle for the Bakassi Peninsula was that of Chief (Dr.) Archibong Edem Young. Young's demise has remained a puzzle that no one has been able to unravel. Did Young die of natural causes or was Young's death the classic case of striking the shepherd to decimate the sheep? That question has remained unanswered. Whatever the case, Young's death decapitated the struggle for the Bakassi Peninsula and decimated the sheep. Young's demise left a huge vacuum in the struggle for the Bakassi Peninsula that no one has been able to fill. Since Young died Bakassi natives have remained fragmented and disorganised.

Young's death was particularly painful because after losing Young's daughter in the boat mishap barely a few years earlier, one could not bear the thought of losing the father. I and the struggle for Bakassi peninsula faced two major handicaps at the inception of Bakassi crisis. Firstly, the struggle lacked a suitable platform from where to launch an offensive. *Mbono Ndito Usakedet*; the association of Usakedet people in Calabar that Young led provided that platform. Secondly, Usakedet people had no prominent persons to lead the struggle. None of those who collaborated with me in the 70s and 80s had a university education. None had a good job. I myself had no name, no social or political status. All I could boast of was the fact that I had managed to get a university education by skipping meals. And apart from the 'big brain' my peers often credited me with I was a 'nobody'. Such handicaps often made my mission extremely difficult. There were too many doors I could not open. It was obvious that to achieve the goal I had set for myself I would need someone with a name.

That platform, name, social and political status was exactly what Young brought to our struggle for the Bakassi Peninsula. Holder of a doctorate degree in chemical engineering; Young had held various positions in the public and private sectors before retiring into politics. A Bakassi native with such a profile and pedigree was undoubtedly what our struggle needed. Young was more than a welcome addition to the struggle and he greatly bolstered the struggle for the Bakassi Peninsula. Young brought a lot more to the struggle. He was a man of firm convictions who openly demonstrated very critical attitude towards all who tried to fraudulently claim ownership of the Bakassi Peninsula; his ancestral motherland. His uncompromising posture and unequivocal commitment to the struggle for the Bakassi Peninsula was unequalled. Young stood head and shoulder high above all in the defence of his people and the Bakassi Peninsula. He was unlike some of our people who though strived to create the impression that they were committed to the struggle seemed not immune from the temptation of begging from the masters' table. Young would never compromise the interests of Usakedet people.

Young's unflinching love and passion for his people made him enemy number one of many who tried to appropriate Bakassi peninsula; his mother's ancestral homeland. He had on several occasions to singlehanded fight battles in defence of his people. I was particularly indebted to Young for many reasons. It was Young who accompanied me to Lagos to confront a state delegation that was going to discuss the future of the Bakassi Peninsula without the inclusion of customary owners of the territory in its delegation. When a certain Bassey Ita; a non-indigene of Bakassi peninsula was foisted on the people as pioneer chairman of Bakassi Local Government Council, it was Young who led the legal battle to unseat the usurper. When Bakassi Local Government Council officials began to engage in corrupt practices and abuse of office, it was Young who dragged them to graft agencies.

For these and for many other reasons there seemed to be no love lost between Young, fishermen communities, corrupt Bakassi council officials and unscrupulous politicians who largely saw Young as a pain in the neck or some dissident who needed to be put away. In spite of the hostility he faced, Young proved to be a true General by the many battles he fought in defence of his people. His strong will and uncompromising stance and often aggressive interventions in defence of his people helped keep many at bay but there was always the fear that the courageous battles Young was fighting for his people could one day bring him harm. Young's sudden and unexpected death confirmed those fears and robbed the struggle for the Bakassi Peninsula of a true General in battle. Young's death not only threw Bakassi natives into confusion and uncertainty, it decapitated the struggle, decimated Bakassi natives and left a great vacuum in the struggle for the Bakassi Peninsula that no one has been able to fill.

CHAPTER NINE

Last Ditched Effort to Save the
Bakassi Peninsula

Against the backdrop of pain and uncertainty, I took the troubles of Bakassi natives back to Abuja in April 2001, convinced that the Bakassi ship was moving dangerously towards the iceberg. In my memorandum to the Chief of Staff to President Obasanjo I recalled that when Nigeria took the first meaningful step ever to regain control of the Bakassi Peninsula, Usakedet people; customary owners of the peninsula frantically welcomed the move and celebrated. They celebrated because for the first time in their over four decades struggle to have their people and territory re-integrated into Nigeria, their dream seemed to begin to materialize. Seven years had elapsed since that momentous event. Seven years in which the euphoria too had naturally died down. Bakassi natives too had had time to reflect on the destiny of their people and territory and the picture that was emerging in the Bakassi Peninsula was dampening their spirit.

I told the Chief of Staff that portions of the Bakassi Peninsula had been liberated and communities living therein were enjoying a degree of freedom and independence hitherto never imagined nor dreamt of. A local council area had also been created and in spite of the many difficulties, Bakassi natives were deriving some form of benefit. But a significant part of the population and a substantial portion of the Bakassi Peninsula remained under the Republic of

Cameroon. In the liberated areas, stranger communities were waging a vicious war against Bakassi natives. The slow progress in reaching a final resolution to the crisis was causing untold hardship and serious deterioration in living conditions in the Bakassi Peninsula. Of grave concern to the corporate existence of Bakassi natives was the proposal to partition the Bakassi Peninsula in a way that would result in the exclusion of some Bakassi natives from Nigeria. Nigeria's apparent refusal to grant recognition to the owners of the Bakassi Peninsula had become a major headache for customary owners of the peninsula.

My memorandum thereafter took a closer look at each of these concerns. It noted that since the outbreak of the crisis in the Bakassi Peninsula, efforts had been made to create the impression that the peninsula was a "terra nullius"; a no man's land. Strong efforts continued to be made to promote that impression and suppress the voice of the legitimate owners of the territory in a desperate bid to sustain falsehood. Thus, while Nigeria and Cameroon had taken their dispute over ownership of the Bakassi Peninsula to the International Court at The Hague, at home, fishermen communities and unscrupulous politicians were waging a totally futile war against customary owners of the peninsula.

For the avoidance of doubt, I categorically reiterated that Usakedet people were the customary owners of the Bakassi Peninsula stressing that Usakedet people had for centuries, exercised unchallenged jurisdiction over every inch of the territory. It was strange; I said that government would continue to disregard such fact despite the availability of a huge body of literature in support of Usakedet claim. My memorandum further provided the Chief of Staff with a brief history of fishing settlements in the Bakassi Peninsula stressing that contrary to the impression being created; fishermen communities were not permanent residents of the Bakassi Peninsula.

Fishermen, I told the Chief of Staff come from various places across Nigeria and beyond to fish in the territorial waters of Bakassi natives during the fishing season. When the season is over, or whenever they like, they return to wherever they came from. No body prior to the outbreak of the crisis ever claimed to come from a fishing settlement in the Bakassi Peninsula. These facts I emphasized were not unknown to the Efik world that curiously had chosen to stand on the side of falsehood. It was indeed a strange irony of fate that fishermen communities who for centuries had benefited from the generosity and hospitality of Bakassi natives would turn around and abuse such kind gestures. I ended the section by re-iterating that the activities of migrant fishermen in the Bakassi Peninsula had become an encumbrance on Bakassi natives.

I noted that the mangrove swamp forests on which itinerant fishermen constructed their temporary huts in the Bakassi Peninsula formed part and parcel of the territorial waters of Bakassi natives and their main source of livelihood. Bakassi natives had no intention, their present circumstances notwithstanding, to surrender an inch of that territory to any stranger. I went ahead to recall that Bakassi natives had had occasions to note that they were not the only people playing host to large communities of strangers. Throughout Nigeria and indeed in many parts of the world, indigenous communities were playing host to large populations of non-indigenes without serious impediments. The only exception appeared to be in the Bakassi Peninsula where the presence of strangers was becoming an encumbrance on customary owners of the land.

Commenting on the proposed partition of the Bakassi Peninsula, I noted that if such a plan were allowed to go ahead, it would abandon principal Bakassi native villages to Cameroon and once again not only separate the people from their kith and kin in Nigeria but this time also separated them from their enormous resources. That, I told the

Chief of Staff was unacceptable. Such a proposal would make our struggle for the Bakassi Peninsula meaningless. It would also not further the cause for peace, stressing that any solution that did not include all Bakassi natives and the entire Bakassi Peninsula in the Federation of Nigeria would be unacceptable.

I told the Chief of Staff that excluding any Bakassi natives from Nigeria would not only worsen the plight of Bakassi natives; it would deepen their economic hardship and increase their political alienation. It would not ease the prevailing sense of insecurity in the Bakassi peninsula and was unlikely to provide Nigeria with secure borders around the peninsula. On the contrary, partition as was being contemplated would create further tensions, fuel animosity and probably engender massive outpouring of anger and hatred towards fishermen communities and the Efik world that Bakassi natives would likely hold responsible for such outcome. Such a solution was not in the interest of Bakassi natives. It was hard to imagine how it could be in the interest of Nigeria.

My memorandum again compared the proposed partition of the Bakassi Peninsula to a poor imitation of the Berlin Wall, a North and South Vietnam, an East and West Germany or a North and South Korea. None of the experiments I recalled had worked. There was no reason to believe that they would work in the Bakassi Peninsula and concluded that it was hard to understand, how Nigeria could in the third millennium when nations were seeking solutions and ways of reuniting families torn apart by those dark events, opt for solutions that would only lead to more hardship and human suffering.

I then seized the occasion to intimate the Chief of Staff about living conditions in the Bakassi Peninsula stressing that life in the peninsula had become a terrible nightmare for Bakassi natives, noting that prior to the outbreak of crisis in Bakassi peninsula, it took Bakassi natives less than an hour or two to get to the market in Ikang or Calabar in Nigeria and lamented that that simple journey now took close to four days, depending on the age of the undertaker of the journey and the means of transportation. Because of the situation, Bakassi natives had to wade through thick and dangerous forest, travel over hills and treacherous mountains, across fast flowing rivers, across turbulent seas and oceans, and through unfamiliar terrain and inclement weather merely to get to the market or reach their loved ones and relations in Nigeria. Meanwhile, their environment continued to experience untold degradation due to the ruthless exploitation of petroleum resources on both sides of the divide without any real benefit to the people.

On the proposed creation of additional local councils in the Bakassi Peninsula, I let the Chief of Staff know that council creation was normally a welcome event but Bakassi natives had nothing to gain from a local council creation demand that was emanating from strangers in the peninsula. I told the Chief of Staff that Bakassi natives were particularly opposed to the proposal to split the Bakassi Peninsula into two councils; a Bakassi North and a Bakassi South local government council because such a creation would legalise and formal transfer of the territorial waters of Bakassi natives together with its enormous petroleum and marine resources to strangers. Bakassi natives would freely be ceding their territory to tenants. The implications of such a development on generations of Bakassi natives could best be imagined.

I told the Chief of Staff that either Nigeria was being continuously misinformed or that Nigeria's own perception of the crisis did not reflect a clear understanding of the situation in the Bakassi Peninsula. My memorandum emphasized the need for government policies to truly be in consonance with the facts on ground as well as in line with the hopes and aspirations of the people in the interest of justice, equity, peace and harmony in the Bakassi Peninsula. I reminded the Chief of Staff that Bakassi natives had had occasion to say that they did not bring up these issues earlier because they considered it wise not to divert attention from the principal goal of total liberation of the peninsula. Although that objective was yet to be fully attained, the activities of unscrupulous politicians and members of fishermen communities in the Bakassi Peninsula were making that good sense of judgement extremely difficult to sustain. I assured the Chief of Staff that Bakassi natives would however continue to exercise restraint in the hope that Nigeria would take meaningful steps to address these concerns.

This final entreaty met a brick wall. The Chief of State did not respond. Nigeria refused to listen. Nothing happened. Bakassi natives' voices remained the lonely voice in the wilderness crying for help that no one was willing to offer. No-one seemed to care. No one seemed to pay attention to the woes of Bakassi natives. In desperation, I would resign myself to fate. Henceforth, I would, not an actor but a spectator be. For me there could be no further action, not even in the shadows. Henceforth, I would watch and be witness and witness I have remained.

CHAPTER TEN

Nigerians Today, Cameroonians Tomorrow

Soon after the outbreak of hostilities in the Bakassi Peninsula, Cameroon took Nigeria to the International Court of Justice at The Hague to determine precisely who between them had sovereignty over the Bakassi Peninsula. I had hoped that Nigeria would take an aggressive posture and overrun Cameroon in a "victorious-little-war" in the Bakassi Peninsula. Nigeria could talk peace thereafter from a position of strength. Nigeria refused to adopt such hard line posture and instead chose the peaceful option of arbitration.

The question of who between Cameroon and Nigeria the law would actually say had sovereignty over the Bakassi Peninsula had been preying on my mind since the outbreak of the crisis. But I could not pay much attention to it because I was preoccupied with how to deal with the threat posed by fishermen communities claiming ownership of the Bakassi Peninsula. The knowledge I had acquired from Pa Leo dealt exclusively with the question of ownership between fishermen communities and my Usakedet people. It did not provide answers to the question of sovereignty between Nigeria and Cameroon. There was good reason to be well prepared for the legal tussle ahead. I was anxious to acquire adequate knowledge on the subject as I had done with immense help from Pa Leo on the ownership controversy between fishermen communities and my people. My first thought was to return to the Bakassi Peninsula and talk to pa Leo but Pa Leo had passed on two months after my meeting with him. Had Pa Leo been alive, Bakassi peninsula would probably have been my first port of call in search of that knowledge.

The matter now seemed truly intriguing as it now became not just a military contest but a legal tussle as well. As far as I was concerned, it was a journey into uncharted territory. Although I am no attorney, my knowledge of international law is more than rudimentary. I wished I could feel the same way about my military knowledge which in my own very humble opinion is below zero. Although it was obvious that I would never be called upon to defend my people at The Hague, I needed to have sound legal knowledge to understand the legal issues involved in the dispute and if need be make good representation on behalf of my people. I had in the past had cause to make representation on the Bakassi Peninsula without being sufficiently informed about the issues. I had felt so embarrassed and demeaned by the ignorance displayed in some of my representations. I was determined not to repeat those mistakes, especially now that the Bakassi Peninsula crisis had become a full blown crisis.

Something inside me kept reminding me that I must not make any more representations that would be based largely on emotions, rumours or gossips. I had felt demeaned and ridiculed when some of my previous statements turned out to be half-truth. I would lose credibility if I ever tried to do that again. Determined to ensure that subsequent memoranda on the Bakassi Peninsula by me were factual and not based on mere assumptions or unproved assertions, I decided that the only way I could avoid a repeat of those mistakes was to undertake thorough study of Agreements and other legal instruments dealing with the Bakassi Peninsula.

Such knowledge was not only necessary for a better appreciation of the crisis; it was a must for anyone involved with the Bakassi

Peninsula ownership controversy between Nigeria and Cameroon. Besides, the story of the Bakassi Peninsula and its peoples could not be fully told and understood without a clear knowledge of the key legal instruments that had shaped the peninsula in time. That way and perhaps that way alone could anyone be in a position to assess the good or damage these instruments had done to the native population of the Bakassi Peninsula. Years of searching would lead me to London, Berlin and Lisbon where long nights and days in libraries would illuminate my mind and provide answers to my many doubts. Valuable help would come from Buea and Enugu where one finds a good collection of colonial records relating to British, French and German colonial rule in Nigeria and Cameroon.

What follow hereunder are the troubling revelations of my research. First, I would confirm that the Bakassi Peninsula was indeed part of Old Calabar in the British Southern Protectorate during colonial rule until Great Britain; in Pa Leo's words "a tiny island nation whose seafaring abilities, worldwide colonisation enterprise, and economic domination brought her great fame and reputation," gave the Bakassi Peninsula in 1913 to Germany; again in Pa Leo's words "a nation renowned for its order, discipline and hard work," whose leaders of the time enormous appetite for power would bring mayhem upon the world on two occasions.

I found it difficult to think through that Great Britain would take such action in spite of the fact that she had in 1884 entered into an agreement with the Kings and Chiefs of Old Calabar to extend to them "Her Majesty's gracious protection and favour". This action by Great Britain to cede part of a territory she held in trust for the Kings and Chiefs of Old Calabar essentially laid the foundation for the Bakassi Peninsula crisis. This March 11, 1913 Agreement with Germany would become the noose round Nigeria's neck in the Bakassi Peninsula that no one would be able to untie. As if enough damage had not been done to Nigeria, other colonial powers and indeed Nigeria herself would through acts of omission or commission go ahead to enter into other agreements that appeared to rely on the validity of the March 11, 1913 Anglo-German Agreement for their own validity.

Professor Ian Brownlie, Nigeria's Co Agent at The Hague in his book *African Boundaries* traces the boundary between Nigeria and Cameroon in a number of documents that include; (i) The German notification to the European powers and the United States on October 15, 1884 concerning the German Protectorate of Cameroon following the July 12, 1884 treaty that established the Protectorate; (ii) Notification to the Signatory Powers of the General Act of the Berlin Conference on June 11, 1885 and May 13, 1885, of the British Protectorate of Lagos; (iii) Exchange of notes dividing British and German Protectorates from April 1885 to July 1886 and the treaty of July 1, 1890; (iv) Delimitation agreements from April 14, 1893 to March 19, 1906 and the Exchange of notes of February 22 and March 5, 1909; (v) The Anglo-German Treaty of April 12, 1913; (vi) The Milner-Simon Declaration of July 10, 1919, which partitioned German Cameroon between the British and the French; (vii) The British and the French Mandates established in 1922; (viii) The trusteeship agreement approved by the General Assembly of the United Nations on Dec. 13, 1946; (ix) The 1959 and 1961 General Assembly Plebiscites held in the territories of Northern and Southern Cameroons respectively and (x) The Anglo-German Treaty of March 11, 1913. (12).

Of all treaties entered into between Great Britain, France and Germany on the Bakassi Peninsula, the Anglo-German treaty of March 11, 1913 is the one that did the greatest harm to Nigeria not simply because it set the contentious border between German administered Cameroon and British administered Nigeria but because Great Britain gave to Germany a portion of land she did not own but held in trust for the Kings and Chiefs of Old Calabar. Although the agreement guaranteed the fishing rights in the area and provided that within six months from the date of marking out the boundary, natives living near the boundary-line could, if they so desired cross over to live on the other side, the Anglo-German treaty of March 11, 1913 contained provisions which not even an act of God could change. Article XX of that treaty for example stipulates;

> "Should the lower course of Akpayefe River so change its mouth as to transfer it to the Rio del Rey, it is agreed that the area now known as Bakassi peninsula shall still remain German territory..." (13)

However, months later Kaiser William II would plunge the world into World War 1 and put an end to Germany's colonial empire but not Germany's colonial ambition. Germany would take on the world again in 1939.

The Franco-British Declaration of July 10, 1919, commonly Known as the Milner-Simon Declaration named after Viscount Milner, Secretary of State for the Colonies of the British Empire, and M. Henry Simon, Minister for the Colonies of the French Republic; and the Declaration made by the Governor of the Colony and Protectorate of Nigeria and the Governor of French Cameroon defined the boundary between British and French Cameroon. Both declarations put the Bakassi Peninsula in Cameroon.

The first attempt by Great Britain and Germany to address the problem of the indigenous people of the Bakassi Peninsula came in 1906. The 1906 Anglo-German treaty not only tried to redefine the boundary in the Bakassi Peninsula area, it made the first effort to address the problem of the indigenous population living in the border area. Not only did it provide for equal fishing and navigation rights on river boundaries, it provided that;

"indigenes who occupied land due to be transferred
to the other power would be free to chose which side of
the boundary they might wish to reside and gave local
representatives of the two colonial powers the discretion
to vary the line by mutual agreement if local circumstances
so demanded." (14)

Although local circumstances actually demanded that there be
fundamental adjustment to this agreement, nothing appeared to
have been done and much of the Bakassi Peninsula remained under
German control. What these treaties tried to do in essence was to
cut off Bakassi natives from their enormous marine and petroleum
resources by abandoning them to Germany. Nigeria appeared to be
heading in the same direction during the Bakassi crisis.

However, despite Anglo-German efforts to separate Usakedet
people from their resources and main source of livelihood, hardly
anything seemed to show that Usakedet people were no longer in
charge in their homeland; the Bakassi Peninsula. Usakedet people
remained in control of the territory, collecting all forms of royalties
and taxes from members of the fishermen community. Usakedet
people continued to carry out their functions including performing
sophisticated traditional rites to appease sea deities in the peninsula.
Usakedet people and the teeming fishermen population continued
to live in peace and harmony as if nothing had happened. Usakedet
people continued to exercise jurisdiction over all the peninsula
and fishermen communities continued to pay allegiance to them
as customary owners of the Bakassi Peninsula. Interaction with
the rest of the Efik world remained unimpeded and as smooth as
ever. Nothing seemed to indicate that there had been any boundary
adjustments in the Bakassi Peninsula.

In spite of numerous Anglo-German agreements on the Bakassi Peninsula that tend to support German possession of the territory there appeared to be no strong evidence to show that Germany actually had effective control of the Bakassi Peninsula at any time. If Germany did, she would not have buried a certain Arthur Biernatzski; a German national who died in the Bakassi Peninsula on 17 February, 1911 in the mangrove swamp forest at Rio del Rey when she could easily have followed British example and given her national a befitting burial on mainland Bakassi peninsula like the British did to Alfred Foreman and John Abend in the catholic church premises in Odon village where one finds three tombstones; two of which carry the following inscriptions;

> 1. In memory of Alfred Foreman,
> Agent for W. D. Woodin & Co. Ltd. Died
> On 17 December 1902 at the age of 41 years
> Designed by Jones and Wills of London

> 2. In memory of John Abend,
> Agent for W. D. Woodin & Co. Ltd
> Died on 14 July, 1904 at the age of 34 year
> Designed by Jones and Wills of London

The third tombstone has so badly been defaced that its epitaph is no longer legible.

Also found in Odon Ambai Ekpa village is a large bell in the 'Leopard Spirit Cult' "EKPE" shrine with the following inscription;

> "ATOKORO- OBONG ODON
> AKWA OBIO USAKEDET
> OLD CALABAR 1892"

Translated;

"ATOKORO- KING OF ODON, USAKEDET CAPITAL CITY OLD CALABAR 1892"

What Britain and Germany did in the Bakassi Peninsula and its environs is hard to understand. Take a walk for example at the Cross River State National Park in Nigeria and you would be amazed to find, conspicuously displayed in the heart of that Park, a German Fort reminding you that the land on which you stand had once been German territory; indeed had once been Cameroon's. In Sokoto and Adamawa regions the trouble the Sultans of Sokoto and the Lamido of Adamawa; traditional rulers of these regions encounter reaching out to their subjects can only be imagined because Europeans chose to put a knife through their territory and spread their subjects out into several countries. Neither Great Britain nor Germany have any idea or have ever been concerned with the trouble these subjects face being separated from their kit and kin nor that which they face going through immigration formalities at various international borders just to pay homage to their traditional leaders.

One man whose analysis of the Bakassi Peninsula boundary controversy I find compelling is Justice Mbuh M in *International Law and Conflict: Resolving Border and Sovereignty Disputes in Africa*. Justice Mbuh reveals that recently made public confidential documents have begun to shed light on some of these boundary controversies. The first noted conflict over the Cameroons and Nigeria coastal area he says can be traced to a dispute between the Germans and the British over German success in signing treaties with the Cameroon Kings of Akwa and Bell Town in Douala on July 14th 1884. The treaties in effect, proclaimed the German Protectorate extending from the Rio Del Rey area to Gabon. Despite this fact, British Consul, Hewett still managed to sign treaties with the same Kings on July 19th 1884. It took German pressure for Britain to withdraw but not before criticizing the German move and perhaps to save face or genuinely to play down the loss of the territory Britain would describe as:

> "the flat, swampy and unhealthy Cameroons-especially as we retain, in the coast of Ambas Bay and the neighbouring mountains, almost the only part of that region that can be inhabited by Europeans."(15)

A second dispute he states arose as a result of the disrespect for German flag where British agents appeared to have incited the natives in Douala to rebel against German rule, and the fact that British explorer Hewett would preside over court cases in Douala as if Germans did not exist equally fuelled tensions between the two European powers. A rebellion of the natives led to the death of one German. Even though it was crushed, it provoked bitter reaction from Germany, compelling the Iron Chancellor; Otto Von Bismarck to demand compensation with land west of Ambas Bay to the Rio del Rey. Britain complied after some hesitation and a new boundary line was made along the Right Bank of the Rio del Rey. Later the British would bargain that Germany surrender claim to St. Lucia in South Africa in exchange for Victoria in the Cameroons. These agreements were contained in exchange of letters dated April 29, 1885 and May 7, 1885. (16).

Justice Mbuh further reveals that all along both the British and the Germans had mistakenly believed that the Rio del Rey was a river. When mapping the Cross River in 1889, Captain Graf Bernstorff discovered with much amazement that:

1) "The Akwayaffe River did not end in the Old Calabar River as the English maps had shown, but rather entered

directly into the sea. Captain Graf also concluded that the Rio del Rey was not a River, but a seaway, and that the Akwayaffe was connected to the Rio del Rey by channels to the east and that the Ndian River on the map prepared by the English Consul Johnson was "unknown to the natives of the Rio del Rey {Isangele} who instead call it the Ofa." (17)

2) Commandant Pullen for Her Majesty's Government confirmed these German findings. These findings provoked maneuvers from both sides in an effort to secure Ndian River on the part of the British, and to secure the acceptance of the Akwayaffe as a substitute for the nonexistent Rio del Rey, on the part of the Germans. Accordingly, Article 4 of the Anglo-German Agreement of 1890 firmly secured the findings.(18)

The importance of these findings, Jurist Mbuh M. believes lies in the fact that the Germans insisted that from 1885, the waterway, whether river or creek, belonged to her and that the 1890 Agreement had changed nothing in this regard. And to this, the British agreed, noting: "There is no doubt that under the agreement of 1885-86 both banks of the river were given to Germany and that from that time to 1890 she held this waterway."(19)

The resulting agreement signed on 14th April, 1893 defined the Rio del Rey boundary with greater clarity. In 1901, an agreement was reached as to the proposed boundary between the Protectorate of Southern Nigeria and the Colony of Kamerun, between the British and the Germans. This agreement reconfirmed the April 29-June 10, 1885; July 27-August 2, 1886; July 1, 1890; April 14, 1893; and November 15, 1893 Agreements on the boundary lines between the Rio del Rey and the rapids of the Cross River. This Agreement was done in Buea, Kamerun on April 1901, and formed the basis of all subsequent boundary Agreements—1906, 1909, and 1913—with minor amendments. (20)

Articles 3 of the Buea Agreement states

> "In lieu of the boundary line commencing in the Rio del Rey at the point given in the maps 'West Pt.' and 'West Huk' respectively, it should commence at the South West Point of *Bakassi* Peninsula marked *'Bakassi* Head' and follow the West Coast Line until *Bakassi* Point at the mouth of the Akpa Iyefe (Akwayefe) River is reached, thence it shall follow the center of the river as far as the Urufian Creek on the left bank of the said river, in such manner as to go through the *Bakassi* Peninsula and the area between the Peninsula and the Creek, formerly in British territory, into the German colony of Kamerun, provided that the engagements in Article 3 of the Agreement of 14th April 1893 (mentioned in Article 3 herein), shall be observed, and no trade settlements be allowed to exist or be erected". (21)

Justice Mbuh equally reveals that declassified documents of the British Archives have shed further light on the nature of border disputes between Great Britain and Germany. These documents have shown that all through British rule of the Cameroons and Nigeria, the boundary pillars laid by the Germans were untouched and that any attempt at redressing the border were resisted. A clear case in point is the dispute over the Obudu Cattle ranch. The question was whether the ranch was on Nigerian soil, or in the Cameroons, or whether it overlapped the border. This dispute was dealt with through the exchange of note in which the British expressed fear of being entangled in a border dispute of the nature of Kashmir between India and Pakistan. (22)

The Obudu Cattle Ranch dispute Justice Mbuh maintains arose from a Shell Company aerial survey map, which showed that part of the Obudu Cattle Ranch was in fact, on the Cameroonian side of the border. Because a team of surveyors from Southern Cameroons had embarked on tracing the borderline of the State, the British feared that if the surveyors saw the Shell map, they might use it to confirm the boundaries of Southern Cameroons. The British believed that this would greatly hurt Nigerian feelings, a thing Great Britain would like to avoid. In an inward telegram to Commonwealth Relations Office, the correspondent advised that the Colonial Office should

> "instruct Southern Cameroons Government to desist forthwith from any attempt to demarcate this boundary."(23)

In 1954 Nigeria is said to have single-handed, but also to her disadvantage, inaccurately redefined the border, leaving out the Bakassi Peninsula and the Obudu cattle ranch which lies inland, north of Bakassi. A document marked WAF 441/110/01 states, "The actual boundary will not be shown on the first editions of the new maps if there is any objection from either side in doing so." (24)

In another document B.J. Greenhill states that although the British could undertake not to show the boundary, or for that matter the position of the existing boundary pillars, on the first edition of the new maps, they

> "find it very hard to resist pressure from the Southern Cameroons Government to stop omitting such essential information from maps of the Southern Cameroons …the

Southern Cameroons Government have asked for mapping of Southern Cameroons to be continued by us after the transfer of power of some form of U.K. Technical Assistance." (25)

Although it was eventually determined that the Obudu Cattle ranch lay on the Nigerian side, Cameroon has tried to raise the Obudu question again at meetings of the Nigeria-Cameroon Mixed Commission and the United Nations set up to demarcate the Nigeria Cameroun borders.

Even though Greenhill observed that the foregoing dispute was due to "lack of liaison between the various departments of the Nigerian Federal Government concerned,' Cameroonian Justice Mbuh believes colonial masters were simply tolerant to Nigeria, and would let Nigeria do as they pleased apparently because D. W. S. Hunt had written to the Colonial Office, asking Geofrey Lamarque to

"...see that Southern Cameroons direct their attention elsewhere. If this particular area is to be mapped let it be done from the Nigerian side. Above all, before any boundary line is printed on the maps, the Nigerian authorities must be fully consulted and given the opportunity of working out their own ideas of where the line should run". (26)

That certainly was an opportunity for Nigeria to deal with the Bakassi peninsula issue. It does not appear Nigeria took advantage of any such opportunities making J. Chadwick, on June 6, 1961, to write to the Commonwealth Office stating,

"After all the Nigerians have given tacit approval to the existing boundary between them and the Southern Cameroons by failing to protest at the time of the Plebiscite,

when the boundary must have been defined as between
those who voted and those who did not...But obviously we
do not wish to offend Nigerians. If they wish to protest ...it
would be better if we were in no way involved in the issue.
If the matter does come to a head and resolve itself into
a possible boundary adjustment dispute, the protagonists
after October 1st would be the Nigerians and, presumably,
the United Federal Cameroon Republic. Must we make our
selves a third party by laying down the boundary at this
stage?" (27)

Great Britain did not want to be involved in another Kashmir
type of crisis. She very well knew that the border she was bequeathing
Nigeria and Cameroon would remain contentious for a long time.
As expected the 1913 Anglo-German treaty remained a contentious
agreement and primary source of conflict between Nigeria and
Cameroon for a long time. In spite of its contentious nature, other
agreements signed thereafter continued to rely on the validity of the
1913 Anglo-German treaty. Soon after Great Britain and Germany
entered into the 1913 agreement, the First World War broke out in
1914. Germany lost the war and lost all her colonies which became
shared between Great Britain and France under the mandate of
the League of Nations. The boundary between British and French
mandated Cameroon were defined by the Franco-British Declaration
of July 10, 1919. That Declaration placed the Bakassi Peninsula as part
of what was then known as British Cameroons. The Declaration was
ratified on December 29, 1929 and January 31, 1930.

The Second World War broke out in 1939 and Germany again lost.
After the war, the British and French League of Nations mandates
over the Cameroons were replaced by Trusteeship Agreements under
the newly created United Nations. In August 1946 Britain divided
the territory under her trusteeship into two; Southern and Northern

Cameroons. And in 1954 British Secretary of State for the colonies issued a legal order defining the border between the Eastern Region of Nigeria and Southern Cameroons. The Bakassi Peninsula was placed in the Southern Cameroons.

In 1960 both Nigeria and Cameroon became independent nations. Nigeria and Cameroon would not only inherit their colonial boundaries without protest, they would go ahead to conclude other agreements on their common border that appeared to rely on the validity of the existing colonial border established by the Anglo-German treaty of March 11, 1913. Nigeria would on attainment of independence, exchanged Notes with Great Britain accepting all obligations and responsibilities arising from any valid international agreement that Britain had entered into on behalf of Nigeria. Such agreements are believed to have included the 1913 Anglo-German treaty. The rights and benefits enjoyed by Britain by virtue of the application of any such international agreement were henceforth to be enjoyed by Nigeria. It turned out that in the case of the March 11, 1913 Anglo-German Agreement there would be no benefits to enjoy.

From available records, Nigeria had never, prior to the outbreak of the Bakassi Peninsula crisis raised any objections over the transfer of the Bakassi Peninsula to Cameroon. Rather, Nigeria, in 1962 sent the infamous Diplomatic Note No. 570 of March 27, to the Embassy of Cameroon in Lagos acknowledging the Bakassi Peninsula to be part of Cameroon. That Note is said to have been accompanied by a map that placed the Bakassi Peninsula in Cameroon. Professor Teslim Elias easily Nigeria's most successful jurist, is said to have proffered an advisory opinion on the Bakassi Peninsula controversy in which he is said to have advised Nigeria to hands off the Bakassi Peninsula because according to him the territory belonged to Cameroon. The learned jurist is also said to have advised, that insisting on Nigeria's ownership of the Bakassi Peninsula would be showing ingratitude to a friend who had come to Nigeria's aid during the nation's difficult moments; a veil reference to Cameroun's assistance to Nigeria during the Nigerian civil war.

In July 1964, both Nigeria and Cameroon joined other African nations to approve the Organisation of African Unity, OAU Cairo Declaration adopting the legal principle of *'utti possedeti'* in which African nations committed themselves to the principle of "inviolability" of boundaries inherited from colonial masters on attainment of national independence. Both nations ratified the Declaration and by so doing restated their commitment to honour borders inherited from their colonial masters.

In spite of all that, legal opinion remained divided with regards to the validity or otherwise of the Anglo-German treaty. Jurists who have commented on the Anglo-German treaty of March 11, 1913 believe that Britain's action amounted to a violation of the fundamental legal principle of *"pacta sunt servanda"*; a fundamental principle of law that requires that once an agreement has freely been entered into, its provisions must be honoured. In their view, Great Britain violated her agreement with the Kings and Chiefs of Old Calabar with whom she had entered into a protection agreement in 1884. These jurists equally maintain that Britain equally violated another fundamental principle of law of *'nomen dat quod non habet'*; meaning 'no one can give what one does not have' insisting that Great Britain had no right to give to Germany a territory she held in trust for the Kings and Chiefs of Old Calabar because the territory was not hers. Great Britain had no right to cede the territory or any part of it to anybody without the consent of the Kings and Chiefs of Old Calabar to whom the territory belonged. That consent they contended was never sought nor granted.

Nigeria's Chief Richard Akinjide, SAN, FCIArb, former Minister and Attorney-General of the Federation and Nigeria's Agent at The Hague for the Bakassi Case, in an article entitled *'Bakassi peninsula whose Bakassi peninsula?'* threw more light on the Bakassi ownership controversy saying;

> "because the Order-in-Council of November 22, 1913, which came into force on January 1, 1914, bringing together the Protectorate of Northern Nigeria and Southern Nigeria into a single Protectorate of the Federation of Nigeria, though still separate from the colony of Lagos, and that because the Anglo-German treaty was signed before this act, the treaty was not binding on the new Federation of Nigeria." Chief Akinjide further stated that because "the British government within months of signing the treaty denounced it, the treaty was not a treaty in force," stressing that "the Anglo-German Treaty of 1913 was not a treaty in force because since something cannot emanate from nothing, the 1913 Treaty cannot therefore be the judicial basis for a claim to Bakassi peninsula by Cameroon." (28)

Whatever the legal arguments for or against, one fact stood out quite distinctly. The Bakassi Peninsula was without doubt an integral part of the Southern Protectorate of Nigeria. But by the outbreak of the Bakassi Peninsula crisis, a lot of water had gone under the bridge. The border between Nigeria and Cameroon around the Bakassi Peninsula had undergone, through sheer negligence and other acts of omission or commission, so much transformation, been so tempered with that sovereignty over Bakassi peninsula in the eye of the law could be said to lay with Cameroon, not simply by virtue of the March 11, 1913 Anglo-German treaty that transferred the territory from British to German rule but also by virtue of other acts by colonial powers, the United Nations, Nigeria and Cameroon that all appeared to rely on the validity of the 1913 Anglo-German treaty for their own legality. However, in spite of these apparent endorsements, the border between Nigeria and Cameroon in the Bakassi Peninsula area continued to generate controversy, making the question of sovereignty over the Bakassi Peninsula a continually contentious issue. The primary responsibility of the Chief Richard Akinjide, SAN, Legal Team at The Hague would be to try to change that perception.

That was a terribly painful conclusion to arrive at. Even more saddening was the realisation of the devastating effect that this shifting nature of the border between Nigeria and Cameroon in the Bakassi Peninsula corridor had had on the native population of the Bakassi Peninsula. This peculiar state of being Nigerians today and Cameroonians tomorrow had literally transformed Bakassi native population; customary owners of the Bakassi Peninsula into a stateless people whose nationality and loyalty like the Bakassi Peninsula itself would swing like a yo-yo from Old Calabar to the Southern Protectorate of Nigeria to Great Britain to Germany to Great Britain again to Nigeria to Cameroon to Nigeria and finally to Cameroon again. This peculiar journey has left huge scars on the Usakedet (Isangele) people; customary owners of the peninsula who seem to be neither Nigerians nor Cameroonians. In the end, despised in Cameroon as Nigerians and rejected in Nigeria; their country of heritage as Cameroonians, the Usakedet people would neither be Nigerians nor Cameroonians. Surely, there is a serious identify problem here. It is in this living like neither bat nor bird wherein lay the veritable dilemma and bizarre tragedy of the Usakedet (Isangele) people; customary owners of the Bakassi Peninsula.

CHAPTER ELEVEN
The Verdict

As internal wrangling and bickering over the ownership of the Bakassi Peninsula between fishermen communities, unscrupulous politicians and Bakassi natives gathered momentum and became intensified, these contenders seemed totally oblivious of the fact that sovereignty over the Bakassi Peninsula was yet to be determined. These contenders appeared to have completely forgotten that at the outbreak of hostilities in the Bakassi Peninsula, Cameroon had taken the dispute to the International Court of Justice at 'The Hague' essentially for the Court to determine the question of sovereignty over the Bakassi Peninsula between the Federation of Nigeria and the Republic of Cameroon. The Republic of Cameroon had accordingly asked the Court to declare that sovereignty over the Bakassi Peninsula lay with Cameroon by virtue of international law, and that the peninsula was an integral part of the territory of Cameroon in accordance with provisions of the Anglo-German treaty of March 11, 1913 that placed the Bakassi Peninsula on the German side. These contenders seemed unaware that the Republic of Cameroon had further requested the Court to declare that the claim of the Federation of Nigeria in the Bakassi Peninsula was a violation of the 1964 Organisation of African Unity; OAU, Cairo Declaration where African nations accepted the principle of *'uti possidetis juris'* requiring African states to honour frontiers inherited from their colonial masters.

The Republic of Cameroon had further asked the Court to adjudge and declare that by using force against the Republic of Cameroon the Federation of Nigeria had violated and was violating its obligations under international treaty and customary law and that in view of these breaches of legal obligations the Federal Republic of Nigeria had the express duty of putting an end to its military presence in Cameroonian territory... Cameroon had also demanded the payment of reparation by the Federation of Nigeria on account of material and non-material damage inflicted upon the Republic of Cameroon.

The Republic of Cameroon further tried to show that upon independence both nations had held series of negotiations aimed at resolving the problem of the Bakassi Peninsula. The outcome of such negotiations, the Republic of Cameroon contended, showed that the Federation of Nigeria had tended to recognize a border derived from the Anglo-German Agreement of March 11, 1913. The Republic of Cameroon further cited Nigeria's Ministry of External Affairs Note No. 570 of 1962, several request for consular visits and other bilateral instruments in support of her claim. The Republic of Cameroon equally drew attention to a significant amount of documentary evidence, including maps drawn in the Federation of Nigeria that consistently placed the Bakassi Peninsula in the Republic of Cameroon as further proof of her claim.

After preliminary objection relating to the Court's lack of jurisdiction, the Federation of Nigeria requested the International Court of Justice to declare that sovereignty over the Bakassi Peninsula was vested in the Federation of Nigerian. The Federation of Nigeria dismissed certain provisions of the 1913 Anglo-German treaty arguing that title in 1913 lay with the Kings and Chiefs of Old Calabar until the territory passed to the Federation of Nigeria upon independence. Recalling that Great Britain and the Kings and Chiefs of Old Calabar had entered into a protection agreement under which Great Britain had undertaken to extend 'Her Majesty's gracious protection and favour' to the Kings and Chiefs of Old Calabar, the Federation of Nigeria insisted that the agreement did not empower Great Britain to alienate all or any part of the territory.

Great Britain, the Federation of Nigeria contended, was therefore unable to pass title to Germany in 1913 because it had no title to pass. (*nemo dat quod non habet*); as a result, the relevant provisions of the Anglo-German Agreement of 11 March 1913 must be regarded as ineffective. In the view of the Federation of Nigeria, the 1913 Anglo-German treaty was further defective because it was inconsistent with the fundamental legal principle of '*pacta sunt servanda*'. The Federation of Nigeria further claimed that the Anglo-German treaty of 1913 was defective on the grounds that it was contrary to the Preamble to the General Act of the Conference of Berlin of 26 February 1885, and that it was not approved by the German Parliament and that it had been abrogated as a result of Article 289 of the Treaty of Versailles of June 28, 1919.

That in a nutshell is the case the Federation of Nigeria and the Republic of Cameroon put before the International Court of Justice for adjudication. The Court's decision is by now common knowledge to all. What may still be news to a good number of people is how the Court came to that decision. What follows are unedited extracts of the proceedings at THE HAGUE as contained in the Report of the International Court of Justice, Year 2002, 10 October, p.99-113. It is our hope that these extracts will help clear lingering doubts and misgivings about the judgement.

195 ["Before addressing the question of whether Great Britain was entitled to pass title to Germany through the Anglo-German Agreement of 11 March 1913, the Court will examine these three arguments of Nigeria concerning the defectiveness of that Agreement.

As regards the argument based on the General Act of the Conference of Berlin, the Court notes that, having been raised very briefly by Nigeria in its Counter-Memorial it was not pursued further in the Rejoinder or at the hearings. It is therefore unnecessary for the Court to consider it.

196 Nigeria further contends that under contemporary German domestic legislation, all treaties providing for cession or acquisition of colonial territory by Germany had to be approved by Parliament. It points out that the Anglo-German Agreement of 11 March 1913 was not so approved. It argues that the Agreement involved the acquisition of colonial territory, namely the Bakassi peninsula, and accordingly ought to have been "approved by the German Parliament at least as far as its Bakassi peninsula's provisions were concerned."

Cameroon's position was that "the German Government took the view that in the case of Bakassi the issue was one of simple boundary rectification, because Bakassi had already been treated previously as belonging de facto to Germany" and thus parliamentary approval was not required.

197. The Court notes that Germany itself considered that the procedures prescribed by its domestic law had been complied with, nor did Great Britain ever raise, any question in relation thereto. The Agreement had, moreover, been officially published in both countries. It is therefore irrelevant that the Anglo-German Agreement of 11 March 1913 was not approved by the German Parliament. Nigeria's argument on this point accordingly cannot be upheld.

198. In relation to the Treaty of Versailles, Nigeria points out that Article 289 thereof provided for "the revival of pre-war bilateral treaties concluded by Germany on notification to Germany by the other party". It contends that, since Great Britain had taken no steps under Article 289 to revive the Agreement of 11 March 1913, it was accordingly abrogated; thus Cameroon "could not have succeeded to the [Agreement] itself".

Cameroon argues that Article 289 of the Treaty of Versailles did not have any legal effect on the Agreement of 11 March 1913 because "the scope of this Article was limited to treaties of an economic nature in the broad sense of the term"_ which in Cameroon's view confirmed by the context of the Article, its position within the scheme of the Treaty, its drafting history and its object and purpose in light of the Treaty as a whole.

199. The Court notes that since 1916 Germany had no longer exercised any territorial authority in Cameroon. Under Articles 118 and 119 of the Versailles Treaty, Germany relinquished its title to its overseas possessions. As a result, Great Britain had no reason to include the Anglo-German Agreement of 11 March 1913 among the "bilateral treaties or conventions" which it wished to revive with Germany. Thus it follows that this argument of Nigeria must in any event be rejected.

200. The Court now turns to the question of whether Great Britain was entitled to pass title in Bakassi through the Anglo-German Agreement of 11 March 1913.

In this regard, Cameroon contends that the Agreement of 11 March 1913 fixed the course of the boundary between the Parties in the area of Bakassi Peninsula and placed the latter on the Cameroonian side of the boundary. It relies for this purpose on Articles XVIII to XXI of the said Agreement, which provides *inter alia* that the boundary "follows the thalweg of Akwayefe as far as a straight line joining Bakassi Point and King Point" (Art. XVIII) and that "[s]hould the lower course of the Akwayefe River so change its mouth as to transfer it to Rio del Rey, it is agreed that the area now known as Bakassi peninsula shall still remain German territory" (Art. XX) Cameroon further states that, since the entry into force of the Agreement of March 1913, Bakassi peninsula have belonged to its predecessors, and that sovereignty over the peninsula is today vested in Cameroon.

201. Nigeria does not contest that the meaning of these provisions is to allocate Bakassi Peninsula to Germany. It does however, insists that these terms were never put into effect, and indeed were invalid on various grounds, though the other Articles of the Agreement of 11 March 1913 remained valid.

Nigeria contends that the title to sovereignty over Bakassi on which it relies was originally vested in the Kings and Chiefs of Old Calabar. It argues that in the pre-colonial era the City States of the Calabar region constituted an "acephalous federation" consisting of "independent entities with international legal personality" It considers that under the Treaty of Protection signed on 10 September 1884 between Great Britain and the Kings and Chiefs of Old Calabar, the latter retained their separate international status and rights, including their power to enter into relationships with "other international persons" although under the Treaty that power could only be exercised with the knowledge and approval of the British Government. According to Nigeria, the Treaty only conferred certain limited rights on Great Britain; in no way did it transfer sovereignty to Britain over the territories of the kings and Chiefs of Old Calabar.

Nigeria argues that, since Great Britain did not have sovereignty over those territories in 1913, it could not cede them to a third party. It followed that the relevant part of the Anglo-German Agreement of 11 March 1913 was "out with the treaty-making power of Great Britain and that part was not binding on the Kings and Chiefs of Old Calabar". Nigeria adds that the limitation on Great Britain's power under the 1884 Treaty of Protection,

"and in particular its lack of sovereignty over Bakassi peninsula and thus its lack of legal authority in international law to dispose of title to it, must have been known to Germany at the time the 1913 Treaty was concluded, or ought to have been on the assumption that Germany was conducting itself in a reasonably prudent way"

In Nigeria's view, the invalidity of the Agreement of 11 March 1913 on grounds of inconsistency with the principle of *nemo dat quod non habet* applied only, however, 'to those parts of the Treaty which purport to prescribe a boundary which, if effective, would have involved a cession of territory to Germany', that is to say essentially Articles XVIII to XXII. The remaining provisions of the Treaty were untainted by that defect and accordingly remained in force and fully effective; they were self-standing provisions, and their application was not dependent upon the Bakassi peninsula provisions, which, being in law defective, were to be severed from the rest of the Agreement.

202. In reply, Cameroon contends that Nigeria's argument that Great Britain had no legal power to cede Bakassi peninsula by treaty was manifestly unfounded.

In Cameroon's view, the treaty signed on 10 September 1884 between Great Britain and the Kings and Chiefs of Old Calabar established a 'colonial protectorate' and, 'in the practice of the period, there was little fundamental difference at international level, in terms of territorial acquisition, between colonies and colonial protectorates'. Substantive differences between the status of colony and that of a colonial protectorate were matters of the national law of the colonial Powers rather than of international law. The key element of the colonial protectorate was the 'assumption of external sovereignty by the protecting State', which manifested itself principally through

'the acquisition and exercise of the capacity and power to cede part of the protected territory by international treaty, without any intervention by the population or entity in question'.

Cameroon further argues that, even on the hypothesis that Great Britain did not have legal capacity to transfer sovereignty over Bakassi peninsula under the Agreement of 11 March 1913, Nigeria could not invoke that circumstance as rendering the Agreement invalid. It points out that, neither Great Britain nor Nigeria, the successor State, ever

sought to claim that the Agreement was invalid on this
ground; in this regard Cameroon states that,

'[o]n the contrary, until the start of the 1990s Nigeria
had unambiguously confirmed and accepted the 1913
boundary line in its diplomatic and consular practice, its
official geographical and cartographic publications and
indeed in its statements and conduct in the political field'.

...Cameroon also contends that, in any event, the
Agreement of 11 March 1913 forms an indivisible whole
and that it is not possible to sever from it the provisions
concerning the Bakassi peninsula. It maintains that 'there
is a strong presumption that treaties accepted as valid must
be interpreted as a whole and all their provisions respected
and applied' and that 'parties cannot choose the provisions
of a treaty which are to be applied and those which are not-
they cannot 'pick and choose'-, unless there is a provision
enabling them to act in that way'

203. The Court first observes that during the era of the
Berlin Conference, European Powers entered into many
treaties with local rulers. Great Britain concluded some 350
treaties with the local chiefs of the Niger Delta. Among
these were the treaties in July 1884 with the Kings and
Chiefs of Opobo and in September 1884 with the Kings and
Chiefs of Old Calabar. That these were regarded as notable
personages is clear from the fact that these treaties were
concluded by the consul, expressly as the representative of
Queen Victoria, and the British undertakings of 'gracious
favour and protection' were those of Her Majesty the Queen
of Great Britain and Ireland.

In turn, under Article II of the Treaty of 10 September 1884, 'The Kings and Chiefs of Old Calabar agreed and promised to refrain from entering into any correspondence, Agreement, or Treaty with any foreign nation or Power, except with the knowledge and sanction of Her Britannic Majesty's Government.'

The Treaty with the Kings and Chiefs of Old Calabar did not specify the territory to which the British Crown was to extend 'gracious favour and protection' nor did it indicate the territories over which each of the Kings and Chiefs signatory to the Treaty exercised his powers. However, the Consul who negotiated and signed the Treaty said of Old Calabar 'this country with its dependencies extends from Tom Shots... to the River Rumby (on the West of the Cameroon mountains), both inclusive'. Some six years later, in 1890 another British Consul, Johnston, reported to the Foreign Office that 'the rule of the Old Calabar Chiefs extends far beyond the Akpayafe River to the very base of the Cameroon Mountains'. The Court observes that while this territory extends considerably eastwards of Bakassi, Johnson did report that the Old Calabar Chiefs had withdrawn from the land east of the Ndian. Bakassi and Rio del Rey lay to the west of the Ndian, an area referred to by Johnston as 'their real, undoubted territory'.

In the view of the Court Great Britain had a clear understanding of the area ruled at different times by the Kings and Chief of Old Calabar and their standing.

204. Nigeria has contended that the very title of 1884 Treaty and the reference in Article 1 to the undertaking of "protection", shows that Britain had no entitlement to do

more than protect and in particular had no entitlement to cede the territory concerned to third States: *"nemo dat quod non habet"*

205. The Court calls attention to the fact that the international legal status of a 'Treaty of Protection' entered into under the law obtaining at the time cannot deduced from its title alone. Some treaties of protection were entered into with entities which retained there under a previously existing sovereignty under international law. This was the case whether the protected party was henceforth termed *"protectorat"* (as in the case of Morocco, Tunisia and Madagascar (1885; 1895) in their treaty relation with France) or "a protected State" (as in the case of Bahrain and Qatar in their treaty relations with Great Britain). In sub-Saharan Africa, however, treaties termed 'treaties of protection' were entered into not with states but rather with important indigenous rulers exercising local rule over identifiable areas of territory.

In relation to a treaty of this kind in another part of the world, Max Huber, sitting as sole arbitrator in the *Island of Palmas* case, explained that such a treaty

"is not an agreement between equals; it is rather a form of internal organisation of a colonial territory, on the basis of autonomy of the natives... And thus suzerainty over the native States becomes the basis of territorial sovereignty as towards other members of the community of nations". (RIIA Vol. II, pp.858-859.)

The Court points out that these concepts also found expression in the *Western Sahara* Advisory Opinion. There the Court stated that in territories that were not *terra nullius* but were inhabited by tribes or people having a social and political organization, 'agreements concluded with local rulers ... were regarded as derivative roots of title' (*Western Sahara, Advisory Opinion, ICJ Reports* 1975, p. 39 para. 80). Even if this mode of acquisition does not reflect current international law, the principle of inter-temporal law requires that the legal consequences of the treaties concluded at that time in the Niger delta be given effect today, in the present dispute.

206. The choice of protectorate treaty by Great Britain was a question of the preferred manner of rule. Elsewhere, specifically in the Lagos region, treaties for concession of land were being entered into with local rulers. It was precisely a reflection of those differences that within Nigeria there was the Colony of Lagos and the Niger Coast Protectorate, later to become the Protectorate of Southern Nigeria.

207. In the view of the Court many factors point to the 1884 Treaty signed with the Kings and Chiefs of Old Calabar as not establishing an international protectorate. It was one of a multitude in a region where the local Rulers were not regarded as States. Indeed, the Court continued, apart from the parallel declarations of various lesser Chiefs agreeing to be bound by the 1884 Treaty, there is not even convincing evidence of a central federal power. There appeared in Old Calabar to have been individual townships, headed by Chiefs, who regarded themselves as owing a general allegiance to more important Kings and Chiefs. Further, from the outset Britain regarded itself as administering the territories comprised in the 1884 Treaty,

and not just protecting them. Consul Johnston reported in 1888 that 'the country between the boundary of Lagos and the German boundary of Cameroon' was 'administered by Her Majesty's Consular Officers, under various Orders in Council' The fact that a delegation was sent to London by the Kings and Chiefs of Old Calabar in 1913 to discuss matters of land tenure cannot be considered as implying international personality. It simply confirms the British administration by indirect rule.

Nigeria itself has been unable to point to any role, in matters relevant to the present case, served by the Kings and Chiefs of Old Calabar after the conclusion of the 1884 Treaty. In responding to a question of a Member of the Court Nigeria stated "It is not possible to say with clarity and certainty what happened to the international legal personality of the Kings and Chiefs of Old Calabar after 1885"

The Court notes that a characteristic of an international protectorate is that of ongoing meetings and discussions between the protecting Power and the Rulers of the Protectorate. In the case concerning *Maritime Delimitation and Territorial Question between Qatar and Bahrain, (Qatar v. Bahrain)* the Court was presented with substantial documentation of this character, in large part being old British State papers. In the present case the Court was informed that 'Nigeria can neither say that no such meetings ever took place, or that they did take place...the records which would enable the question to be answered probably no longer exist...'

208. As to when the Kings and Chiefs ceased to exist as a separate entity, Nigeria told the Court it "is not a question susceptible of a clear-cut answer".

The Court notes in this regard that in 1885 Great Britain had established by proclamation a 'British Protectorate of the Niger Districts' (which subsequently changed names a number of times), incorporating in a single entity the various territories covered by the treaties of protection entered into in the region since July 1884. The Court further notes that there is no reference to Old Calabar in any of the British Orders in Council, of whatever date, which list protectorates as protected States. The same is true of the British Protected Persons Order of 1934, the Schedule which refers to "Nigerian Protectorate and Cameroons under British Mandate". Nor is there any reference to Old Calabar in the Second Schedule to the British Protectorates, Protected States and Protected Persons Order in Council, 1949, though in the First Schedule there is a reference to the Nigerian Protectorate.

Moreover, the Court has been presented with no evidence of any protest in 1913 by the Kings and Chiefs of Old Calabar; nor of any action by them to pass territory to Nigeria as it emerged to independence in 1960.

209. The Court thus concludes that under the law at the time, Great Britain was in a position in 1913 to determine its boundaries with Germany in respect of Nigeria, including the southern section.

210. The Court will now examine the treatment, in the period 1913 to 1960, of the southern sector of the boundary as defined by the Anglo-German Agreement of 11 March 1913.

Cameroon contends that the mandate and trusteeship period, and the subsequent independence process, show recognition on the part of the international community of Cameroon's attachment to the Bakassi Peninsula.

Following the First World War, it was decided that the German colony of Cameroon should be administered in partitioned form by Britain and France under the framework of the League of Nations mandate arrangements. Bakassi is said to have formed part of the area of the British Cameroons termed Southern Cameroons. This territorial definition is said to have been repeated in the trusteeship agreements which succeeded the mandates system after the Second World War. According to Cameroon, there was never any doubt in the minds of the British authorities that Bakassi formed part of the mandated and trusteeship territory of the Cameroons since Bakassi had formed part of German Cameroon pursuant to the Anglo-German Agreement of 11 March 1913. Moreover, although the British Cameroons Order in Council of 1923 established the Northern and Southern Cameroons would be administered 'as if they formed part of' Nigeria, Cameroon emphasized that this was merely an administrative arrangement which did not lead to the incorporation of these territories into Nigeria. Cameroon produces documentary evidence, British Orders in Council and maps which, it claims, evidence that Bakassi is consistently placed within the British Cameroons throughout this period.

Cameroon further recalls that the United Nations plebiscites, held on 11 and 12 February 1961, resulted in a clear majority in the Northern Cameroons voting to join Nigeria, and a clear majority in the Southern Cameroons voting to join Cameroon. It maintains that the process of holding the plebiscite meant that the areas that fell within the Northern and Southern Cameroons had to be ascertained. Cameroon points out that the map attached to the Report of the United Nations Plebiscite Commissioner shows that the Bakassi Peninsula formed part of the Victoria South West plebiscite district in the south-east corner of Cameroon. This would show that the peninsula was recognized by the United Nations as being a part of the Southern Cameroons. Cameroon also emphasizes the absence of any protest by Nigeria to the proposed boundary during the independence process and the fact that Nigeria voted in favour of General Assembly Resolution 1608 (XV) by which the British trusteeship was formally terminated.

Cameroon further refers to the maritime negotiations between Nigeria and Cameroon since independence, which resulted in instruments under which Nigeria is said to have recognized the validity of the Anglo-German Agreement of 11 March 11, 1913, the boundary deriving from it, and Cameroons sovereignty over Bakassi Peninsula. These instruments included the Nigerian Note No.570 of 27 March 1962, the Yaounde II Agreement of 4 April 1971, the Kano Agreement of 1 September 1974 and the Maroua Agreement of 1 June 1975.

Cameroon finally refers to its granting of permits for hydrocarbon exploration and exploitation over the Bakassi Peninsula itself and offshore, commencing in the early 1960s as well as to a number of Consular and Ambassadorial visits to the Bakassi region by Nigerian Consuls and Ambassadors, whose conduct in requesting permission and co-operation from Cameroonian local officials and expressing thanks for it is said to corroborate Cameroon's claim to sovereignty over Bakassi.

211. Nigeria for its part argues that, at all times while the 1884 Treaty remained in force, Great Britain continued to lack power to give Bakassi away. As such, it claims that no amount of British activity in relation to Bakassi in the mandate or trusteeship periods could have severed Bakassi from the Nigeria Protectorate. It draws additional support from the fact that, in practice throughout the period from 1913 to 1960, Bakassi was administered from and as part of Nigeria, and was never administered from or as part of Cameroon. Nigeria also asserts that there is no documentary evidence that the population of Bakassi Peninsula participated in the United Nations Plebiscite; the description of the Victoria South West plebiscite district in the Commissioner Report does not refer to any areas situated in the Bakassi Peninsula.

Nigeria further denies the binding nature of the delimitation agreements referred to by Cameroon, in particular the Maroua Declaration, whose adoption, it claims, was never approved by the Supreme Military Council in contravention of Nigeria's constitutional requirements. It also denies the evidentiary value of the visits to the Bakassi region by Nigerian dignitaries referred to by Cameroon, on the basis that consular officials are not mandated to with issues of title to territory, nor to make assessments of questions of sovereignty, and, as such, their actions cannot be taken to impact upon these questions. Finally on the issue of granting of oil exploration permits and production agreements, Nigeria argues *inter alia* that 'the area in dispute was the subject of competing exploration activities' and that 'the incidence of oil-related activities was not… regarded (by the Parties) as conclusive of the issues of sovereignty'

212. The Court notes that after the First World War Germany renounced it colonial possessions. Under the Versailles Treaty the German possessions of Cameroon were divided between Great Britain and France. In 1922 Great Britain accepted the mandate of the League of Nations for 'the part (of the former German colony) of Cameroons which lay to the west of the line laid down in the (Milner-Simon) Declaration signed on the 10th July, 1919'. Bakassi was necessarily comprised within the mandate. Great Britain had no powers unilaterally to alter the boundary nor did it make any request to the League of Nations for any such alteration. The League Council was notified, and did not object to, the British suggestion that it administer Southern Cameroon together with the eastern region of the Protectorate of Nigeria. Thus the British Order in Council of 26 June 1923 providing for the Administration of the Mandated Territory of the British Cameroons stipulated that British Cameroons lying southwards of the line described in the schedule would be administered 'as if it formed part of' the southern provinces of the Protectorate of Nigeria. The Court observed that the terminology used in the Order in Council preserves the distinctive status of the mandated territory, while allowing the convenience of a common administration. The Nigerian thesis must therefore be rejected.

When, after the Second World War and the establishment of the United Nations, the mandate was converted to a trusteeship, the territorial situation remained exactly the same. Then 'as if' provision continued in place, and again the Administering Authority had no authority unilaterally to alter the boundaries of the trusteeship territory. Thus for the entire period from 1922 until 1961 when the trusteeship was terminated, Bakassi was comprised within British Cameroon. The boundary between Bakassi and Nigeria, notwithstanding the administrative arrangements, remained an international boundary.

The Court is unable to accept Nigeria's contention that until its independence in 1961, and notwithstanding the Anglo-German Agreement of 11 March 1913, the Bakassi Peninsula had remained under the sovereignty of the Kings and Chiefs of Old Calabar. Neither the League of Nations nor the United Nations considered that to be the position.

213. Equally, the Court has seen no evidence that Nigeria thought that upon independence it was acquiring Bakassi from the Kings and Chiefs of Old Calabar. Nigeria itself raised no query as to the extent of its territory in this region upon attaining independence.

The Court notes in particular that there was nothing which might have led Nigeria to believe that the plebiscite which took place in the Southern Cameroons in 1961 under United Nations supervision did not include Bakassi.

It is true that the Southern Cameroons Plebiscite Order in Council, 1960 makes no mention of any polling station bearing the name of a Bakassi village. Nor, however, does the Order in Council specifically exclude Bakassi from its scope. The Order simply refers to the Southern Cameroons as a whole. By that time it was already clearly established that Bakassi formed part of the Southern Cameroons under British Trusteeship. The boundaries of that territory had been precisely defined in the 'Northern Region, Western Region and Eastern Region (Definition of Boundaries)

Proclamation, 1954' issued pursuant to the Nigerian (Constitution) in Council, 1951. That Proclamation, repeating the provisions of the Anglo-German Agreement of 11 March 1913, provided in particular: 'From the sea the boundary follows the navigable channel of the River Akpa-yafe; then follows the thalweg of the aforesaid River Akpa –Yafe upstream to the confluence with the Rivers Akpa-Korum and Ebe'. That the 1960 Order in Council applied to the Southern Cameroons as a whole is further confirmed by the fact, as noted in the Report of the United Nations Plebiscite Commissioner for the Cameroons under the United Kingdom Administration, that the 26 'plebiscite districts' established by the 1960 Order in Council corresponded to the 'electoral constituencies for the Southern Cameroons House of Assembly'.

The United Nations map indicating the voting districts for the plebiscite also reflected the provisions of the Agreement of 11 March 1913 reiterated in the above mentioned 1954 Proclamation.

The Court further observes that that frontier line was acknowledged in turn by Nigeria when it voted in favour of the General Assembly resolution 1608 (XV), which both terminated the trusteeship and approved the results of the plebiscite.

214. Shortly after, in Note Verbale No. 570 of 27 March 1962 addressed to Cameroon, Nigeria referred to certain oil licensing blocks. A sketch map was appended to the Note, from which it is clear that the block 'N' referred to lie directly south of the Bakassi Peninsula. The block was described as offshore Cameroon. The Note Verbale further

stated 'the boundary follows the lower courses of the Akpa-yafe River, where there appears to be no uncertainty, and then out into the Cross River estuary'. Nigeria clearly regarded the Bakassi peninsula as part of Cameroon. The Court further notes that this perception was reflected in all Nigerian official maps up until 1972.

This common understanding of where title lay continued through until the late 1970s, when the Parties were engaging in discussions on their maritime frontier. In this respect Article XX1 of the Anglo-German Agreement of 11 March 1913 provided:

"From the centre of the navigable channel on a line joining Bakassi Point and King Point, the boundary shall follow the centre of the navigable channel of the Akpayafe River as far as the 3-mile limit of territorial jurisdiction. For the purpose of defining this boundary, the navigable channel of the Akwayafe River shall be considered to lie wholly to the east of the navigable channel of the Cross and Calabar Rivers"

Article XXII provided that: "The 3-mile limit shall, as regards the mouth of the estuary, be taken from a line 3 nautical miles seaward of a line joining Sandy Point and Tom Shot Point".

In 1970 Cameroon and Nigeria decided to carry out a total delimitation and demarcation of their boundaries, starting from the sea. Under the terms of Article 2 of the Yaounde 1 Declaration of August 14 1970 and the agreement reached in the Yaounde 11 Declaration of 4 April 1971 with its signed appended chart, it was agreed to fix the boundary in the Akwayafe estuary from point 1 to point 12 (see paragraph 38 above). Then by declaration signed at Maroua on 1 June 1975, the two Heads of State "agreed to extend the delineation of the maritime boundary between the countries from Point 12 to Point G on the Admiralty Chart No. 3433 annexed March 1913 Anglo-German to this Declaration" It precisely defined the boundary by reference to maritime co-ordinates (see paragraph 38 above). The Court finds that it is clear from each of these elements that the Parties took it as a given fact that Bakassi belonged to Cameroon. Nigeria, drawing on the full weight of its experts as well as its most senior political figures, understood Bakassi to be under Cameroon sovereignty.

This remains the case quite regardless of the need to recalculate the co-ordinates of point B though an exchange of Letters of 12 June and 17 July 1975 between the Heads o State concerned; ...quite regardless whether the Maroua Declaration constituted an international agreement by which Nigeria bound. The Court addresses these aspects at paragraph 262 to 268 below.

Accordingly, the Court finds that at that time Nigeria accepted that it was bound by Articles XVIII to XXII of the Anglo-German Agreement of 11 March 1913, and that it recognized Cameroonian sovereignty over the Bakassi Peninsula.

215. In the view of the Court, this common understanding is also reflected by geographic patterns of the oil concessions granted by the two Parties up to 1991. While no ... offshore delimitation lines were adhered

to in the grants made, their underlying assumption was that Cameroon had the right to the resources in those waters that depended on the land boundary as fixed in the Anglo-German Agreement of 11 March 1913. It is true, as Nigeria insists that oil licensing "is certainly not a cession of territory". The Court finds however, that the geographic pattern of licensing is consistent with the understanding of the Parties, evidenced elsewhere, as to pre- existing Cameroon title in Bakassi. Nor can this striking consistency (save for a very few exceptions) be explained by the contention that the Parties simply chose to deal with matters of oil exploitation in a manner wholly unrelated to territorial title.

216. In assessing whether Nigeria as an independent State, acknowledged the applicability of the provisions of the Anglo-German Agreement of 11 March 1913 relating to Bakassi, the Court has also taken account of certain formal request up until the 1980s submitted by the Nigerian Embassy in Yaounde, or by the Nigerian consular authorities, before going to visit their nationals residing in Bakassi. This Nigerian acknowledgement of Cameroon sovereignty is in no way dependent upon proof that any particular official visit did in fact take place.

217. For all these reasons the Court finds that the Anglo-German Agreement of 11 March 1913 was valid and applicable in its entirety. Accordingly, the Court found no need to address arguments advanced by Cameroon and Nigeria as to the severability of treaty provisions, whether generally or as regards boundary treaties.

Equally, the Court has not found it necessary to pronounce upon the arguments of *uti possidetis* advanced by the Parties in relation to Bakassi.

218. The Court now turns to further claims to Bakassi relied on by Nigeria. Nigeria advances 'three distinct but interrelated bases of title over the Bakassi peninsula':

'(i) Long occupation by Nigeria and by Nigerian nationals constituting an historical consolidation of title and confirming the original title of the Kings and Chiefs of Old Calabar, which title vested in Nigeria at the time of independence in 1960;

(ii) Peaceful possession by Nigeria, acting as sovereign, and an absence of protest by Cameroon;

and

(iii) Manifesting of sovereignty by Nigeria, together with acquiescence by Cameroon in Nigerian sovereignty over the Bakassi Peninsula.

Nigeria particularly emphasizes that the title on the basis of historical consolidation, together with acquiescence, in the period since the independence of Nigeria, 'constitutes an independent and self sufficient title to Bakassi'. Nigeria perceived the situation as comparable to that in the *Minquiers and Ecrehos case,* in which both parties contended that they retained an ancient title (*ICJ Report 1953, p. 53*) but the Court considered that "What is of decisive importance ... is... evidence which relates directly to the possession of the Ecrehos and Minquiers groups" (ibid p. 57) Nigeria also presents evidence of various State activities, together with other components of historic consolidation of title. It contends *inter alia* that Nigerian authorities had collected tax as part of a consistent pattern of activity, that Nigeria had establish health centres for the benefit of the communities in Bakassi, often with the assistance of local communities, and that it health centre at Ikang on the other side of the Akpa-yafe treated patients from Bakassi. Nigeria also refers to a number of other miscellaneous State activities during the post-independence era, including the use of Nigerian currency for both public and commercial purposed or the use of Nigerian passports by residents of Bakassi.

219. Cameroon for its part argues that a legal treaty cannot be displaced by what in its view amounts to no more than a number of alleged *effectivites*. It contends that after the conferral of the Mandate, Great Britain's administration of the area was carried out, not on behalf of the Kings and Chiefs of Old Calabar, nor on behalf of Nigeria, but as the mandatory Power under Article 22, paragraph 1, of the League Covenant acting on behalf of the international community and the inhabitants of the Southern Cameroons. Cameroon further denies the existence of historical consolidation as a separate basis of legal title. What Nigeria brings under this concept is in Cameroon's view nothing more than 'the establishment of title by adverse possession, which has traditionally been labelled as 'acquisitive prescription'. Cameroon also contends that, in order to establish prescription, the acts of the State which does not hold title must be carried out in a sovereign capacity, under a claim of right, openly, peacefully, without protest or competing activity by the existing sovereign, and for a sufficiently long time. In Cameroon's view if these

criteria were applied to the evidence adduced by Nigeria, this would eliminate the whole of Nigeria's list of *effectivites*. Referring to the Judgement in the *Frontier Dispute (Burkina Faso/Republic of Mali)*, Cameroon finally maintains that, in a case of prescription, if there is a conflict of effectivites, "preference should be given to the holder of the title".

220. The Court first recalls its finding regarding the claim to an ancient title to Bakassi derived from the Kings and Chiefs of Old Calabar. It follows there from that at the time of Nigeria's accession to independence there existed no Nigerian title capable of being confirmed subsequently by "long occupation" (see paragraph 212 above). On the contrary, on the date of its independence Cameroon succeeded to title over Bakassi as established by the Anglo-German Agreement of 11 March 1913. (see paragraph 213-214 above).

Historical consolidation was also invoked in connection with the first of Nigeria's further claimed bases of title, namely peaceful possession in the absence of protest. The Court notes that it had already addressed these aspects of the theory of historical consolidation in paragraph 62 to 70 above. The Court thus finds that invocation of historical consolidation could not in any event vest title to Bakassi in Nigeria, where its 'occupation' of the peninsula is adverse to Cameroon's prior treaty title and where, moreover, the possession has been for a limited period.

The Court cannot therefore accept this first basis of title over Bakassi relied on by Nigeria.

221. The Court will now deal with other aspects of the second and third bases of title advanced by Nigeria, and

finds it convenient to deal with these interrelated matters together. Localities in Bakassi will be given either their Nigerian or their Cameroonian names as appropriate.

The Court finds that the evidence before it indicates that the small population of Bakassi already present in the early 1960s grew with the influx from Nigeria in 1968 as a result of the civil war in that country. Gradually sizeable centres of population were established. The Parties are in disagreement as to the total number of Nigerian nationals living in the peninsula today, but it is clear that it has grown considerably from the modest numbers reported in the 1953 and 1963 population censuses. Nor is there any reason to doubt the Efik and Effiat toponomy of the settlements, or their relationship with Nigeria. But these facts of themselves do not establish Nigerian title over Bakassi territory; nor can they serve as an element in a claim for historical consolidation of title, for reasons already given by the Court (see paragraphs 64-70).

222. Nigeria has relied before the Court, in consideration detail, often with supporting evidence, on many activities in Bakassi that it regards as proof both of settled Nigerian administration and of acts in exercise of sovereign authority. Among these acts are the establishment of schools, the provision of health facilities for many of the settlements and some tax collection.

It is true that the provision of education in Bakassi settlements appears to be largely Nigerian. Religious schools were established in 1960 at Archibong, in 1968 at Atabong and in Abana in 1969. These were not supported by public funds but were under the authority of the Nigerian examination and education authorities. Community schools were also established at Atabong East in 1968, Mbenmong in 1975 and Nwanjo in 1981. These schools established in Abana in 1992 and in Archibong and Atabong in 1993, were Nigerian government schools or State secondary schools.

There is evidence that since 1959 health centres have been established with the assistance of local communities receiving supplies, guidance and training for personnel in Nigeria. The ten centres include centres established at Atabong in 1959, Nbenmong in 1960, Atabong West in 1968, Abana in 1991 and Atabong East in 1992.

There was also some collection of tax, certainly from Akwa, Archibong, Mben Mong, Wanjo, Atabong and Abana.

Nigeria notes that Cameroon failed actively to protest these administrative activities of Nigeria before 1994 (save, notably, the building by Nigeria of a primary school in Abana in 1969). It also contends that the case law of this Court, and certain arbitral awards, makes clear that such acts are indeed acts a titre de souverain, and as such relevant to the question of territorial title *(Minquiers and Ecrehos, Judgment, I.C.J Reports 1953; Western Sahara, Advisory Opinion, I.C.J Reports 1975; Ram of Kutch, Arbitral Award, 50 ILR 1; Beagle Channel Arbitration, 52 ILR 93)*

223. The Court observes, however, that in none of these cases were the acts referred to acts *contra legem;* those precedents are therefore not relevant. The legal question of whether effectivites suggest that title lies with one country rather than another is not the same legal question as whether

such effectivites can serve to displace an established treaty title. As the Chamber of the Court made clear in the *Frontier Dispute (Burkina Faso/ Republic of Mali)*, where there is a conflict between title and effectivites, preference will be given to the former *(.IC.J. Reports 1986, judgement, pp.586-587, Para. 63)*.

In the view of the Court the more relevant legal question in this case is whether the conduct of Cameroon, as the title holder, can be viewed as an acquiescene in the loss of the treaty title that it inherited upon independence. There is some evidence that Cameroon attempted, *inter alia* to collect tax from Nigerian residents, in the year 1981-1982, in Idabato I and II, Jabane I and II, Kombo Abenimo, Naumsi Wan and Forisane (West and East Atabong, Abana and Ine Ekoi) But it engaged in only occasional direct acts of administration in Bakassi, having limited material resources to devote to this distant area.

However, its title was already established. Moreover, as the Court has shown above (see paragraph 213), in 1961-1962 Nigeria clearly and publicly recognized Cameroon title to Bakassi. That continued to be the position until at least 1975, when Nigeria signed the Maroua Declaration. No Nigerian effectivites in Bakassi before that time can be said to have legal significance for demonstrating a Nigerian title; this may in part explain the absence of Cameroon protests regarding health, education and tax activity in Nigeria. The Court also notes that Cameroon had since its independence engaged in activities which made clear that it in no way was abandoning its title to Bakassi. Cameroon and Nigeria participated from 1971 to 1975 in the negotiations leading to the Yaounde, Kano and Maroua Declarations, with the maritime line clearly being predicated upon Cameroon's title to Bakassi. Cameroon also granted hydrocarbon licences over the peninsula and its waters, again evidencing that it had not abandoned title in the face of the significant Nigerian presence in Bakassi or any Nigerian *effectivites contra legem*. Any protest was immediately made regarding Nigerian military action in 1994.

The Court considers that the foregoing shows that Nigeria could not have been acting '*a titre de souverain*' before the late 1970s, as it did not consider itself to have title over Bakassi; and in the ensuing period the evidence does not indicate an acquiescence by Cameroon in the abandonment of its title in favour of Nigeria.

For all these reasons the Court is also unable to accept the second and third bases of title to Bakassi advanced by Nigeria.

The Court accordingly concludes that the boundary between Cameroon and Nigeria in Bakassi is delimited by Articles XVIII to XX of the Anglo-German Agreement of 11 March 1913, and that sovereignty over the peninsula lay with Cameroon."] (29)

CHAPTER TWELVE

Cameroonians Celebrate as Shock and Anger Trail World Court Decision in Nigeria

That World Court judgement shattered our dreams. Melancholy spirit filled the air; a sense that something was over; that an opportunity had been lost enveloped my being. After all the energy, time and resources I had put into the struggle, after all the hope I had pinned on Nigeria regaining control of the Bakassi Peninsula, it was devastating to come to the realisation that it was all over. I remained in a mood of dashed hope and utter desperation for weeks. In spite of the alienation and unacceptable treatment of my people, I had quietly hoped and prayed that Nigeria would win the legal battle for the Bakassi Peninsula. Bakassi natives would thereafter take on anyone falsely claiming ownership of the peninsula and its enormous resources without jeopardizing Nigeria's chances at the Court. With the mountain of literature in favour of Bakassi natives, I was certain Usakedet people could easily win that battle. Now that hope was dashed. It all seemed like a bad dream but it was true. The curtain came down on October 10, 2002.

Anyone who had dispassionately subjected the Bakassi Peninsula to some kind of scrutiny from the inception of the crisis might have seen it coming. Such persons may not have failed to observe that Nigeria's many acts of omission and commission in the Bakassi Peninsula may have inadvertently accumulated evidence in favour of

Cameroon. Such persons may equally not have failed to realise that the heavy burden imposed on Nigeria by provisions of Articles (18-22) of the March 11, 1913 Anglo-German Agreement would make it extremely difficult if not impossible for Nigeria to win a legal battle for ownership of the Bakassi Peninsula. Article 20 of that treaty for example stipulates;

> "Should the lower course of the Akwayafe so change its mouth as to transfer it to the Rio del Rey, it is agreed that the area now known as the Bakassi Peninsula shall still remain German territory..."

This irrevocable provision as can be observed ensures that not even an act of God could bring the Bakassi Peninsula back to Nigeria.

Analysts may equally not have failed to conclude that an international environment in which Nigeria was largely seen as a pariah nation by western democracies at the outbreak of hostilities in the Bakassi peninsula was unlikely to favour Nigeria's claim over the peninsula. It must also have been pretty clear to any impartial observer that France, Cameroon's colonial master and biggest beneficiary of the enormous petroleum deposits in the Bakassi Peninsula would not give Nigeria any support. It could easily have been concluded too that not even the fact that French investment in Nigeria estimated to be over ten times her investment in Cameroon would make France dump her former colony for Nigeria. The fact too that France maintains a defence treaty with Cameroon would have made it obvious that France was unlikely under any circumstance to support Nigeria against Cameroon in the Bakassi Peninsula in the event of a war.

As for Great Britain and Germany there could be no doubting on whose side these nations would stand. Nigeria's attempt to regain sovereignty over the Bakassi Peninsula was essentially a challenge to Great Britain and Germany who had created the Bakassi Peninsula problem in the first place. Undoing what these colonial powers had done would in essence have caused Britain and Germany considerable embarrassment. Under such circumstances, it was obvious that representatives of France, Great Britain and Germany at THE HAGUE would vote against Nigeria, regardless of the strength of Nigeria's legal arguments. It was also probable that the United States would support her allies and vote against Nigeria. It should also have been expected that these big powers would use their influence to cajole less powerful nations at THE HAGUE to vote against Nigeria. Nigeria's own Bakassi policies that tended to alienate Bakassi natives would further compound an already miserable situation. It should have been pretty obvious from the very beginning that Nigeria was unlikely to win the legal battle for the Bakassi Peninsula. In fact Nigeria had no business going to The Hague. It does however appear that either people were ignorant of these facts or that some naive old fashion and outdated patriotism had blurred visions, as the overwhelming reaction from Nigeria would seem to suggest.

In Cameroon the judgement was hailed as 'a victory for international law' and Cameroonians as would be expected reacted, to the judgement with pomp and fanfare. The people's jubilation knew no bounds. Cameroonians shed tears of joy as they gulped down drums of beer and 'majonga' red table wine. Cameroonians rolled out their drums, blared trumpets, bells rang, guns boomed and Cameroonians danced to the tune of 'makosa' and 'beromo' across streets till dawn. That was to be expected. In spite of legal evidence that weighed heavily in Cameroon's favour, most Cameroonians saw their country's claim over a Bakassi peninsula that is owned by a people of Nigerian extraction and over ninety-five percent populated by Nigerians as a mere gamble. The World Court proved them wrong.

In Nigeria the World Court verdict caused consternation eliciting angry reactions from many. Nigerians overwhelmingly and unequivocally rejected the decision with some describing the verdict as full of fundamental errors. The nation became awash with seemingly unending virulent criticism of the International Court of Justice. The ruling caused wide spread discontent and aroused vitriolic comments from several commentators. Angry and acrimonious reactions greeted a decision which Chief Richard Akinjide, SAN, declared was '50% international law, 50% international politics,' 'blatantly biased and unfair,' 'a total disaster,' 'a complete fraud.'(30)

The Nigerian Guardian newspaper went even further declaring the judgement 'a rape, an unforeseen potential international conspiracy against Nigeria's integrity and sovereignty' and 'part of Western ploy to foment and perpetuate trouble in Africa.' Fishermen communities and their politicians threatened to break away from Nigeria. Such reactions by an overwhelming majority of Nigerians summed up the general feeling of despair about the judgement and led to allegations of partiality against the presiding French Judge Guillaume. As a result, not a few Nigerians would have wished President Obasanjo to renege on his decision to honour the judgement. But while these criticism and threats raged, there arose the feeling that Nigeria may have been too economical with the truth about the Bakassi Peninsula leading critics to question and pick holes in what they had been made to believe about the Bakassi Peninsula. Needless to say such discordant voices were quickly tagged as ignoble and unpatriotic.

Nigeria nevertheless accepted the decision albeit not without hesitation. Nigeria's President Obasanjo went on to sign the Greentree Agreement with Cameroon's President Biya in what seemed a bid to find an honourable way to exit the territory and ensure the protection of Nigerians in the peninsula. This act notwithstanding, implementing ICJ judgement proved to be quite a challenge to Nigeria for obvious reasons. Nigeria found that decision so difficult to swallow that it took nearly four years of foot-dragging and tedious negotiations before the Greentree Agreement was signed on June 12, 2006. The United Nations, Germany, United Kingdom, United States of America and France witnessed the agreement. Two months later, in August, 2006 Nigeria quietly pulled out of portions of mainland Bakassi she had occupied; an area that incidentally happened to be where Bakassi natives reside. Nigeria held on to the part of Bakassi peninsula where the overwhelming population of fishermen carry out their businesses; around Abana, Atabong and surrounding fishing ports. This area happened to be the jewel of the Bakassi Peninsula where most of the hydrocarbon and marine resources are found. Bakassi natives once again felt cheated and betrayed. Not a finger was raised against the handover of that section of the Bakassi Peninsula in August 2006. No objections were raised anywhere. By this singular act, Nigeria and the Efik world once again demonstrated their preparedness to take Bakassi native territory and abandon Bakassi natives.

Nigeria delayed the handover of the area largely occupied by fishermen communities for another two years until August 14, 2008. Such delay however did nothing to convince critics who believed that President Obasanjo acted too hastily in handing over the Bakassi Peninsula to Cameroon. Opponents of the handover wanted Nigeria to hold on to the remaining part of the peninsula and risk possible United Nations sanctions which they believed had never been effective anywhere. Besides, they contended that Nigeria's friends would come to Nigeria's aid if it became necessary and stressed Nigeria's in-built mechanism to weather any threats. In their view President Obasanjo's apparent hasty handover of the territory stemmed from the President's desire to get the support of Western Democracies for his abortive third term ambition. Supporters of the handover held a completely different view. They praised President Obasanjo's action claiming it was driven by the desire to prove to the world that Nigeria was a responsible member of the international community that respects international law and treaty obligations. They commended the President for the posture which they believed would boost Nigeria's chances of obtaining a permanent seat at the United Nations Security Council.

Many Nigerians disagreed and continued to heap blame on President Obasanjo for the loss of the Bakassi Peninsula. Yet, neither President Obasanjo nor General Yakubu Gowon who at different times have been accused of selling the Bakassi Peninsula were born when Great Britain gave the Bakassi Peninsula away to Germany in 1913. Obasanjo's critics appeared not to care about such facts. They simple appeared to equate President Obasanjo's remarkably colourless-low-profile-posture and quasi total abhorrence of flamboyance for lack of dept and substance. Those who have had the privilege to closely watch Obasanjo at work strongly disagreed. They insisted that Obasanjo had on more than one occasion proved that he was not just endowed with a sharp and analytical mind he was also a doggedly patriotic Nigerian. They advised those who still had any doubts to ask Barclays Bank plc or Shell B.P.; a clear reference to Nigeria's nationalisation of these multinationals when Obasanjo was Nigeria's military Head of State. As a matter of fact, few Nigerians can boast of the experience Obasanjo has acquired, not in the four walls of a university but through years of involvement with state affairs at the highest level. However, when it comes to the Bakassi Peninsula, few Nigerians believe Obasanjo did well. Obasanjo has kept everyone guessing by his uncharacteristic silence over the Bakassi Peninsula. It is our hope that Obasanjo will someday break this silence and throw some light on the Bakassi Peninsula saga.

Although most Nigerians seemed united in their condemnation of the judgement and the Greentree Agreement, legal luminaries on the other hand appeared to be split down the line on the World Court's ruling. Few critics however provided a compelling and unbiased analysis of the judgement. Most merely succumbed to old fashion patriotic sentiments and took the occasion to do mischief. They vilified political opponents and professional colleagues and poured out their emotions, ignorance and misconceptions. As no efforts were made to enlighten the public about the real issues involved, most Nigerians went to bed with conflicting and inconsistent views about the judgement and the Greentree Agreement.

In an interview granted THE PUNCH newspaper, Chief Richard Akinjide, Senior Advocate of Nigeria, SAN, astute politician and erstwhile Attorney General of the Federation and Minister of Justice and Nigeria's Agent at the International Court of Justice, ICJ for the Bakassi Peninsula case declared that ICJ decision on Bakassi was 'fifty percent law and fifty percent politics'. Chief Akinjide, told the world

> "I have always believed that that judgement was perverse because you don't transfer to others what you do not have. There is no doubt at all that Bakassi is part of Nigeria because one of the kingmakers who always appoint the Obong of Calabar is one of the senior chiefs from Bakassi... In 1913 without consulting the Obong of Calabar and the people of Calabar, Britain went ahead and entered into Anglo-German treaty, purporting to transfer Bakassi to Germany. You don't give what you don't have... Now, look at the scenario, Britain purportedly gave to Germany what it did not own. At that time, Bakassi and Nigeria were British protectorates and in a protectorate, the radical title of the territory belongs to the chiefs and the people who own that territory, whereas in a colony the root of title is in the imperial power. So the root of title of Bakassi, being part of Nigeria Protectorate, was not in Britain. So, Britain had no right to transfer what it didn't

have to Germany in 1913. That is the base of the issue. And there are settled judgements in International Law which support that view." (31)

Reacting to accusations that Nigeria's legal team mishandled the case, Chief Akinjide had this to say.

"We did our best for the country. But a lot of things were stacked against us. In the first place, mysteriously, the President of the ICJ at that time was a Frenchman. And it is an open secret that France was openly supporting Cameroon. It is also an open secret that Britain was not supporting Nigeria because the Anglo-German Treaty of 1913 embarrasses Britain. We have a situation where Britain was supporting Cameroon, where France was supporting Cameroon and where a Frenchman was President of the ICJ... The lawyers who argued Nigeria's case were some of the finest brains in International law... The judgement was a great injustice which started in 1913 and which was being perpetuated under the guise of the International Court of Justice. When you have a biased tribunal or a tribunal with unconscious bias, either conscious or unconscious bias, there is no way you can win." (32)

Prince Bola Ajibola, SAN, erstwhile Attorney General of the Federation and Minister of Justice, Retired Judge of the International Court of Justice and Nigeria's Judge Advocate on the Bakassi Peninsula case seemed to differ strongly with Chief Akinjide. He told The Nation newspaper that Bakassi had never been part of Nigeria.

"Nigeria had no genuine case...The court based its judgement on the agreement of March 11, 1913 which was between Great Britain and Germany. In that agreement, if you look at it from Articles 18 to about 23 or 24, it irrevocably gave to Germany the whole of Bakassi peninsula which in turn was surrendered to France and from France to Cameroun. That was it and that agreement was very clear beyond any doubt. It ceded the whole of Bakassi to Cameroun and that is why all along, Cameroun had been fighting and quarrelling with Nigeria because that area belonged to it. But there is more to it than that. Even before Cameroun filed that action against Nigeria, as far back as around 1962, our own minister of Foreign Affairs then had written a verbale note to Cameroun confirming that the entire Bakassi peninsula belonged to Cameroun. But that was not all. Systematically, we have in fact been surrendering our claim on Bakassi to Cameroun. From the time of our independence, particularly if you look at the map of 1977, you will see that the map of Nigeria was there without Bakassi, reflecting that Bakassi was even part of Cameroun."(33)

Such divergent views from two of Nigeria's most distinguished legal luminaries did not seem to help matters very much. Rather, it threw the debate open and into greater confusion. Nigerians disagreed and insisted that Bakassi being part of Old Calabar was without doubt part of Nigeria; its people, culture, deities being very much Nigerian. Note even Prince Ajibola's allusion to the infamous Verbale Note No. 570 of 1962 from Nigeria's Ministry of External Affairs to the Embassy of Cameroon in Lagos affirming that the Bakassi Peninsula belonged to Cameroon or Nigerian maps that consistently put the Bakassi Peninsula in Cameroon before 1977 or even the many agreements between Nigeria and Cameroon that systematically surrendered sovereignty over the Bakassi Peninsula to Cameroon or the Cairo Declaration where African states recognized the sanctity of boundaries inherited from colonial masters would make Nigerians change their minds on the judgement.

According to Prince Ajibola, by these acts of omission or commission, Nigeria systematically surrendered the Bakassi Peninsula to Cameroon and Cameroon of course took advantage of the situation,

> "...and raked a lot of things generally and conclusively against Nigeria's claim over Bakassi peninsula'. 'When it comes to Bakassi, we (Nigeria) did not do well ourselves. Our homework was poor, bad. Quite frankly we bastardized the case. We in effect disclaimed Bakassi." (34)

Responding to those opposed to the hand over of the Bakassi Peninsula to Cameroon, Prince Bola Ajibola, lamented that

> "...people were either acting mischievously or were ignorant of the situation."(35)

Reacting to the National Assembly's opposition to the hand over of the Bakassi Peninsula, Prince Bola Ajibola attributed the Assembly's reaction to a lot of misconception and ignorance saying;

> "At the moment, Cameroon is fully on 85 percent of the Bakassi peninsula. Has the refusal of the National Assembly changed anything? You see, the supremacy of the international law is clear once you have entered into it." (36)

Professor Itse Sagay who believed legal 'blunder' costs Nigeria the Bakassi Peninsula opined that Nigeria had in her usual 'nonchalant, irresponsible manner' accumulated evidence in favour of Cameroon. Sagay blamed Nigeria in the first place for accepting the compulsory jurisdiction of the International Court of Justice when Cameroon only accepted it a few days before filing its case against Nigeria. Although Sagay shared Prince Bola Ajibola's opinion that there could be no appeal of ICJ judgement and equally subscribed to the view that in conflicts between international obligation and municipal law, international obligation always prevailed, Professor Sagay still wanted Nigeria to put Bakassi handover on hold. (37)

A Port Harcourt based lawyer, Mr. Sabastine Hon was more emphatic. Hon argued that not even a court injunction restraining the handover could prevent Nigeria from meeting its international obligation. Hon based his argument on the judgement delivered in 2002 by the International Court of Justice, ICJ, under its compulsory jurisdiction and the June 12 2006 Greentree Agreement signed between Nigeria's President Olusegun Obasanjo and Cameroon's President Paul Biya. Citing Articles (5)(6)(7) and (94) of the United Nations Charter, Hon warned that should Nigeria disregard the judgement she could face different forms of hostile reactions from the international community ranging from imposition of sanctions to outright military action to enforce the judgement. (38)

ICJ judgement and the handover controversy provided a window of opportunity for many to pour out their emotions and ignorance. For others it was simply an opportunity to play dirty politics. Greentree provided an occasion for die-hard critics and politicians to castigate, if not vilify political opponents and professional colleagues. President Olusegun Obasanjo and erstwhile Attorney General of the Federation, Prince Bola Ajibola, in particular appeared to have been the primary targets of this tongue-lashing. Interestingly, few people heaped much of the blame on erstwhile Attorney General of the Federation, Chief Richard Akinjide who actually was Nigeria's Agent at The Hague. If anyone had to be held responsible for whatever legal 'blunder' and 'bastardization' of the case, many thought it should be Chief Richard Akinjide, SAN, who was Nigeria's Agent at The Hague.

At a point attention became almost entirely focused on the question of the supremacy of international law over domestic law.

Lawyers in support of the supremacy of international law gave their nod to the final handover of the Bakassi Peninsula to Cameroon. In defence of that position they relied on Articles (60) and (61) of the Statute of the International Court of Justice whose Article 60 states:

> "The judgement is final and without appeal. In the event of a dispute as to the meaning or scope of the judgement, the Court shall construe it upon the request of any party."

While Article 61 stipulates;

> "An application for revision of a judgement may be made only when it is based upon the discovery of some fact of such a nature as to be a decisive factor, which fact was, when the judgement was given, unknown to the Court and also to the party claiming revision, always provided that such ignorance was not due to negligence...The Court may require previous compliance with the terms of the judgement before it admits proceedings in revision. The application for revision must be made at least within six months of the discovery of the new fact. No application for revision may be made after the lapse of ten years from the date of the judgement."

Not a few Nigerians expected Nigeria to avail herself of this provision before October 10, 2012 when that window would close. Nigerians must have been disappointed that despite orchestrated campaigns at the sharp end of that window by diverse political forces to compel the Federal Government to seek a review of ICJ's decision, Nigeria ignored all such calls and pressure for a review until the window closed on October 10, 2012.

Exponents of the supremacy of municipal law over international law saw the final handover of Bakassi peninsula as a flagrant violation

of Nigeria's Constitution and of an Abuja High Court injunction
restraining Nigeria from going ahead with the transfer. They cited
Article (46)(1) of the Vienna Convention on the Law of Treaties to
buttress their argument. Article (46) (1) provides;

> "A state may not invoke the fact that its consent to
> be bound by a treaty has been expressed in violation of
> a provision of its internal law regarding competence to
> conclude treaties as invalidating its consent unless that
> violation was manifest and concerned a rule or its internal
> law of fundamental importance"

Many Nigerians, including Senator Bassey Ewa Henshaw who
represented Bakassi people in Nigeria's Senate, strongly believed
that the Nigerian Constitution was 'an internal law of fundamental
importance' and that it had been violated by President Obasanjo's
unilateral implementation of the Greentree Agreement. Nigeria's
Senate passed a resolution demanding the ratification of the Greentree
Agreement in accordance with Article (12) of the 1999 Constitution
of Nigeria before the handover could go ahead. Article (12) of the
Constitution of Nigeria 1999 stipulates;

> "No treaty between the Federation and any other
> country shall have the force of law except to the extent to
> which such treaty has been enacted into law by the National
> Assembly."

And because the Greentree Agreement had not been so
domesticated members of the National Assembly insisted that until
that was done the Greentree Agreement was not binding on Nigeria
and its provisions therefore could not be implemented. To go ahead
with the handover before ratification was obtained, in the view of
the National Assembly and exponents of the supremacy of domestic

law over international law, was tantamount to a violation of the Constitution of Nigeria 1999. On November 27, 2007 Senate passed a resolution declaring withdrawal from Bakassi peninsula illegal. Government took no notice.

Nigeria's military was not left out of the controversy. The military seemed clearly uncomfortable with the handover and made its feelings known. At a public hearing organised by the National Assembly the military gave Nigerians a few hints about the implication for Nigeria of the Greentree Agreement. They told Nigerians that the country's naval warship would have hard times accessing the Calabar port. The military particularly believed the Greentree Agreement was 'dangerous' and a disaster for national security and raised particular concerns over Article 4(d) of Annex 1. They painted a gloomy picture of how the movement of the nation's naval warships could be impeded if not encumbered and demanded that Article 4(d) of annex 1 of the Greentree Agreement be expunged or amended. It took the timely intervention of the Naval Chief to calm nerves. Article 4(d) of Annex one

> "allows innocent passage in the territorial waters of the Zone to civilian ships sailing under the Nigerian flag, consistent with the provisions of the Agreement, to the exclusion of Nigerian warships."

Had anyone taken the time to critically look at the Anglo-German treaty of 11 March 1913 on which the International Court had so heavily relied on in arriving at its decision they may have discovered that certain provisions of that treaty had taken care of such navigational worries. Articles (23)(24)and (25) of the March 11, 1913 Anglo-German Treaty regulate navigation in the area. Its Article 23 provides,

> "Nothing in this Agreement shall prevent British or German vessels, whether public or private, from using the

most convenient course between the open sea and the Akwayafe River, and from navigating that river without any differential treatment whatever."

Nigeria could easily avail herself of this provision or have recourse to relevant provisions of the United Nations Law of the Sea (UNCLOS) 1982, on the 'Right of Innocent Passage' and 'Transit Passage' if the provisions of Article 23 of the March 11 Anglo-German treaty proved inadequate.

Most Nigerians however remained anxious and opposition to the handover grew stronger. The Bakassi handover controversy continued to swing to and fro like a yo-yo. Opposition of the Greentree Agreement increased as the deadline for the hand over got closer. Nigerians continued to base their claim on the 1884 Anglo-Efik treaty that the ICJ had rejected. Nigerians simply refused to accept ICJ's rejection of the 1884 Anglo-Efik treaty. Supporters of the Greentree Agreement and Nigeria's withdrawal however dismissed the Anglo-Efik treaty and drew attention to some three hundred and sixty similar agreements that Britain had concluded with other Nigerian communities. They noted in particular the agreement with the Dosumu family in which King Dosumu of Lagos gave 'Lagos and its environs to the Queen of England and her heirs for ever and ever'. They reasoned that had such agreements been valid, Lagos and many other parts of Nigeria that had entered into such agreements with Great Britain might probably never have been part of the Federation of Nigeria. Whatever the arguments for or against ICJ's decision, most Nigerians seemed to agree that Nigeria's preparation and her many acts of omission or commission cost Nigeria the Bakassi Peninsula.

As August 14, 2008 final handover deadline drew nearer, Bakassi peninsula began to experience a new form of crisis. Opponents of the handover seemed quite desperate and determined to scuttle the handover. Militancy, a hitherto unknown phenomenon in the peninsula suddenly emerged and armed militants began to carry out unwholesome activities in the peninsula. People mounted rigorous campaigns and employed highly questionable tactics in their efforts to make conditions unfavourable for the handover. They took their campaign to the fishermen population, painted pictures of the looming disaster and catastrophe that would befall the fishermen population if Nigeria went ahead with the handover. They spoke in bold terms of the anticipated huge influx of refugees that would swamp and overwhelm Nigeria on the handover day and threatened that violence would consume the Bakassi Peninsula. To ensure their apocalyptic predictions came to pass, they sneaked into the Bakassi Peninsula and spread their message urging innocent fishermen to abandon the fishing settlements and flee the Bakassi Peninsula.

These apostles of doom contrived refugee crisis and invented conflicts in the peninsula to create confusion and put the handover on hold. Gradually life in the Bakassi Peninsula was becoming very unsafe as militants began to have some firm grip of the peninsula. As Nigeria approached the sharp end of her rule in the Bakassi Peninsula, news of armed skirmishes between some unidentified persons and Cameroon soldiers stationed in the peninsula began to emerge. Cameroon played into the hands of those responsible for these provocative attacks by expelling innocent members of the fishermen population. Such reaction only helped to further heighten tension between the two nations. Political racketeers who had turned the Bakassi Peninsula into a big business venture were quick to rake huge profit from the incidents. They blew the incidents out of proportion, exaggerated the number of fleeing fishermen to justify fabulous amounts that might be needed to feed and accommodate the so-called refugees.

Such incidents emboldened opponents of the Greentree Agreement who now saw the harassment and molestation of fishermen communities as a reason to justify their demand for Nigeria to put a hold on the handover. But the real danger in a post-Greentree Bakassi Peninsula was no longer the harassment and molestation of fishermen communities; it was the threat to life and property posed by militants to the entire Bakassi population and to innocent traders and passengers commuting between Nigeria and Cameroon through the Bakassi Peninsula. These faceless people who operated under the cover of darkness did not limit their activities to attacks on Cameroon military. They went about the maze of creeks in the peninsula kidnapping and extorting money from everyone including the very fishermen communities they claimed to be fighting for. They harassed innocent passers-by, dispossessing them of their valuables and occasionally killed their victims. The situation was quite reminiscent of the post-civil war era when renegade soldiers from the conflict inflicted heavy suffering and hardship and occasional death on the inhabitants of Bakassi peninsula and on those commuting between Cameroon and Nigeria through the Bakassi Peninsula.

At a point militant activities seemed likely to threaten the handover. But if the intention of these militants and their sponsors had been to force Nigeria to put a permanent hold on the handover, they probably might have been terribly disappointed because President Umaru Yar'Adua on whose shoulders the enormous burden of resolving this contentious issue rested left no one in doubt as to what direction Nigeria was heading. Receiving the Letters of Credence of Ambassador Salaheddine Abbas, the first Cameroonian High Commissioner to Nigeria in some fourteen years, President Yar'Adua gave the assurance that Nigeria would certainly honour the Greentree Agreement. President Yar'Adua told the Envoy, 'We must ensure that the August 14 handover goes ahead, in accordance with the Greentree Agreement.'

Cameroon reciprocated the gesture and sent a Special Envoy to Abuja the following week. Cameroon had, at the outbreak of the

Bakassi Peninsula crisis taken the seemingly unwise decision to recall her High Commissioner from Nigeria; an intermediate diplomatic demarche, short of severing diplomatic relations to indicate serious displeasure about Nigeria's conduct in the Bakassi Peninsula. Diplomats believe that although states commonly adopt the demarche, it is indeed an unwise decision because it really makes no sense to maintain diplomats on the scene when things are going relatively very well and pull them out when you really need them. It was against this backdrop that one could appreciate the significance of moves by both countries to re-establish friendly relations. Nigeria and Cameroon were beginning to rediscover the warmth and fraternity that the long years of Bakassi crisis and distrust had rendered impossible.

Thus; although security concerns led to the sudden and unexpected change of venue of the final handover ceremony, President Umaru Yar'Adua on August 14, 2008 amidst serious security concerns kept his word and handed over the rest of the Bakassi Peninsula to Cameroon in a solemn ceremony in Calabar, leaving thousands of fishermen who had been deceived to leave their fishing settlements to come to Ikang to disrupt the handover stranded in the cold at Ikang. This historic though mournful handover, it is hoped will bring an end to decades of unease, suspicion and sometimes hostile relations between Cameroon and Nigeria. No serious thought however, appears to have been given to the future of Bakassi natives besides vague promises in Nigeria of relocation and resettlement.

CHAPTER THIRTEEN
Uncertain Future

One would think that following the ruling of the International Court of Justice, the signing of the Greentree Agreement and the successful though controversial and mournful handover of the Bakassi Peninsula to Cameroon, the peninsula crisis would have come to an end. That would be a grave mistake. ICJ's decision has far reaching ramification for many people. Firstly, the territorial frontiers of the Efik world and indeed, Nigeria have shrunk considerably. Culturally, the origin of "Ekpe"; undeniably the most important symbol of Efik tradition and culture is now confirmed Cameroonian. Nigeria's Cross River State has not only lost enormous petroleum resources; it has also become a land-locked state. The long-term impact of this judgement is yet to unfold. Only time will tell how far and for how long the repercussions of the judgement will reverberate through the Efik world, Nigeria and indeed, Cameroon. Will ICJ's decision put a definitive end to the shifting nature of Nigeria-Cameroon borders around the Bakassi Peninsula corridor? Again, only time will tell. From every indication, the Bakassi Peninsula crisis appears far from over. Bakassi peninsula has all the trappings of an on-going drama. Both in Cameroon and in Nigeria the battle for the Bakassi Peninsula is raging on several fronts and it appears to be just beginning.

Cameroon won the legal battle for the peninsula and is now ruthlessly exploiting Bakassi petroleum resources but Yaounde still seems pretty unsure how to proceed in the territory. Besides the ruthless exploitation of resources in the territory, Cameroon is still contemplating what to do with a territory that provides over ninety percent of Cameroon's petroleum exports and is over ninety percent populated by Nigerians or people of Nigerian extraction. What status can she give such a territory? Can she turn the Bakassi Peninsula into a division in Cameroon? The answer appears to be a unanimous "No". Cameroonians seem united on the matter. They just do not seem to like the idea. The reason is simple. It would mean creating a division for Nigerians in Cameroon. Cameroon is apparently casting for Cameroonians to come, occupy and own the Bakassi Peninsula. Yaounde is constructing expansive plantation-style housing estates where possible in the Bakassi Peninsula for this purpose. But Cameroonians do not yet seem enthusiastic about living in the Bakassi Peninsula. Some of the houses as would be expected are already rotting away or being vandalized. Cameroon will have to do a lot more to attract her own people to the peninsula. That could only complicate matters very much in the future.

Some Cameroonian ethnic groups do not seem to want to help their nation. They are apparently adding to the confusion and making it harder for their government to come to terms with the Bakassi Peninsula situation. An incredible number of Cameroonian ethnic groups, prominent among them being the Balondos suddenly seem to have awoken from a deep slumber to discover that the Bakassi Peninsula belongs to Balondo people. They are waging a vicious war against the Usakedet (Isangele) people just like fishermen communities and clans of Efik ancestry did in Nigeria. Bakassi ownership controversy continues to rage in Cameroon where indigenes of ethnic groups, some of which do not even share common maritime or land boundaries with the Bakassi Peninsula continue to mount pressure on their government to create chiefdoms for them in the Bakassi Peninsula as if the territory were a no man's land. The reason is obvious. They all have their eyes firmly fixed on the rich marine and petroleum resources in the peninsula. Cameroonians continue to clamour for any role in the Bakassi Peninsula that would enable them to assume some form of authority over Bakassi resources. Those posted to the peninsula are known to embark on bold action in an effort to try to dispossess Bakassi natives. Yet, there is no record anywhere to show that any Cameroonian ethnic group had at any time in history ever laid claim to any portion of the Bakassi Peninsula. Post Greentree Bakassi peninsula is however witnessing a surprising upsurge of Cameroonian ethnic groups claiming ownership of the Bakassi Peninsula. For the Usakedet (Isangele) people; customary owners of the peninsula, this is déjà vu.

In spite of her victory, Cameroon remains quite uneasy with the fact that the territory is over ninety percent populated by a Nigerian people or Nigerians. Cameroon remains quite uncomfortable with this demography and continues to make relentless efforts to alter the demographic landscape of the peninsula. Cameroon's commitment to this objective is beginning to look like an obsession. Fishing settlements that for centuries had borne names that reflected their origin and the tradition and culture of their founders have long had their names changed into Cameroonian names. There is need for these places to revert to their original names because of the grave implication such changes could have on the territory's history. The future is clearly uncertain.

Since the handover, Cameroon has embarked upon massive construction of houses in Bakassi peninsula in the hope of attracting thousands of Cameroonians into the peninsula and although Cameroonians do not yet seem to feel at home in the peninsula the few that have answered their nation's call are struggling to take control of vital sections of Bakassi politics and economy. At Ngosso and Atabong for example where you find huge oil installations,

Cameroonians are making their presence increasingly felt. They are not only getting involved with the business of oil production, they are sponsoring candidates and getting themselves elected into the local council and filling positions that should be reserved for Bakassi natives. It is clear what the ultimate intention of these Cameroonians is; disinherit Bakassi natives. Therein lay the real trouble. The future is surely uncertain.

No aspect of life in the peninsula appears to have escaped Cameroon's effort to assimilate customary owners of the peninsula. The onslaught seems to be total. The Efik language, tradition and culture which are common to Bakassi natives have been and continue to be under attack. The Efik language and the local dialect of Bakassi natives which children commonly speak from birth in the peninsula are under tremendous pressure from an aggressive assimilation policy. Efik language, like Efik names, tradition and culture are now on the decline amongst Bakassi natives. Children born in Bakassi peninsula no longer seem able to express themselves in Efik or even in the local dialect as was the habit prior to the advent of Cameroon in the peninsula. Those who try, mix the local dialect so dangerously with French and Pidgin English that they hardly make sense. Attention is now focused on the promotion of French and English; none of which are spoken correctly among a largely illiterate population of a people of Efik extraction.

Bakassi natives continue to be psychologically subjected to a number of indignities and pressure. It is no longer fashionable for Bakassi natives to give their newly born babies names their ancestors bore. Names that reflect their Efik ancestry are clearly discouraged and an illiterate population has stupidly bought into the idea as a survival strategy. Consequently, names such as Okon, Effiong, Edet, Asuquo, Etim, Iquo, Arit, Atim, etc are disappearing among the Usakedet (Isangele) people. The older generation that already bear these names, confronted with the dilemma is going round the problem by adding prefixes and suffixes to their names as a survival strategy. Thus, Edet becomes edetson, Effiong-effiongson, Effiom-effiomson, Okon-okonson, etc while persons bearing names like Nyong have simply found a new way of going round the problem by changing the 'y' in Nyong to 'j' in order to be accepted as Cameroonians. The younger generation has reacted even more strangely. They now seek family names that have obscure origins. Those not so lucky to find such names in their family lineage resort to more radical solutions. They are turning short phrases and sentences in the local dialect into names. As a result Usakedet children today bear names such as 'Chema' meaning 'good morning', 'Nyemadem' 'I too have got it' 'Orami' 'mine', etc. Others have simply chosen to bear two different names; one in Cameroon, the other in Nigeria in order to maintain both nationalities. No thought is given to how what they now see as a solution could affect their identity in the long term. The future is undoubtedly uncertain.

Childhood games, songs and dances; the very essence of the tradition and culture of the people are gradually disappearing because they are frowned at and discouraged for being too Nigerian. Bakassi natives are systematically being transformed into a people without a tradition; a people without a culture. Yet, Bakassi peninsula is the home and birth place of the 'Leopard Spirit Cult' known as "EKPE" in Efik language. Cameroon will need to provide guarantees to the Usakedet (Isangele) people that they can bear names such as Okon, Effiong, Edet, Asuquo, etc that their ancestors bore and that they do not need to change their names to something that appeals to the imagination of Cameroonians or their way of life to be accepted in their homeland. Cameroon needs to accept the Bakassi Peninsula as is. Clearly the future is uncertain.

Cameroon needs to put a stop to policies and actions aimed at rewriting the history of the Bakassi Peninsula. That history was written several centuries ago. Of the four sub-divisions Cameroon has created in the Bakassi Peninsula only one bears a name that reflects the location and ownership of the sub- division. The other three sub divisions, like fishing settlements bear strange names. The numerous oil wells in the Bakassi Peninsula equally have names that do not reflect their location or ownership. There is need for Cameroon to take a hard look at these names because of the potential long-term negative impact on Bakassi natives. Military and civilian personnel posted to the Bakassi Peninsula seem to be leaving no stone unturned in what seems like a holy mission to assimilate and re-engineer the indigenous population of the peninsula. They are doing everything imaginable to ensure that they father a good number of children in the area. At the rate they are going, Bakassi natives, as a people, may be extinct sooner rather than later in Cameroon. The future is clearly uncertain.

When these functionaries are not engaging in such 'holy' missions, they busy themselves minting conflicts between the different Bakassi native clans. Until recently, Cameroonian officials sent to work in the Bakassi Peninsula were wont to interfere in a subversive way in disputes involving Bakassi natives. One crisis that Cameroonian officials posted to the peninsula have appeared to exploit is the age-old controversy over who first arrived in the peninsula between the village of Efut Inwang (Bateka) that claims its origin from the Balondo people of Cameroon and the Oron and Amoto stock that are of Nigerian heritage. Claiming to be a Cameroonian in Bakassi peninsula seems a convenient way to gain favour from Cameroonian officials in the peninsula. This 'who-first-arrived' controversy has remained the most intractable and principal source of conflict in the Bakassi Peninsula for centuries. Cameroonian authorities' continued exploitation of this centuries-old antagonism has hardly helped peace building efforts in the community.

There is however some cheering news. There are encouraging signs that Cameroon may be changing her attitude towards Bakassi natives; thanks to Bakassi crisis. In recent times, Cameroon has made significant effort to integrate Bakassi natives; the Usakedet (Isangele) people into mainstream Cameroon politics. In a surprised but extremely pleasant move, Cameroon appointed a Bakassi native; Governor of one of her regions. This was quickly followed by the election of another Bakassi native into Cameroon's premier Senate. There are today Bakassi natives who have been appointed District Officers in Cameroon. These are very encouraging signs but Cameroon will need to do more to assuage the concerns of Bakassi natives especially in those critical concerns that have been highlighted here. Bakassi natives need to retain their identity as a people of Efik extraction. More importantly, Bakassi natives must be made to derive some benefit from the enormous resources on their land. It cannot continue to be "RICH BAKASSI PENINSULA; POOR BAKASSI NATIVES. Unless deliberate attention is given to these concerns in Cameroon, the future could be truly uncertain.

In Nigeria the story cannot be said to be too different. The Bakassi Peninsula has been lost but amazing efforts continue to be made to create the impression that the Bakassi local government council is still in existence. The battleground has also shifted to Ikang; purported new location of the local government; recognized by the Government of the Cross River State but not by the Independent Electoral Commission. (INEC) The battle is also no longer between Bakassi natives, fishermen communities and unscrupulous politicians. The battle now is for the heart and soul of a Bakassi local government that has neither territory nor people; that only exists in space and in the minds of those promoting the falsehood. The Bakassi Peninsula, it is common knowledge has been ceded in its entirety to Cameroon. Its inhabitants remain on the peninsula carrying out their usual trade. There has been no unusual movement out of the peninsula in spite of the change in sovereignty. Yet, Bakassi local government by some mysteriously turn of events is said to be in existence. This is just one of the many wonders that we on this side of the planet are capable of performing. The main challenge today is to sustain the falsehood that Bakassi local government is still in existence. The other challenge is to convince the world that there are thousands of 'displaced Bakassi people' that need to be relocated and resettled. The goal in both cases is to ensure the continued flow of funds from Abuja to sustain a non-existent local government council. These twin conspiracies remain the driving force behind the actions of architects of Bakassi politics. How long these great lies can be sustained remains to be seen. The future is clearly uncertain.

As would be expected, the relocation of a non-existent 'displaced Bakassi people' would create considerable upheaval. Not surprisingly the relocation project has run into serious trouble. Several years after Nigeria withdrew form the Bakassi Peninsula no Bakassi native has been relocated. Yet, huge sums of money are said to have been expended on the relocation of a so called 'displaced Bakassi people'. That is hardly surprising. The fact is there are no persons to relocate from the Bakassi Peninsula.

The idea of relocation of the native population of the Bakassi Peninsula is however not a new one. The 1906 Anglo-German treaty not only redefined the boundary around the Bakassi Peninsula, it made the first attempt to address the problem of the indigenous population of the area. Besides regulating navigation and fishing rights in the area, the 1906 Anglo-German treaty made provision for indigenes who occupied land due to be transferred to the other power to choose which side of the boundary they wished to reside. The treaty equally gave local representatives of the two colonial powers the discretion to vary the line by mutual agreement if local conditions so demanded. Similar provisions were contained in the contentious March 11, 1913

Anglo-German Agreement for the relocation of members of the indigenous population who did not wish to belong to the German or British side. Article 27 of the 1913 Anglo German treaty provides;

> "It is agreed that within six months of marking out the boundary, natives living near the boundary-line may, if they so desire, cross over to live on the other side, and may take with them their portable property and harvesting crops."

Greentree Agreement merely replicates this provision and as can be observed the provision relates exclusively to the native population. This provision was never intended for itinerant fishermen communities who as a matter of fact, have never needed any such provisions to move out of the Bakassi Peninsula and return home. They have always returned to their homes in Bayelsa, Rivers, Delta, Ondo, Akwa Ibom and Cross River states, etc whenever the fishing season was over or whenever they felt the need to go home.

Bakassi native population on the other hand who did not wish to live under German rule did take advantage of such provisions to abandon the Bakassi Peninsula, return to Nigeria, melt into the wider Efik world or establish new settlements along the banks of River Akpayafe or deep inland. This is how the people of Aqua came to co-found present day Ikot Nakanda; Headquarters of Akpabuyo Local Government Area. That too is how the people of Oron Ambai Ekpa came to found Esuk Okon, Ikot Affiong Asuquo Anjeh Usim, Ikot Offiong Ambai, etc. That is equally how the people of Amoto became so integrated into the Efik world that they almost completely lost touch with their ancestral homeland. As a result of these movements people of Usakedet ancestry can be found in virtually every Efik hamlet today.

This is equally how the people of Ifiang came to abandon their original home along-side Aqua on the right bank of the River

Akpayefe, and moved over to the left bank of the same river to found new settlements in present day Ifiang Ayong and Ifiang Nsung. Prince Archibong Edem of Calabar would much later attempt the reverse movement and relocate temporarily from Calabar to the very site vacated by Ifiang people along side Aqua. Prince Archibong Edem would call his new home Obufa Obio; new Calabar in his continued defiance of his brother; King Orock to whom he had lost the throne in Calabar. Archibong Edem's unsuccessful attempt to transfer the concept of Efik home and headquarters from Calabar to his new settlement in the Bakassi Peninsula would come to an end when he abandoned the peninsula and returned to home in Calabar, in a bid to try to regain the throne following the death of his brother. The place that gave him refuge in the Bakassi Peninsula would become known as Archibong Town.

A small percentage of Bakassi natives; the Usakedet people however chose to remain in the Bakassi Peninsula to protect the homeland their ancestors had founded in the fifteenth century. These people have since then not only been regarded but also been treated as Cameroonians; Nigerians claim of the territory notwithstanding. These people would be the only people who might deserve to be relocated and resettled if they so desire. But from every indication, it does not appear these Bakassi natives deserve or desire any form of relocation. Faced with a basket of unpalatable options, these Bakassi native have accepted Cameroonian nationality as a necessity not only because it is the only reasonable option in the basket but equally because it is the wisest option on the table. It would make no sense for Bakassi natives to abandon the stupendous wealth their peninsula harbours for any other place on this planet.

It is evident that there are absolutely no people to relocate or resettle from the Bakassi Peninsula. Fishermen communities all have villages in Nigeria and beyond. With the exception of a handful of individuals, Bakassi natives now seem to have fully embraced Cameroonian nationality and will not abandon their rich homeland. Given this scenario, the talk about relocation and resettlement seems meaningless.

Who does Nigeria truly intend to relocate and resettle? I doubt exponents of this policy would want to publicly provide answers to such queries. The reason is obvious. There are no people to relocate and resettle from the Bakassi Peninsula. All the talk about relocation and resettlement is purely to make money. And given the falsehood that the Bakassi Peninsula had been transformed into, relocation and resettlement have become the latest means of lining the pockets of unscrupulous politicians and corrupt public servants. Relocation, like the Bakassi Peninsula itself, has been bastardized and transformed into the latest money spinning enterprise in post-Greentree Bakassi politics. Several years after the initial handover of the Bakassi Peninsula to Cameroon in 2006, no Bakassi native has been relocated or resettled. And there are no refugee camps any where in Nigeria swarming with thousands of displaced persons from the Bakassi Peninsula awaiting relocation and resettlement. This reason is clear. There are no persons to relocate or resettle in spite of claims to the contrary and contrived refugee camps. Bakassi peninsula fishermen are in their fishing settlements carrying out their legitimate businesses. They freely return to their homes in Nigeria and go to the Bakassi Peninsula as they please. It has always been this way regardless of who is in charge in the peninsula. Nothing has changed.

Come to think of it, if truly there were displaced Bakassi people one would expect government to resettle such persons in other local government areas since the Bakassi Peninsula has been lost in its entirety. Instead, a lost Bakassi peninsula local government and a 'Bakassi traditional ruler and his council have been superimposed on Ikang Ita communities in Akpabuyo Local Government Area and the area purportedly renamed Bakassi Local Government Area. Bakassi traditional institutions have equally been imposed on the people of Ikang Ita as if the people of Ikang Ita had no traditional institutions of their own.

All over the world, when monarchs are deposed or compelled to leave their Kingdom temporarily or for good for whatever reason, they remain condemned to live in exile as refugees for the rest of their life or until their situation is remedied. Dethroned monarchs do not become kings on someone else's land. The only exception in history can be found in Nigeria where a so-called traditional ruler who has lost his supposed territory has been imposed as traditional ruler on the people and territory that provide him refuge. And the Cross River State Government made great efforts to shore up the arrangement. It passed its law No. 007 of 2007 ostensibly to adjust boundaries between a Bakassi Local Government Area that was already lost and the neighbouring Akpabuyo Local Government Area whereas in reality the state government simply created a new local government to ensure continued flow of funds from the Federal Government to a lost and non-existent Bakassi Local Government Area.

However, after taken such bold steps to sustain the falsehood, the state government failed to stay on top of the situation and allowed the situation to spiral wildly out of control. It failed to take necessary measures to obtain federal government endorsement for its initiative, thus making it possible for aggrieved politicians and other disenchanted persons to challenge its law No. 007. These aggrieved politicians have gone ahead to establish their own Bakassi Local Government Area at some mosquito infested mangrove swamp forest called Day Spring and Qua Islands. To prove their seriousness, these politicians would not only get the Independent National Electoral Commission (INEC) to conduct voters' registration in Day Spring peninsula and Qua Islands, they would in a show of strength actually make INEC conduct some of the 2011 general elections for Bakassi Local Government Area in Day Spring and Qua Islands in what appears to be a show of strength and absolute contempt for Cross River State Law No. 07 of 2007. You can hardly imagine the confusion. As we write no one can say with any degree of certainty where Bakassi Local Government Area is located even though the 2015 General Elections were conducted largely in this Day Spring jungle.

Supporters of Day Spring and Qua Islands would go ahead with such bold action despite the fact that the state government had constructed some two hundred housing units in Ikang Ita for the resettlement of the so-called displaced persons from Bakassi in what it calls 'Bakassi resettlement camp'. One would think the state was anticipating a huge influx of refugees since resettlement camps are generally holding zones where displaced persons and refugees may stay temporarily until they were integrated into the community or were repatriated. That hardly seems to be the expectation with the so-called 'displaced Bakassi persons'. Government is ignoring the facts and proceeding with the falsehood.

Even in this atmosphere of falsehood, relocation and resettlement needed to be done in a way that would guarantee a minimal preservation of elements of the tradition and culture of displaced persons. The lumping of a people of diverse origins like the Ijaws, Ibibios, Efiks, Ilajes, Effiats, Orons and Okobos people, etc; the main fishermen communities in the Bakassi Peninsula in a single camp can hardly achieve that objective. To make matters worst the state again allowed the situation to spin out of control making it possible for militants, hoodlums and other unauthorized persons to invade the camp and take possession of the resettlement camp. Bakassi resettlement camp increasingly risked becoming a sanctuary for militants and criminals. Bakassi resettlement is clearly becoming an interminable exercise designed to line the pockets of unscrupulous politicians and corrupt bureaucrats.

Not surprisingly, efforts to relocate and resettle a 'displace Bakassi people' that actually does not exist has run into a different kind of trouble. While the people of Ikang Ita; the landlords and principal beneficiaries; indeed heirs of the purported relocation of Bakassi Local Government Area have on one hand displayed great enthusiasm in enjoying the benefits and privileges arising from the purported relocation of Bakassi Local Government to their land, they have on the other hand demonstrated great unwillingness to accommodate any of the so-called 'displaced Bakassi people'. This is hardly surprising and should have been expected. The people of Ikang Ita are no strangers to the Bakassi Peninsula. Ikang Ita shares common maritime borders with Bakassi peninsula and its peoples. They know the history of the peninsula and its peoples. They cannot be fooled. Ikang Ita is aware that the so-called 'displaced Bakassi people' all have homes and states of origin in Nigeria. A significant number of these so-called 'displaced Bakassi people' are actually permanent residents of Ikang Ita. It is from Ikang Ita that they go to the Bakassi Peninsula to fish. The call for the relocation and resettlement of such persons in Ikang Ita; the very community where they reside is meaningless.

The question now is 'Does Bakassi Local Government actually exists?' 'Where is the actual location of Bakassi Local Government Area? Some of these questions may need to be submitted to the National Assembly or the Supreme Court for determination. For now opinion is divided as to whether Ikang Ita that the Constitution of Nigerian, 1999 as amended recognizes as constituting a Federal ward in Akpabuyo Local Government Area can become Bakassi Local Government Area without a constitutional amendment? The state government seems to believe it can. The Independent National

Electoral Commission (INEC) while recognizing the power of the state government to adjust local government boundaries thinks it can not. The real problem however is not INEC's disagreement. What truly seems disturbing is that the Independent National Electoral Commission (INEC) does not just disagree, the Agency claims that Day Spring and Qua Islands; that militant and mosquito infested mangrove swamp forest on the west bank of the Akpayefe River south of Ikang is a part of the Bakassi Peninsula that was not ceded to Cameroon and on that basis INEC justifies its conduct of elections for Bakassi Local Government Area in Day Spring and Qua Islands.

This is again great imagination! No one, not even the International Court of Justice is aware of any part of the Bakassi Peninsula that was not ceded to Cameroon. The result of course of INEC's ingenuity in the matter is that Bakassi people did not take part in some of the 2011 general elections. Although INEC conducted voters' registration for Bakassi Local Government in Day Spring and Qua Islands, its decision to hold elections in that uninhabited and inaccessible jungle was successfully challenged in Court. INEC apparently does not seem to be alone in this adventure. It seems to have the support of powerful and influential bureaucrats and politicians who indeed may have written the scrip for INEC. The dust is yet to settle as there are strong indications that the masterminds of the plan have not given up the idea. It does not seem we have heard the last of this Bakassi Local Government Area location controversy.

Nigeria needs to close this relocation and resettlement chapter and deal with more pressing fallouts of the Bakassi Peninsula crisis. For this to happen, the lie that Bakassi peninsula had become must first be dismantled. There is need to put an end to the falsehood that Bakassi peninsula had become from the inception of the Bakassi crisis. Until this is done, Nigeria would be unlikely to make significant progress in handling fallouts from the Bakassi Peninsula crisis. To do so, Nigeria must first settle the question of who qualifies, if any for relocation and resettlement. For that to happen, Nigeria needs to go back to the drawing board and recognize basic fact about the territory. This will enable Nigeria to stop wasting the nation's resources to line the pockets of unscrupulous politicians and corrupt public servants. Nigeria must bear such facts in mind in decision relating to the Bakassi Peninsula. Nigeria must not feel encumbered by the past or the result would be no different.

Fishermen communities have always come from their various homes across Nigeria and beyond to fish in the Bakassi Peninsula and beyond. They also have always returned to their various homes at the end of every fishing season. It has been this way for centuries regardless of who is in command in the Bakassi Peninsula. Our unsuccessful effort to bring the peninsula back to Nigeria has changed nothing. Fishermen will not leave the Bakassi Peninsula because the peninsula guarantees them a sure and honest means of livelihood; momentary difficulties notwithstanding. The call for the relocation and resettlement of fishermen is not only meaningless; it is fraudulent. Exponents of the policy have other intentions. Government should disregard such calls. Fishermen living in Bakassi peninsula are no refugees. They all have homes and villages in Nigeria.

There is of course the indigenous population of the Bakassi Peninsula; the Usakedet (Isangele) people that have their ancestral home and permanent residence in the Bakassi Peninsula. These are the ones whose parents and ancestors are resting in peace in the Bakassi Peninsula. They, and they alone may be considered for relocation and resettlement if they so desire. But as we have already noted, these people with the exception of perhaps a handful do not appear to desire any form of relocation or resettlement. If there are any, Nigeria is unlikely to encounter any problem with the handful that might want to be relocated and resettled. Finding a place to resettle them can hardly pose any difficulties. In the first place the number is unlikely to be more than a few dozens. Such a number can hardly constitute a local government. Besides, there are villages in Nigeria that were established by their ancestors. They can easily re-integrate these villages or found new ones along Akpayefe River. In a worse case scenario, they could return to their last home in Nigeria at Udah in Mbo Local Government Area of Akwa Ibom State.

Experience has shown that any attempt to resettle fishermen communities from across Nigeria in the Cross River State is likely to encounter serious difficulties if not outright hostility. If the experience in Ikang is anything to go by; host communities are most likely to view such policy with suspicion. The experience in Bakassi resettlement camp at Ikot Effiom has clearly shown that no people in Nigeria want to swell their population with the injection of a large population of strangers. Such a policy is fraught with danger. The fear of the domination of minority ethnic groups by majority ethnic groups is real, not fiction. Such a community risk waking up one morning to discover that it has become a minority on its own land. Such a policy also runs contrary to the principle and spirit of laws creating states and local governments in Nigeria. These laws have served Nigeria well. If nothing else these laws have to a very large measure helped minimize minority fear of marginalisation and domination. It is in the interest of the nation for Nigeria to do everything to maintain them in principle, spirit and practice because Nigerians have a spiritual attachment to their land.

Continued calls in Nigeria for the creation of more states and local government councils are clear indications that the phantom of domination and marginalisation is still very much alive. Dumping the fishermen population that come from across Nigeria to fish in the Bakassi Peninsula in a particular state has grave implications for the inhabitants of such a state. It could automatically turn strangers into indigenes of such states. It is not advisable in the Nigeria of today. Fishermen communities living in the Bakassi Peninsula are not refugees. They all have villages in Nigeria. If living conditions become unbearable in the peninsula or wherever Nigerians may be outside Nigeria, one would think that the right thing to do should be to return home and allow Nigeria time to resolve any irritant through the usual diplomatic channels. There is absolutely no reason whatsoever to justify the relocation and resettlement of fishermen communities in the Bakassi Peninsula in the Cross River State. It cannot work. Acceding to such demands would be playing into the hands of unscrupulous politicians whose only intention is to continue to exploit the Bakassi situation and sustain the falsehood.

It is time to dismantle the lie that Bakassi had been turned into. Bakassi peninsula no longer exists as a territory in Nigeria. The continued existence of a local government that has no territory is an aberration and an unjustifiable drain on the nation's economy. There is need to put an end to this falsehood. Abuja should explore other demarche to regain control of the territory; try a buy-back or explore some more imaginative ideas. If all effort should come to naught, Abuja should find a noble and equitable way to compensate the Cross River State for the loss of the territory. Abuja must stop sustaining an ignoble falsehood whose only objective is to line the pockets of unscrupulous politicians and corrupt bureaucrats at the expense of Bakassi natives and the Nigerian nation.

Besides the relocation controversy, Bakassi peninsula inhabitants continue to face more dangerous challenges. It does appear opponents of the handover are taking their frustration to new heights. The peninsula has witnessed an increase in nefarious activities since the handover. It appears diehard opponents of the ruling are continuing to embark on unwholesome activities in a desperate move either to try to reverse the Court's decision or to make Bakassi peninsula ungovernable. Opponents of Bakassi handover seem to be embarking on bolder action in a bid to achieve this objective. Since the final handover of the Bakassi Peninsula on August 14 2008, the Bakassi Peninsula has witnessed an alarming rate of piracy, armed robbery, armed confrontations and kidnappings. Some of these incidents that have involved Cameroon soldiers and some unidentified gunmen believed to be 'militants' have resulted in significant casualties. There have been reports of kidnappings of oil workers and molestation of fishermen and traders in the Bakassi Peninsula. Gradually, kidnapping and sea piracy are becoming common features of life in post-Greentree Bakassi peninsula. And gradually too, the Gulf of Guinea is becoming the second most unsafe and dangerous waterway in the world; second only to the Somalia coastline. The future is surely uncertain.

The intention of the sponsors of these unwholesome activities is unclear but if their desire is to chase Cameroon out of the territory by making the Bakassi Peninsula ungovernable, they had better think again. Change in the Bakassi Peninsula will be brought about by Bakassi natives; not by strangers. Peace will come via peaceful means not through violence. Besides, Cameroon is no stranger to fighting guerrilla war-fare. Cameroon spent the 1950s and 60s; her pre and early post independence years fighting an internal insurgency led by Bameliki tribesmen who wanted to chase President Ahmadou Ahidjo out of office. The army Generals that led that war are still in active service in a Cameroon army where Generals do not retire from the army. They could be more than a match for a rag-tag gang operating on someone else's land.

Militant activities are hampering efforts to enable Bakassi inhabitants return to a perfectly normal life in the peninsula. The situation in Bakassi peninsula needs to return to the status quo ante bellum. Without peace in the peninsula, it is difficult to see a bright future for Bakassi people, given all that has happened. These so called militants also need to realise that only their kith and kin will bear the brunt of unwholesome activities in the Bakassi Peninsula. They are unlikely to harm Cameroon in any significant way. Cameroon soldiers, oil workers and oil installations in the peninsula are getting more and more professional protection. Targeting this group will increasingly become more hazardous if not suicidal.

Militants seem to have already realised this fact as they now seem to turn their attention inward. They now seem to direct their operations largely in the maritime zones of the Cross River and Akwa Ibom States where they focus on the molestation and harassment of border inhabitants, members of the fishermen communities and persons commuting in the zones. Militants have been known to block the Ikang Calabar road and besiege the Bakassi Local Government Headquarters at Ikang forcing workers to take to their heels. The people most likely to bear the brunt of these senseless acts whether in the Bakassi Peninsula or anywhere else remain those living in the area and those that commute between Nigeria and Cameroon through the Bakassi Peninsula; again over ninety five percent Nigerians. They are also the ones who are most likely to be victims of Cameroon's rage if militant activities become too provocative and Cameroon decides to take more robust action. The future is clearly uncertain.

Militant activities are not only disrupting normal life in the Bakassi Peninsula, militant activities are threatening trade between Nigeria and Cameroon and could compromise current efforts to restore normal bilateral relations between the two countries. The situation calls for collective response that in the past has been hampered by political tensions and distrust. Now that Nigeria and Cameroon appear to be rediscovery excellent relations, there is need for closer collaboration through increased joint surveillance and joint patrols to check maritime crime and piracy in the Bakassi Peninsula. Happily, efforts seem to be on going to check the menace. The Yaounde initiative that envisages security for the entire Gulf of Guinea region and has the support of the big powers and the United Nations appears to be a move in the right direction. But warships alone will not provide the full answer. Maritime crimes and piracy have deep roots in weak governance and poor management of the oil sector. A system where oil production paradoxically creates poverty and social tensions; where oil incomes only benefit governments, oil companies and a few elites needs to be reviewed. People who feel excluded from such a system will resort to violence. Nigeria and Cameroon will need to do more to bring calm and peace to the inhabitants of the Bakassi Peninsula.

Nigeria and Cameroon may have settled their territorial dispute over the Bakassi Peninsula. But as we have observed, nothing truly seems to have been settled for owners of that territory. Bakassi natives have once again been betrayed and abandoned by Nigeria, the Efik nation; fishermen communities and the international community just like Great Britain did in 1913. This time however, Bakassi natives have not only been abandoned, they have been literally stripped of their petroleum and marine resources that are now being exploited without any real benefit to the people. It is also no longer a question of who has sovereignty over the Bakassi Peninsula. Surely, the question of sovereignty over the Bakassi Peninsula has been put to rest. Both Nigeria and Cameroon are beginning to enjoy the warmth and fraternity that once characterized relations between these two brotherly nations. Bakassi natives too may also not have the intention or indeed the capacity to resurrect the Bakassi Peninsula question, not with the experience they have been through; not when their kith and kin have betrayed and deserted them; not when their country of heritage has disclaimed and turned her back on them. Clearly, there are still some dark clouds over the Bakassi Peninsula. Bakassi peninsula looks more like a 'ticking bomb' and until fundamental issues affecting the well-being of Bakassi natives begin to be addressed, we may be setting the stage for a new Bakassi peninsula crisis, the consequences of which we may not be able to anticipate. Until this "RICH BAKASSI PENINSULA; POOR BAKASSI NATIVES" image begins to change, the Bakassi Peninsula crisis could be far from over. Surely, the future is uncertain.

BIBLIOGRAPHY

1. Exchange of Notes between the Secretary of State for Foreign Affairs and General De Gaulle concerning commercial and economic relations between the United Kingdom and the Cameroons under French Mandate. London, January 21, 1941 [Cmd.6249, P(1940-1)VIII 445.]

2. Exchange of Letters and memorandum of Agreement between the Secretary of State for Foreign Affairs and General De Gaulle Concerning Commercial and Economic relations between the United Kingdom and the Cameroons under the French mandate. London March 18, 1942 [Cmd. 6345; P.(1941-2)IX605]

3. Cameroon under United Kingdom trusteeship; text of Trusteeship Agreement, Dec. 1946-New York [T.S.20(1947)Cmd.7082; P.(1946-7)XXV377; 148 B.S.P. 281] Under French: [T.S. 66(1947), Cmd. 7198; P.(1946-7)XXV371; 148 B.S.P.258]

4. Exchange of Notes with Germany confirming Protocols defining boundaries between British and German territories in Africa-Gorege to Lake Chad, Feb. 12, 1907; Uba to Maio Tiel, March 11, 1907. Berlin Feb. 22/March 5, 1907. [T.S. 17(1909), Cd.4699; P.(1909) CV445; 102 B.S.P.93; 26 HCT.172; 2 Martens V.700]

5. Agreement with Germany respecting (1) the settlement of the frontiers between Nigeria and the Cameroons from Yola to the sea and (2) the regulation of navigation on the Cross River. London. ETF imm. March 11, 1913 [TS. 13(1913), Cd.6681; P.(1913) LXXX1325; 106 B.S.P.787; 27 H.C,T. 227]

6. Convention with France supplementary to Declaration of March 21, 1899 and Convention of June 14, 1898 respecting boundaries west and east of the Niger

7. Mandate for the administration of part of the former German territory of the Cameroons, Conferred upon His Britanic Majesty, confirmed and defined by the Council of the League of Nations. ETF imm. Lon. July 20, 1922. [Cmd. 1794; P.(1923)XXIV 484; 116 BSP.832]

8. Exchange of Notes between His Majesty's Government in the United Kingdom and the French Government respecting the boundaries between French and British Cameroons. London Jan. 9, 1931 ETF imm. [TS 34 (1931), Cmd.3936; P.(1930-1)XXXIII 387; 134 B.S.P. 238]

9. Protocol with Germany for the settlement of British claims in territories under German protection in South West Africa. Berlin July 15, 1886 [77 B.S.P.1042; 17 HCT.1172; M.A.T 608]

10. Arrangement between Great Britain and Germany supplementary to the Agreement of 29 April, 7/16 May, 2/10/16 June, 1885 relative to the respective spheres of action of the two countries in the Gulf of Guinea. London July 27, August 2 1886. Supplemented by Agreement of November 15, 1893. [77 B.S.P. 1085; 18 H.C.T 283]

11. Agreement with Germany respecting the Rio Del Rey on the West Coast of Africa. Berlin: April 14, 1893 [TS 9(1893), C. 7026; P.(1893-4) CIX 105; 85 B.S.P. 38; 19 HCT239; M.A.T654; 20 Martens (IV) 235.

12. Agreement with Germany respecting boundaries in Africa. Berlin, November 15 1893. [TS.17(1893), C.7230; P.(1893-4) CIX 125; 85 B.S.P.4; 19 HCT.253; M.A.T 658 20 Martens (IV)276].

13. Agreement with the Chiefs and natives of Batanga for the better regulation of trade and the further protection of the British merchants and their property wreck etc. July 18, 1860 ETF imm. [65 B.S.P. 1182; 14 H.C.T 967]

14. Agreement with Creek Town, Old Calabar. (Substitutionary punishment) January 18, 1861 ETF imm. [55 B.S.P. 182; 11 H.C.T. 31]

15. Agreement between the British and other super cargoes and the native traders of Old Calabar. May 5, 1862 [55 B.S.P.186; 12 H.C.T94]

16. Agreement with the King and Chiefs of Old Calabar (Duke Town) for the abolition of Substitutionary punishment. Old Calabar, April 26, 1871 [61 B.S.P.202; 13 H.C.T 25]

17. Treaty with the king and Chiefs of Creek Town, Old Calabar (recognition of King and ratification of former treaties) Calabar, Feb. 27, 1874 [65 B.S.P.1185; 14 HCT. 24]

18. Agreement with King William and John of Batanga for the protection of lives and property of British traders. 23 March, 1880 [71 B.S.P.310; 15 H.C.T 538]

19. Treaty with King and Chiefs of New Calabar. Calabar July 4, 1884 [17 H.C.T 131]

20. Preliminary treaty with King and Chiefs of Creek Town, Old Calabar, Calabar July 23rd 1884. [17 H.C.T. 134]

21. Preliminary treaty with King and Chiefs of Duke Town, Old Calabar, Calabar July 24th 1884 [17 H.C.T 136]

22. Treaty with King and Chiefs of Old Calabar, Calabar September 10, 1884 Accessions, Efut Sept. 8, 1884; Idombi, Sept. 9, 1884; Tom Shot Sept. 11, 1884 [17 H.C.T. 154

23. General Act of the Conference of Berlin [76 B.S.P. 4; 17 H.C.T. 62; M.A.T 20; 10 Martens (14) 414]

24. Agreement between Great Britain and Germany relative to their respective spheres of action in portions of Africa. London April 29, /7/16 May; 2/10 June 1885. Supplemented by arrangement of 27th July/ 2nd August 1886. Modified by agreement of 5/9 May, 1893 [76 B.S.P.772; 17 HCT 77; 23 HCT 494]

25. Daily Sun, Dec. 09, 13, 2007, Friday, August 15, 22, 25, 29, 2008

26. The Bakassi Story by Dr. Nowa Omoigui; http://www.omoigui.com

27. Nigerian Army Journal, Vol. 9 No. 1, 1999

28. West Africa, March 28-3rd April, 1994

29. The Guardian, 27th March, 1990; Dec. 16, 2007

30. Weekly Trust, Dec. 13-19, 2002

31. Nigerianet Newline (Int), Nov. 18, 2002

32. The PUNCH, Feb. 15, 1999, November 26, 2007, August 14, 2008 Sept. 27th, 2008

33. INDEPENDENT, January 22, 2007

34. Greentree Agreement-12th June, 2006

35. Cross River State of Nigeria Law No. 7 (2007)

36. TELL magazine, August 4, 2008

37. National Life, Sat. 19th July, 2008

38. Chippla's Weblog-Thoughts on Issues

39. Socialistworld.net

40. Europaworld.org

41. Nigeriaworld.com

42. THISDAY, Sun. Dec. 09, 2007, Sat. August 05, 14, 12, 15, 16, 2008, June 24th, 2009

43. THE NATION, Feb. 3, 2008; April 15, 2009

44. SATURDAY SUN, August 2, 2008

45. Anderson, H.O, Intelligence Report on the Isangele Community.

46. Goodliffe, F. A, Public Records Office, London

47. Latham, A. J. H; 1973, Old Calabar 1600-1891, Clarendon Press, Oxford.

48. Hertslet, Map of Africa by Treaty, Vols. 1,2,3

49. International Court of Justice, Year 2002, 10 October, General List 94

50. General Act of the Conference of Berlin-February 26, 1885

51. Treaty of Versailles-June 28, 1919

52. United Nations Convention on the Law of the Sea (UNCLOS) 1982

53. Africa Confidential, "Nigeria/Cameroon: Blundering into battle," Vol. 35, No. 8 p.6, April 16, 1994, London.

54. Jeune Afrique, "Cameroun/Nigeria...*La guerre secrete*," *No. 1871, 13-19 Nov. 1996, p.13.*

55. Ian Brownlie, African Boundaries, (London: C. Hurst & Company, 1985), p.553-555

56. J. L. O. Ekpenyong, "Potentials of Nigerian Boundary Corridors as Sources of International Economic Conflict," in *Borderlands in Africa*, (Eds.) A. Asiwaju, & P. O. Adeniyi, (Lagos: 1989), p.293-305.

57. Y. Bologun in, "The Process of Cartographic Definition of Nigerian Boundaries,"

58. Weladji, C. (1975) "The Cameroon-Nigeria Border (2) Cross River to the Sea," in *Abbia,* 29/30, p.165.

59. Justice M. Mbuh; International Law and Conflicts: Resolving Border and Sovereignty Disputes in Africa, iUniverse INC., 2004 ISBN 0595297072

60. Jeune Afrique, Nov. 13, 1996 "L'alternative du diable"

NOTES AND REFERENCES

1. Dr. Nowa Omoigui,
   http://www.omoigui.com

2. H. O. Anderson,
   Intelligence Report on Isangele community

3. ibid

4. ibid

5. ibid

6. Dr. Keith Nicklin
   Ekpe in Rio del Rey

7. Goodliffe F. A
   Public Records Office, London

8. ibid

9. ibid (correspondence Ref: No. 212.A.80)

10. ibid

11. Anderson H. O
    Intelligence Report on Isangele community

12. Ian Brownlie,
    African Boundaries, (London: C. Hurst & Company, 1985, p.553-555)

13. Hertslet E.
    The Map of Africa byb Treaty

14. ibid

15. Weladji, C.
    (1975) "The Cameroon-Nigeria Border (2) Cross River to the Sea," in *Abbia,* 29/30, p.165

16. ibid

17. ibid

18. ibid

19. Mbuh M, (Justice)
    International Law and Conflict: Resolving Border & Sovereignty Disputes in Africa. iUniverse INC 2004, ISBN 0595297072

20. ibid

21. Directorate of Overseas Surveys, Doc. C O 554/2452 B. J. Greenhill, May 9, 1961. Public Records Office

22. ibid

23. ibid

24. B.J. Greenhill
    Correspondence Ref: No.503/3/4 of May 9, 1961

25. ibid

26. D. W. S. Hunt,
    Correspondence Re: No. NIG 40/240/1 May 10, 1961

27. J. Chadwick,
    Correspondence Ref: No. CO554/2452, June 6, 1961

28. R. Akinjide,
    "Bakassi whose Bakassi" West Africa April, 1994

29. International Court of Justice, Year 2002, 10 October

30. This Day-Thursday August 14, 2008

31. The PUNCH, November 26, 2007

32. ibid

33. Tell Magazine, August 4, 2008 & National Life, Saturday July, 2008

34. ibid

35. ibid

36. ibid

37. Saturday Sun, August 2, 2008

38. This Day, August 5, 2008